LeeWards *Illustrated Library of*

Arts and Crafts

FULLER & DEES
TIMES MIRROR
New York • Los Angeles • Montgomery

Table Of Contents

©FULLER & DEES MCMLXXIV
3734 Atlanta Highway, Montgomery, Alabama 36109
Library of Congress Cataloging in Publication Data
Main entry under title:

The Illustrated Library of Creative Arts and Crafts

1. Handicraft.
TT157.I43   745.5   74-22068
Complete Set ISBN 0-87197-076-7
Volume IV ISBN 0-87197-080-5

FULLER AND DEES

PRESIDENT
James Lueck

PROJECT EDITORS
Pat Warner
Nell McInnish

THOMAS A. CHACHARON & ASSOCIATES AND SYNTHEGRAPHICS CORPORATION

EXECUTIVE EDITOR
Richard G. Young

CONSULTING EDITORS
Thomas A. Chacharon
Sidney Lewis

PROJECT EDITOR
Bonnie Oberman

ART DIRECTOR
Will Gallagher

PICTURE EDITOR
Holly Harrington

ASSOCIATE PICTURE EDITOR
Barbara Metzger

LAYOUT STAFF
John Mahoney
Deloras Nicholas
Joseph Petek

ILLUSTRATIONS

Joanna Adamski-Koperska
Victor Brecher
Joe Chmura
John Draves
Ken Hirte
Margalit Matso
Will Norman
Joe Petek
Gabriel
David Meyer

COPY RECORDERS
Nancy Bonfield
Linda Noel

ASSIGNMENT PHOTOGRAPHY
Larry Gregory
Wayne Lennenbach

LEE WARDS

CONSULTANTS
Ward Beck
Ken Bieschke

CONTRIBUTING AUTHORS

Barbara R. Cohen (Knitting)
Vice-President, The Yarn Shop, Inc.
Latham, New York

JoAnn Fiore DeRose (Boutiquing)
Art Instructor
John F. Kennedy School, Sherwood School

Doris H. Fry (Early American Decorative Painting)
Coordinator of Craft Classes
Albany Institute of History and Art
Albany, New York

K. Riccio Guerin (Design in Crafts)
Teaching Assistant
Northern Illinois University

Lily D. Klump (Scrap Art)
Author of Handicraft Books

Harvey Magitz (Candlemaking)
President, The Candle Patch, Inc.

Lisa E. Schlossberg (Crocheting)
Instructor, Syracuse Yarn Company

Joan Mandeltort (Mosaics)
Art Instructor
Lincoln School
Highland Park, Illinois

Mahboab Shahzamon (Weaving)
Professor of Art
Art Department
Northern Illinois University

Stephen D. Thurston (Basketry and Straw)
Assistant Professor of Weaving and Textile Design
Northern Illinois University

Pages 812-813 BUTTERFLIES 'N FLOWERS MEMORY BOX
LeeWards

Pages 790-793 BABY ANIMAL CANDLES LeeWards

This Egyptian pottery jar, decorated with gazelles and stylized ostriches, dates back to the predynastic period. (Courtesy, The Metropolitan Museum of Art, Rogers Fund, 1920.)

Pottery *and* Clay Modeling

Making pottery and molding clay by the technique of wheel throwing is one of the most difficult of all craft skills to learn. Yet, it is one of the most satisfying.

Much of man's knowledge of early civilizations has been derived from studying remaining clay artifacts. Fired clay is an almost indestructible historical record — objects break but the shards remain as evidence of man's past actions and ideas.

Pottery formed without the use of a spinning wheel was made as early as 5000 B.C. in eastern Mediterranean areas. A thousand years passed before a wheel was used to assist the potter in the forming process. It was then discovered that shaping a symmetrical (or nearly symmetrical) form was easier while turning the clay on a platform supported by a rotating vertical axis. At first man used the wheel only to scrape and refine a form that had previously been hand-built. By 3000 B.C., however, Middle Eastern pots were formed by applying pressure with the hands to clay that was spinning on a fast-turning wheel.

Figure 1. This piece of pottery was unearthed by archaeologists in the Nazca Valley in Peru. (Courtesy, Field Museum of Natural History, Chicago.)

Almost all ancient civilizations have made pottery. While some cultures learned the craft independent of others, most cultures learned about pottery making from migrating people or from tradesmen. As already mentioned, the earliest pottery originated in the Middle East about 5000 B.C., reaching southeastern Europe by 2500 B.C. Pottery making in China began approximately 3500 B.C.

The development of pottery in the New World was entirely free of any influence from the rest of the world. Although the potter's wheel was not known to early New World civilizations, their work in clay was very sophisticated. The earliest pottery (2500 B.C.) in the Americas has been found in Central and South America.

The forming and firing of clay forms has been going on all over the world for thousands of years because of the availability, the functionality, and the plasticity of the material. Clay, which is found everywhere in the world, was used by primitive agrarian societies in making storage containers and cooking vessels. While the initial reason for interest in pottery was a practical one, the lasting fascination and love of clay forms developed through a sense of the aesthetic possibilities of this plastic material. Clay is a medium for the expression of ideas: clay forms are concrete extensions of the hands and the mind.

In the United States, since the beginning of the second half of the twentieth century, extraordinary attention has been given to the making of pottery. University classes in ceramics are overflowing with students. Even elementary and secondary schools are offering courses in pottery

Figure 2. An 18th-century Wedgewood chocolate set (below) exemplifies English skill in relief pottery. (Courtesy, The Metropolitan Museum of Art, Gift of Ferdinand Hermann, 1912.)

Figure 3. This Greek black-figured amphora (below) dates from the 6th-century B.C. (Courtesy, The Metropolitan Museum of Art, Rogers Fund, 1917.)

Figure 4. An Athenian red-figured amphora (above), 5th-4th century B.C., shows a satyr and a maenad. (Courtesy, The Metropolitan Museum of Art, Fletcher Fund, 1944.)

Figure 5. An ancient musician adorns this Greek vase (below) from the 5th-century B.C. (Courtesy, The Metropolitan Museum of Art, Fletcher Fund, 1956.)

Figure 6. A modern stoneware tea set and casserole by Laura Andreson (above). (Courtesy, American Craftsmen's Council, New York.)

Figure 7. This 19th-century English tea set (above) exhibits elaborate surface decoration. (Courtesy, The Metropolitan Museum of Art, Gift of the Rev. W.P. Eigenbrodt, 1894.)

Figure 8. This 18th-century Meissen chocolate pot uses a Chinese motif. (Courtesy, The Metropolitan Museum of Art, Gift of Alfred Duane Pell, 1902.)

Figure 9. This precious Chinese porcelain jar dates from the Ming dynasty. (Courtesy, The Metropolitan Museum of Art, Gift of Edgar Worch, 1950.)

making. More and more adults are seeking instruction in pottery making at art centers and evening schools. There is an unprecedented interest in all crafts. People want to make useful, beautiful objects with their own hands. They want and need a connection between themselves and their work — a connection that starts with an idea and continues to the finished product.

Common Terms Used In Pottery and Clay Modeling

Bisque Fire: the firing prior to the glaze fire. Although the bisque fire hardens the object, it is still porous enough for the glaze to adhere.

Black Hard: a stage in the drying process after leather hard (see below); lacks sufficient moisture to maintain a cohesive bond between two joined pieces of clay.

Ceramics: the art and technology of making forms of clay or glass treated by fire.

Clay Body: a mixture of clay (or clays) and water into a workable consistency for use in pottery.

Earthenware: the lowest fired ware of the three categories of pottery (see also porcelain and stoneware); fired below pyrometric Orton cone 6 (2246° F).

Grog: fired clay that has been crushed and ground to various particle sizes and added to the clay for porosity.

Handbuilding: forming clay forms by hand without the use of the potter's wheel.

Kiln: a firing chamber for pottery.

Knuckle Pull: the process of lifting the clay wall in the forming process called throwing.

Leather Hard: a stage in the drying process of clay when there is sufficient moisture content to bond clay to clay.

Plasticity: the quality of clay that allows it to be manipulated and to maintain its shape.

Porcelain: the highest fired ware of the three categories of pottery; fired above pyrometric Orton cone 10 (2381° F).

Porosity: the openness of the clay body; also refers to the hardness and vitrification (see below) of the clay.

Pyrometric Cone: a small (1⅛" or 2⅝" in height) tetrahedral cone composed of ceramic materials compounded to bend at a given amount of work heat when placed in a kiln, thus enabling the potter to determine when to complete the firing.

Scoring: scratching the surface of the clay before joining clay to clay.

Sherd or Shard: a broken piece of fired pottery.

Slip: a combination of clay and water.

Stoneware: the middle fired ware of the three categories of pottery; fired between pyrometric Orton cone 6 and 10.

Throwing: forming on the potter's wheel.

Turning, Trimming, or Tooling: the technique of removing excess of support clay from wet clay forms.

Vitrification: fire hardening of ceramic materials.

Wedging or Kneading: the hand mixing of clay into a homogenous mass free of air pockets.

Wheelhead: the wheel on which clay is formed; part of a potter's wheel.

Wheel Wedging: the centering technique of forcing the clay up and down on the wheelhead.

Basic Equipment And Supplies

For the purposes of this discussion, attention will be restricted to the clay and potter's wheel. Discussion of decoration, firing, and other forming techniques are too comprehensive for the limitations of this article. The purpose here will be to introduce the new craftsman to one aspect of ceramics — throwing on the potter's wheel. For additional information, please refer to the reading list at the end of the article.

CLAY BODY

Clay is mixed with other clays to form a body suited to the manner in which it will be molded. The potter may wish to handbuild instead of throw, or to work with stoneware rather than earthenware or porcelain. In each case, the composition of the clay body is different. For throwing purposes, it is essential that the clay body be plastic (meaning that it will maintain the given shape). In addition to categorizing by use, clay bodies are classified according to the temperature range at which they mature into a hard, rock-like state. There are three such categories: (1) porcelain, the highest temperature range; (2) stoneware, a temperature range not as high as porcelain; and (3) earthenware, a relatively low temperature range. Categorization is also determined by the purity of the clay bodies — porcelain being the purest (free of metallic oxides) and earthenware being the least pure. Porcelain is always white in color while stoneware and earthenware may vary from white to dark earth tones. The novice should avoid porcelain as a throwing body because it is difficult to manipulate on the wheel.

Once the beginner is aware of the categories of clay, it will be possible for him to select the correct type for a given project. The determination of clay body should be based on the firing limitations of an available kiln. If the kiln will only fire to an earthenware temperature range (2000° F), it would be foolish to model stoneware or porcelain.

PURCHASED CLAY

Clays may be purchased dry from large refractory companies throughout the United States. But, it is usually sold in one ton or more loads and then must be mixed. It is suggested that the novice begin by purchasing a premixed clay body. Check with a nearby university ceramics department or a professional potter to find out where quality premixed clay can be purchased inexpensively (one should not pay more than $0.15 per pound plus shipping).

FOUND CLAY

Many sites contain found clay, which will be most likely suitable for throwing earthenware. Found clay should be free of humus (organic impurities) and coarse particles of stone. The unwanted particles can be eliminated by liquifying the clay with water and then pouring it through an old screen. The water may then be eliminated by placing the slip (liquified clay) in a large shallow container under the sun. If cracking results in the drying or firing, the clay particles may be too fine. An addition of 10 percent of 20-mesh grog should eliminate the problem. Grog can be made by pulverizing bisque fired pots or it may be purchased from refractory companies or ceramic supply dealers. The term "mesh" refers to the number of holes per inch in a screen. The greater the mesh number, the finer the particle. Firing tests must be made to determine the maturation temperature range. Put a small amount of clay in a kiln, fire to a given pyrometric cone, and see what happens. Does the clay harden or does it melt? If it does not harden, it was not fired at a temperature high enough. On the other hand, if it melts, the temperature was too high. Start low (2000° F) and work higher through a series of tests.

THE POTTER'S WHEEL

In the Western world, three types of potter's wheels are used: the treadle wheel, the kick wheel, and the electric wheel. The treadle wheel, as the name implies, is a horizontally moving treadle propelled by foot. This is connected to a crank shaft which supports the wheelhead. The

Figure 10. The kick wheel is operated by pushing the bottom of the foot against the large flywheel. This motion turns the vertical shaft which moves the wheelhead.

kick wheel is propelled by kicking or shoving the bottom of the foot against a heavy horizontal fly wheel. This moves a vertical shaft which supports the wheelhead. The electric wheel has a wheelhead driven either by a belt or by a gear; the source of power is an electric motor.

Each type of wheel has an advantage and a disadvantage when compared to the other types. The treadle and kick wheels cost less and have fewer maintenance problems than the electric wheel. After years of use, the bearings are the only parts that need to be replaced. A good electric wheel, costing over $400, is the easiest on which to throw large forms. An excellent kick wheel may be purchased for under $200, while a treadle ranges in cost between $200 and $300. The mechanisms of the treadle wheel provide the potter with direct control: the potter's foot controls the speed of the wheelhead. The action of the kick wheel is a bit smoother with less vibration. But the control is not as direct because the potter first kicks the flywheel, then begins to throw on the wheel. The clay turns on the wheelhead until the momentum falls off. The electric wheel should have a variable speed range from 0 rpm to approximately 180 rpm. Those electric wheels with a switch from low to high speed should be avoided.

When considering the purchase of any type wheel, get several opinions from knowledgeable potters. And, of course, use personal judgment when evaluating craftsmanship of the construction and quality of products.

THROWING TOOLS

The preference and number of tools used in throwing varies, but certain tools are very helpful to the beginner.

1. Water bowl: a flat-bottomed container (approximately one quart) used to hold water necessary for lubricating clay during the throwing process.

2. Elephant ear sponge: used to apply and remove water and to smooth the rims of thrown forms; may be purchased at ceramic supply houses.

3. Clean-up sponge: a foam-rubber sponge placed beside the wheelhead while throwing

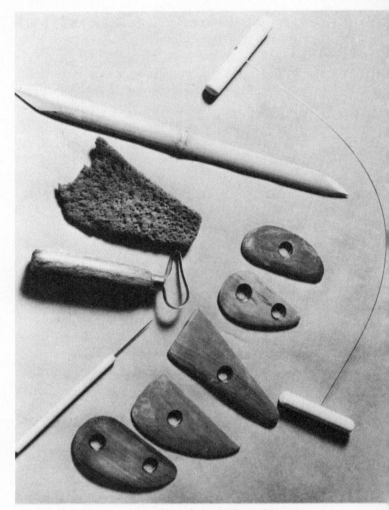

Figure 11. Among the throwing tools a beginning potter needs are a dowel rod and needle, a pear pitter, an elephant ear sponge, a bamboo stick, a wire cutter, and an assortment of ribs.

to catch the slip thrown off by centrifugal force; sponge should be approximately 10" x 6" x 2".

4. Needle: serves as a cutting tool to level or shorten a thrown cylinder. Actually, it is a 6" length of 3/8" or 1/4" wooden dowel rod with a sewing machine needle forced into one end.

5. Rib: a hardwood shaping tool that pushes positive and negative curves into a clay wall while throwing.

6. Bamboo and cutting wire: used to cut a 45° bevel in the circumference of the outside bottom of a pot after throwing is complete. The cutting away of this area removes excess clay and also provides a gripping groove

which enables the potter to remove the thrown form from the wheelhead. The thrown form must be cut away from the wheelhead by cutting wire. This stranded, stainless steel wire about 1/32″ in diameter is secured between two 1/2″ x 4″ dowel rods. A source for the proper wire, called lead out wire, is model airplane hobby shops.

7. Pear pitter: a trimming tool for removing excess support clay. (Trimming or turning is described in detail later.) The pear pitter or trimming tool — as well as the needle, the ribs, the bamboo, and cutting wire — may be purchased from a good ceramic supply house. A paring knife, which may be substituted for the bamboo, can be purchased at any dime store.

Basic Procedures

There are prevailing myths about throwing on the potter's wheel that should be dispelled. It is believed by some that an inherent talent is required to learn the technique — this is not so. Any reasonably coordinated person can learn this skill. What is required is self-tolerance, patience, and tenacity during the early stages of development. One must be willing to spend many hours of practice over a long period of time to acquire the skill. The rate of development varies with the individual. After much practice, the novice should be able to begin to make rudimentary cylinder and bowl forms — a feeling of freedom and confidence arrives only after a great deal of experience in working with the material.

PREPARATION FOR THROWING — WEDGING THE CLAY

Before the throwing process begins, it is necessary to wedge the clay. Wedging or kneading is a technique for mixing the clay into a homogeneous mass free of air pockets. Any trapped air will become an annoying bubble in the clay wall while throwing. The clay should have an equal moisture content throughout and the consistency should be soft, but not sticky.

Find a strong table on which to do the wedging. The table should be about 6″ above the knee cap. A good surface for the tabletop is one that is hard and slightly absorbent. Asbestos board, transite, and prepoured concrete slabs work very well and are usually available at lumber yards. Canvas or plaster surfaces are not recommended.

The two most effective wedging methods are known as the European wedge and the Oriental screw wedge. The European wedge is the easiest to learn but the least effective. This method, as shown in the accompanying illustrations, is much like the technique used for kneading bread dough. Take a large ball of clay (15 to 20 pounds) and force the top of the mass into the center with the heels of the hands. Use the entire body weight as a pushing force. Keep the arms stiff from the shoulders down. Now recover by reaching the extended fingers over the top and again forcing the top into the center. The body moves in a rocking, rhythmic motion. When the clay forms an elongated loaf, stand the loaf up vertically and fold the top into the center. Continue until the clay is well mixed.

Figure 12. Using the European wedge method, fold and push the outer clay into the center.

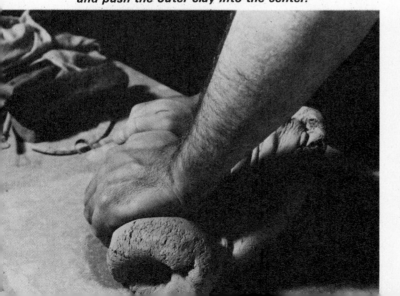

Figure 13. After folding and pushing, the clay mixture becomes smooth and fairly soft (below).

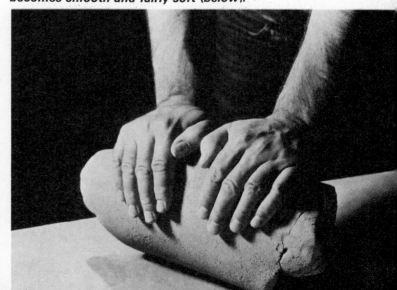

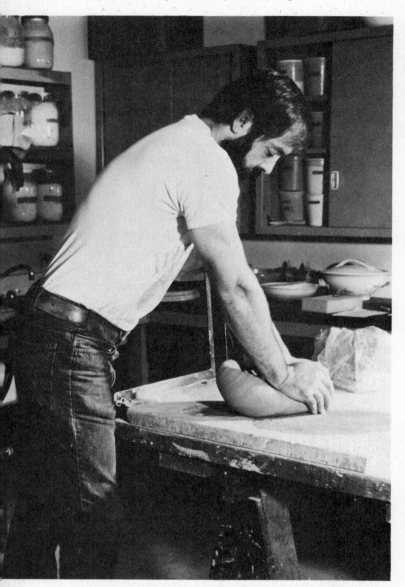

Figure 14. This photograph (above) shows the correct body position for wedging the clay. Keep the arms stiff from the shoulders down when kneading.

Since the Oriental screw wedge is much more difficult to master, use the European technique as a working method while gradually learning the other. The Oriental is similar to the European technique except that the top of the clay is rolled into the center with a very slight clockwise twist, with the left hand exerting a little more pressure than the right. It is necessary to maintain a ball shape at the top of the mass in order to correctly effect the kneading action. The recovery, after forcing the clay into the center of the mass, is to position the right hand behind the top right of the ball while the left hand is positioned on the left side of the top ball. The kneading should continue

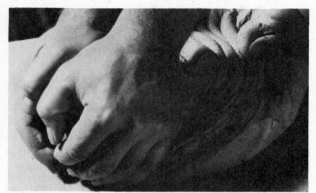

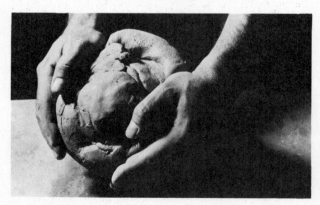

Figure 15. In preparing clay by the Oriental wedge method, first lift the top of the clay from the center (A), then push it back down with a twisting motion (B). Maintain the ball shape during kneading (C), and, finally, slap the clay into shape (D).

for about five minutes once the wedging techniques have been mastered.

The only true test to determine if the clay has been wedged well is to throw with the kneaded clay. If air bubbles are trapped in the clay, they will be felt when pulling up the clay wall. There is a quick test to give some indication as to the condition of the clay: cut through a wedged loaf of clay with the cutting wire and examine the cross sections. If the clay appears to be well mixed, with no air pockets visible, it is probably ready to throw.

POSITION AT THE WHEEL

As a general rule of thumb, the height of the seat should be adjusted to about the same height as the wheelhead. A simple four-legged stool will suffice. One should be able to bend comfortably over the clay. Brace the elbows on the thighs near the groin. This method of bracing applies only when working with the electric and kick wheels. Many potters, using an electric wheel, will elevate their left foot on a block. This places the left arm in a more advantageous position for bracing. The height of the block depends on the size of the thrower — average height is from 6″ to 8″.

When sitting on the treadle wheel, brace the wrists on the top box rim that surrounds the wheelhead. The assumed position should be a comfortable one. Try to keep the back straight and do not roll the shoulders forward into a slouch. Many potters over the age of 40 have back problems due largely to lifting incorrectly when loading and unloading kilns. Another cause of back trouble stems from assuming an incorrect position while throwing at the wheel.

TURNING THE WHEEL

Now it is time to begin throwing. The kick wheel must be kicked in a counterclockwise direction. Using the bottom of the right foot, push the heavy flywheel away from yourself. Continue a shoving kind of kick to achieve a maximum speed for centering (approximately 150-200 rpm). Some potters use a kicking and pawing method. This requires a simultaneous pushing out against the flywheel with the right foot (a kick) and a pulling in toward oneself with the left foot (a paw). It may be necessary to grasp the seat in order to kick with more vigor.

Figure 16. When using an electric wheel, elevate the left foot on a block and brace the elbows on the thighs. The stool and the wheelhead should be the same height.

The treadle wheel also requires a start in the right direction, as the wheel is capable of turning in either direction. The direction of the wheel determines the side on which form finger pressure will be exerted while throwing. (In the western world, traditionally, the wheel turns in a counterclockwise direction and therefore throwing is accomplished on the right side of the clay form.)

The electric wheel turns in a counterclockwise direction, except for those manufactured in the Orient, which are capable of turning in either direction.

WHEEL WEDGING — A PRELUDE TO CENTERING

Wheel wedging is the process of forcing the clay in and upward, then down and outward by exerting hand pressure against the clay while the wheel is turning. This process leads to centering. Not all potters begin by wheel wedging — many go directly to centering. However, wheel wedging is a good way of becoming familiar with the clay and its workable characteristics. Wheel wedging also helps to align the clay particles, making the centering and forming process easier.

Start with six balls of clay about the size of a softball. Cover all except one ball of clay with a thin film of plastic (dry-cleaning bags) to keep the clay from drying out. Beginners should use a softer consistency of clay for learning to center.

Forcing the Clay up

Set the water bowl next to the wheelhead at the farthest point from you. Place a moistened clean-up sponge next to the bowl and against the wheelhead. Thus, it will absorb the slip flying off. Force the clay down on the center of the wheelhead. Begin turning the wheelhead at high speed. When using the kick wheel, kick the flywheel to high speed. Then, rest the feet while making contact with the clay. Do not kick and throw at the same time. On the other hand, when using the treadle wheel, one does treadle and throw simultaneously.

Moisten the hands by dipping them in the water bowl. Then place them on the turning clay — the left hand first and the right thumb over the left as illustrated. Force the clay down hard enough to insure its adherence to the wheelhead. If either the wheelhead or the clay ball has a film of water on it, the clay will not adhere.

Next, with the muscle part of the thumb and heel part of the left hand, push the ball of clay toward the center of the wheelhead. With the lower right hand, pull the clay toward the center. Move the clay up to a height of about 4″ or 5″. Always release the clay gradually by moving the hands to the outside. Beginners usually release so quickly that the clay adheres slightly to the hands, causing it to move in an elliptical path off center. As the clay moves upward, force the hands closer to-

Figure 17. When forcing the clay up on the wheelhead (top) and applying downward pressure (center), the hands should be positioned as shown. The clay will adhere to the pressure points on the hands (bottom).

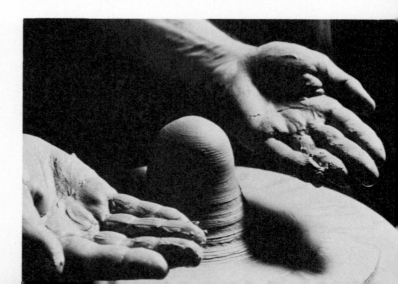

ward the center, thereby forming a cone shape. If a hollow forms in the center of the clay, it must be squeezed out using the inward pressure. If allowed to remain, the hollow will cause weaknesses and air pockets in the clay wall. For the beginner using the kick wheel, it may be necessary to rekick the wheel before forcing the clay down. As one becomes more experienced, it is not necessary to kick the wheel as frequently during the wheel wedging process.

Downward Pressure on Clay

The downward pressure on the clay is a more critical maneuver than forcing the clay up. The hand position is basically the same but the emphasis given to particular pressure points along the hands changes. Begin with the left hand. Apply the muscular pad at the base of the thumb on top of the clay. Try to keep the fingers as vertical as possible while wrapped around the top of the cone of clay. The right thumb pad is placed over the left and the fingers of the right hand are wrapped over those of the left hand. If using an electric or kick wheel, keep the forearms braced on the legs (the wrists braced on a treadle wheel) while applying pressure downward on the clay.

As the cone flattens out, continue to maintain pressure with the fingers along the vertical wall of the clay while applying a downward pressure with the muscular base of the thumbs. The hands will open up as the base of the clay becomes wider. The movements of the hands should be gradual and fluid without quick readjustments in position. Hold the downward pressure of the thumbs and the inward pressure of the fingers for a few turns of the wheel after feeling the clay coming into center. One senses this only after many hours of practice. Force the clay up and down approximately three times, or until the clay flows smoothly, then center the clay on the third downward motion. Remember to release the clay gradually. The centered clay need not be absolutely true, but it should not have a visible wobble.

POSITION OF HANDS

There are several different hand positions that potters use for throwing. For a starting point, only one basic position will be explained here. As one becomes more experienced, a variation of this position may be more comfortable for your hands. Take the position by first making the letter C with the thumb and the first finger of the left hand. The thumb should be pointing down. Then tuck the entire right hand (right thumb first) into the hollow formed by the C. Point the fingers away from yourself. The C clasps the right hand as shown in the accompanying illustrations. Next, rotate the right wrist clockwise slightly and bring the right thumb up between the first two fingers of the left hand. Now roll the right fingers into a fist. Lastly, project the knuckle of the first finger of the right hand away from yourself.

If these instructions seem a bit complex, perhaps an explanation of the position's function is in order. When two hands are braced together, each has more stability — thus the clasping C of the thumb and finger of the left hand. The right thumb braced next to it provides added strength. When lifting the clay wall (knuckle pull), the tip of the middle finger of the left hand is on one side of the wall and and the first knuckle of the first finger of the right hand is on the opposite side of the wall. These two points are the pressure areas of the fingers that do the throwing.

OPENING A CYLINDER

When learning to throw, it is best to practice developing one simple form before attempting another. The basic short cylinder (often referred to as the dog dish) is a good introductory form. The clay is first centered. Now, with the wheel turning at high speed, brace the forearms on the thighs, lean over the clay, and take the hand position. The knuckle of the first finger of the right hand should ride along the right outside wall of the turning centered clay. With the tip of the middle finger of the left hand, make contact with the center of the clay and force an opening into the clay. Do not point the fingers into the clay, thereby causing the forearms to be lifted from the thighs. Rather, pivot the fingers from the wrists. It is much easier to maintain a center if one pulls slightly toward oneself with the opening fingers.

Allow the third and little fingers of the left hand to follow the middle finger into the opening, thus forming an inverted cone well. (If a wobble in the clay results, use the cutting wire to remove the clay and start centering again with a new ball of

A

B

Figure 18. Begin throwing the clay by forcing an opening into the center (A), then deepening it to ¼ " from the bottom (B) and widening it to ¾ " across the base (C). The walls are then carefully lifted (D).

C

D

clay.) Open the clay to approximately 4" from the bottom — simply estimate the depth of the opening. Look down over the clay and compare the depth of the wheelhead with the depth of the opening. Another method is to gauge the depth with the needle. Once the proper depth is reached, widen the opening by exerting pressure on the bottom of the opening toward the right pressure point (first knuckle of the first finger of the right hand). Attempt to maintain an equal thickness across the bottom.

When the opening has reached three-quarters across the base of the centered clay, begin to exert an equal pressure at the left pressure point, thereby squeezing the clay up into a wall. Now the speed of the wheel should be decreased to about half the speed used for centering. If the squeezing pressure is too great, the wall will weaken and eventually tear away from the base. If this happens, begin again.

As the wall is lifted again, the motion should be deliberate and fluid. Do not hesitate and do not allow the hands and forearms to pivot from the elbows. Keep the elbows braced on the thighs.

The beginner will have a tendency to widen the form while lifting the wall. This is a mistake. Since it is much easier to widen than to close the form, it is wise to maintain a closed form when throwing a cylinder.

While lifting the wall, lean the pressure points toward the center of the opening so that the top

Figure 19. A knuckle pull (below) is used to make final adjustments on the clay. The index fingers of both hands apply pressure to the outside wall, while the fingers of the left hand exert force on the inside walls.

A

C

B

Figure 20. The right thumb is positioned on the rim (A) and the other fingers on the walls (B), as shown. The first knuckle pull strengthens and controls the shape (C).

will be narrower than the bottom. When near the top of the wall, do not continue to squeeze — just maintain the space between the left and right pressure points. Hold this position for a few turns of the wheel, allowing the clay to adjust itself.

The final touch of the first pull is to level out the top of the wall with the underside of the first joint

of the right thumb as illustrated. These three pressure points strengthen and control the top of the clay wall.

SECOND KNUCKLE PULL

The second knuckle pull is executed to further thin and heighten the clay wall. (A thrown form

Figure 21. In the second knuckle pull, the thumb action (below) levels the top.

Figure 22. As the thumb evens out the top, the fingers apply pressure to heighten the wall (below).

Figure 24. Pressure is also applied to smooth the bulge that forms (above).

Figure 23. The knuckle pull is repeated to further lift and thin the wall (above).

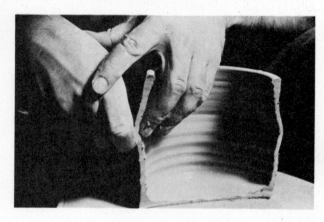

Figure 25. This pulling action creates uniformly thin walls (right).

with a thin wall is usually one indication of a well-crafted piece.) With the left pressure point, exert force on the inside bottom corner. A bulge will form on the outside wall. Just below that bulge, press in with the right pressure point. Hold this squeezing action for two complete turns of the wheel, then lift with a fluid motion. A collar of clay should precede the pressure points if the clay is being lifted properly.

More pressure must be exerted at the bottom of the wall. Then, as the lifting action rises, the pressure points should relax gradually. The top is again finished with the assistance of the thumb, as mentioned previously. The knuckle pull is re-peated until the wall is thin enough (approximately 1/4" thick for a small pot).

The clay wall may be straightened by using the vertical rib. Hold the rib in the right hand and gently press the flat side of the rib against the outside clay wall. With the left pressure point, apply pressure to the bottom corner of the cylinder. Push the clay into the rib and slowly move the left pressure point up along the inside wall of the cylinder — bottom to top. Upon reaching the top, reach over with the left thumb and hold it against the top of the rib as a brace. Hold this position for a few revolutions, then release gradually. This should straighten the cylinder wall.

Figure 26. A vertical rib is held against the outside to straighten the walls (left). The left thumb braces the top of the rib as the cylinder completes a few rotations (right).

EVALUATING ONE'S WORK

The basic cylinder is usually considered an exercise in learning the throwing technique. Further development is required to complete the form. Instead of drying and firing the cylinder, it makes more sense to evaluate one's progress by carefully examining this work. Take the cutting wire and cut between the bottom of the cylinder and the wheelhead. Then slice the cylinder in half vertically and check the cross section. Look for a uniform wall thickness throughout. It is normal for the wall to be thicker in the bottom corner. Beginners may find it necessary to trim excess clay away from the bottom wall with the pear pitter. As skill increases, less trimming or tooling is required.

REMOVING CYLINDER FROM THE WHEELHEAD

To remove the cylinder from the wheelhead, first cut a 45° bevel with the bamboo as illustrated. Hold the bamboo in the right hand as holding a pencil. Turn the sharp edge near the point into the clay so that it is actually cutting the clay away. Place the needle under the cut-away clay as the wheel revolves. Remove the excess clay from the wheelhead. Cut across the bottom of the pot, using the cutting wire as the pot turns one revolution. Then remove the pot as shown — i.e., the right hand closest to you; the pot between the thumb and first finger; and, the left hand on the opposite side of the pot with the heel of the hand and little finger gripping the cut-away bevel. Give the pot a slight twist and lift. Place the pot on a board to dry.

TRIMMING, TOOLING, OR TURNING

The potter should strive to throw a thin clay wall so that only a minimum amount of trimming is necessary. Some small functional forms, such as pitchers and mugs, should be thrown so that absolutely no tooling is required. As mentioned earlier, the beginner may need to trim excess clay from the bottom of a cylinder in order to achieve a thin, even-walled form. The pot must also reach a drying stage called leather hard in order to be handled without distorting. At this point the pot has dried so that the surface is firm enough to be picked up without leaving fingerprints. If the pot

Figure 27. To trim the piece, hold the bamboo at a 45° angle and cut a bevel at the base with the sharp edge (top). The needle is then placed under the cut-away piece to remove the excess clay (bottom).

dries to the point that the clay is no longer pliable, it has reached a stage called black hard. At this stage the pot is too dry for trimming or for adding moist clay parts like handles to the thrown form.

The leather hard form is placed on a moist wheelhead. If a thin film of water is rubbed on first, the pot will adhere to the wheelhead after a short

Figure 28. Grasp the handles of the cutting wire and slide it under the bottom of the clay pot. As the wheel makes one final revolution, cut the cylinder away from the base of the wheelhead.

drying period. (If the pot is not sticking properly, use a small coil of clay around the base of the form.) The pot is again centered by rhythmically tapping the left side of the form with the left fingertips as the pot turns slowly on the wheel. This technique requires further practice.

After the pot is centered and adhered to the wheelhead, grasp the handle of the pear pitter in the right hand and push the thumb against the cutting loop of the tool. The trimming is done on the right side of the pot; the fingers of the left hand support the left side of the pot, with the left thumb placed against the right thumb as an additional brace. Brace the elbows as in throwing. Begin cutting the clay with the loop of the tool, moving slowly down along the bottom side of the pot. Repeat the process until the clay wall appears to be an equal thickness throughout.

Projects You Can Do

All thrown forms are based on an understanding of how to throw the basic forms — the plate, the bowl, and the cylinder. The cylinder is usually the starting point. Once the basic cylinder is mastered, the bowl and plate forms are much easier to learn. Many beautiful and useful objects can be mde from a simple cylinder form.

FLOWER POT

Throw two cylinders that are approximately the same size. Dry them to leather hard and trim if necessary. Cover the cylinders with plastic to keep them from further drying.

A

B

Figure 29. To begin the flower pot project, flatten clay between the hands (A), then press a textured object into it (B), and stretch the slab by pulling and slapping it (C).

C

A

B

Figure 30. When the slab has dried to the leather hard stage, score the surface by scratching the areas to be joined (A), then apply slip to the scored areas of the base and top (B). Place the slab and cylinder together and tap in place (C). Cut an opening in the finished flower pot (D).

C

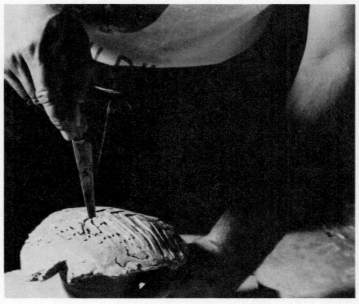

D

Now take a ball of clay the size of an orange and flatten it out with the heel of the hand. Texture the flattened ball with anything that has the possibility of developing an interesting pattern in clay — everything from fingernails to the bottom of tennis shoes. Press a texture into the clay or press the clay onto a textured surface. Experiment. After pressing the texture, stretch the clay out by pulling the slab toward you while slapping it down on an absorbent surface. Pick up the clay by gently moving both hands under the slab. Give the slab a quarter turn and repeat the slapping technique. Repeat the whole process until the slab is nearly 3/8" thick. If the slab is sticking to the surface, the clay is being slapped too hard or directly downward. The stretching action, which comes from pulling the clay toward you while slapping it down, transforms a texture that is often very rigid and sterile into a lively, organic surface. Next, allow the stretched slab to dry to the leather hard stage. Then join a portion of the stretched slab to the top of one of the thrown cylinders. It is necessary to score and cover with slip those areas of clay that are to be joined. (Scoring is the process of scratching into the surface of the clay. Slip is formed by combining water with clay that is in a liquid state and stirring.) Score and apply slip to the rim of the cylinder. Tear off from the stretched slab a section that is larger than the opening of the cylinder. The actual size and configuration of the slab are personal decisions. Place the slab over the cylinder. The wet slip on the rim of the cylinder will indicate where to score and apply slip to the underside of the slab. Join the slab to the cylinder with a gentle tapping of a paddle (any flat-sided object held in the hand will function as a paddle). Cut a large opening or a number of small openings in the slab. Soften any sharp edges caused by cutting or tearing. Repeat the technique for the second cylinder. Decorate and fire the pieces and then arrange them together.

Figure 31. The finished flower pots use a cylindrical base. The shape of the tops may be varied. Dried flowers or weeds look attractive in these pieces.

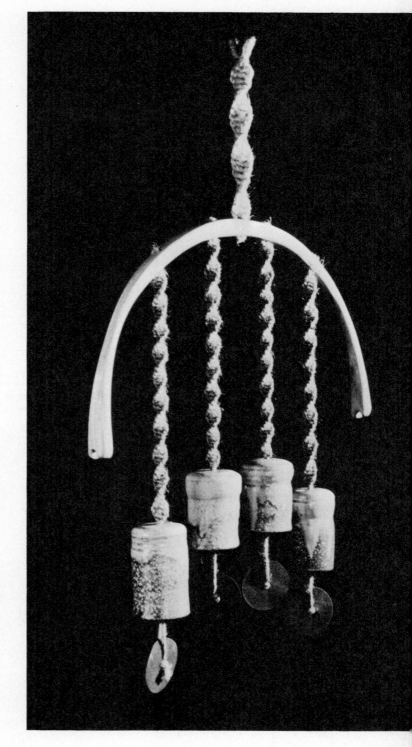

Figure 32. A fired clay cylinder and a flat disc or clapper (above) are the pottery segments of the wind chimes. When several of these pieces are assembled with appropriate connecting materials, they make a striking room accent (right).

WIND CHIMES

Throw four cylinders of any size. When leather hard, poke a small hole through the center of the bottom of each cylinder. The hole must be large enough for the tether or rope that will hold the clapper of the chime. Using small balls of clay, pinch out the clay into flat discs with diameters slightly smaller than the opening of the cylinders.

Poke holes of the same size through the centers of the discs in the same manner as the cylinders. Fire the discs or clappers — then assemble after firing. Tie the clappers into the cylinders as shown. The sails that catch the wind and the tether should be made up of materials that are related to the clay. A plastic sail and a chrome chain tether would not be appropriate. Dry, decorate, and fire.

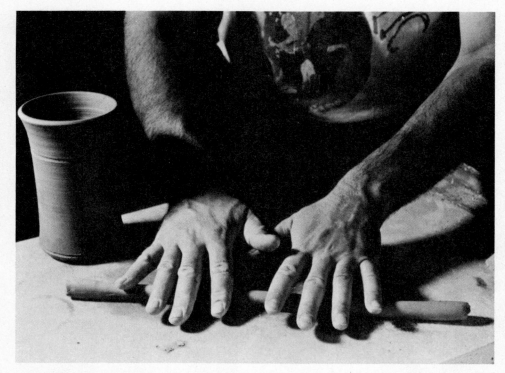

Figure 33. To make handles for a mug, roll out a piece of clay into a coil shape (above). Score and slip the areas to be joined, then attach the handle to the mug (below). The finished salt-glazed mug (opposite) may now be proudly displayed.

A MUG

Throw a cylinder about 20 percent larger than the desired size of the finished mug. Make an effort to throw the wall thin, keeping in mind that the function of the mug is to hold a heavy liquid. Smooth the rim by draping the elephant-ear sponge around the rim. Flare the rim outward so the form will be more comfortable to drink from. Allow the cylinder to dry to the leather hard stage and trim if necessary. Use coils to form a handle. Experiment and attempt to make a unique handle based on a coil technique. Roll out several small coils, then roll the small coils together into a larger one while preserving the resulting texture. Score and apply slip to areas where the handle will be attached. Dry, decorate, and fire.

For Additional Reading

Cardew, Michael, **Pioneer Pottery,** St. Martin's Press, 1969.

Leach, Bernard, **A Potter's Book,** Transatlantic Arts, Second Edition, 1967.

Nelson, Glen C., **Ceramics: A Potter's Handbook,** Holt, Third Edition, 1971.

Rhodes, Daniel, **Kilns: Design, Construction, and Operation,** Chilton, 1968.

Mobiles

One of man's newest art forms, mobiles reflect the energy and vibration of everyday living and can be an added feature to any home or office.

The original idea for mobiles is attributed to a well-known contemporary artist, Alexander Calder. Prior to Calder's innovations, little had been attempted in changing the form or content of sculpture. Anything that was not solid was not considered sculpture.

The Impressionists and Post-Impressionists both experimented with new artistic methods, primarily in painting, as a rebuttal against the redundancy of nineteenth-century work. As a result, they inspired a group known as the Futurists, who in turn renounced everything that did not move or vibrate. The Futurists created paintings and drawings which were solely of such moving objects as speeding cars and people in motion. They wanted to portray the idea that nothing ever stands still — man is set in motion and progress will not stop.

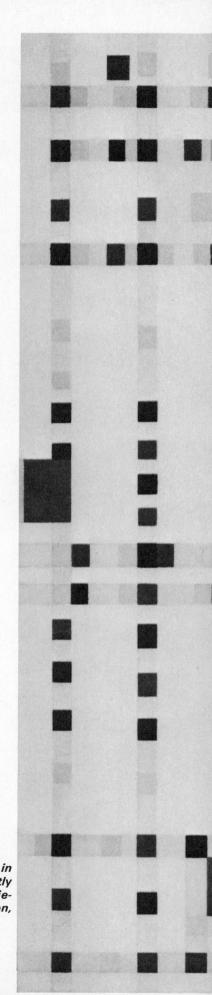

Figure 1. Mobile-maker Alexander Calder's interest in geometric shapes and primary colors was partly inspired by paintings like "Broadway Boogie-Woogie" by Piet Mondrian. (Courtesy, Collection, The Museum of Modern Art, New York.)

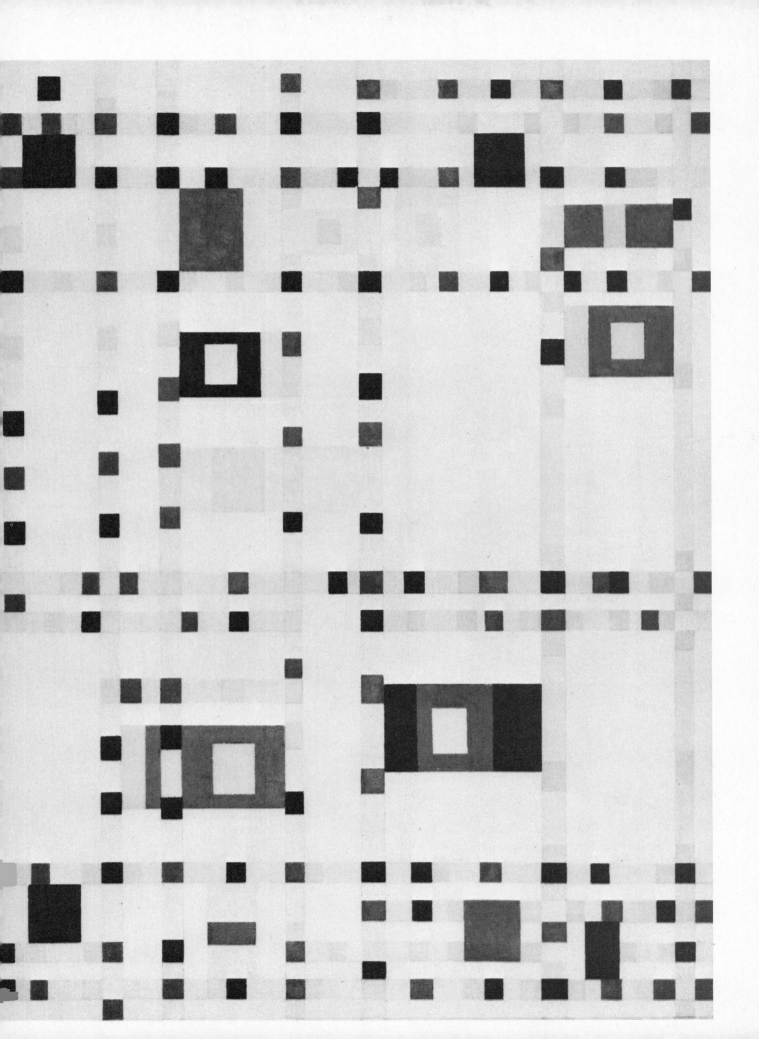

Figure 2. Alexander Calder designed this interesting hanging mobile, titled "Lobster Trap and Fish Tail." (Courtesy, Collection, The Museum of Modern Art, New York, Commissioned by the Advisory Committee for the Stairwell of the Museum.)

Calder's work stemmed from the relief sculptures and collages generated by the Cubists. Their new and fresh approach to pure form and "pure" (primary) color encouraged Calder to work in geometric shapes and colors. Calder's first small sculptures were inspired by puppet circuses. These small, animated people and animals seemed alive and full of motion. Made from small scraps of cork and wire, the figures were skillfully pulled together to create an impression of circus performers. The more Calder strived for motion in the figures, the more he became entranced with motion alone. Finally, after a visit with Mondrian, whose paintings were of primary colors and black and white, Calder was inspired to make his first attempt at moving sculpture. By using only geometric shapes and primary colors, he created the first true mobile, a sculpture in which each part moves independently of the other parts.

Mobiles today are used for many purposes: some are purely decorative to delight a child or enhance the home; others are used for such educational purposes as representing the solar system. Mobiles can be created by everyone and can symbolize any subject or can be abstract. They are improvisational, delightful, and easy to make. When completed, a mobile adds life and motion to a room, not only by its movement but also by the shadows it casts and the light that radiates from it.

Figure 3. Sheet metal and brass wire were used by Alexander Calder in his lively 1951 mobile "Streetcar." (Courtesy of The Art Institute of Chicago, Gift of Mr. and Mrs. Samuel A. Marx.)

Common Terms Used In Making Mobiles

Arms: the lengths of wire used to suspend objects in air; keeps them swinging and moving without hitting each other.

Attachment Methods: the various ways of attaching pieces to the arms of a mobile (see also *Construction* under "Basic Procedures").

Balance: to hang a mobile so that the sides are level.

Balance Loop: the loop made in the arm of a mobile at the determined balance point.

Laminate: to glue veneer wood to other pieces of wood.

Mobile: a hanging, moving sculpture.

Smoothing an Arc: the process of running a hand over the arc arms of a mobile to make them bend down at the ends of the arc.

Stabile: a static sculpture which has the appearance of being mobile or moving.

Static: characteristic of a composition which is lifeless and uninteresting, but may be used for special effects.

Symmetrical: being the same on both sides, as if an imaginary line were drawn down the center; the mirrored equal sides will contain the same parts.

Table Mobile: a mobile suspended from a small sculpture on a table or the floor rather than one hung from the ceiling.

Basic Equipment And Supplies

Many materials can be used in mobiles. However, before one attempts the construction of a mobile, it is best to consider materials which are easily handled and then experiment as desired. There is also a range of materials which should not be used since they can cause complications. Such materials include very light papers, such as tissue paper, and very heavy items, such as huge chunks of wood.

CARDBOARD

Cardboard is extremely versatile: it can be cut in any desired shape and painted. Things can be glued to it; it can be covered with wrapping paper, ribbons, bows, or fabric.

One type of commercial cardboard is known as illustration board. This is available in several thicknesses and is made from layers of gray cardboard glued together with a layer of white drawing paper on top. The drawing paper is excellent for pencil drawings, draftings, or watercolors. Try to find the double thickness weight. This is durable and will not warp.

Another type of board to look for is poster board or railroad board. A lightweight board which has a medium-texture surface, poster board is usually less expensive and more porous than illustration board. Because it is more porous, poster board will accept spray paint readily and is more suitable for one-color shapes that are either brush or spray painted. Railroad board is often just a colored poster board, but it is available only in a limited selection of colors. Therefore, it is usually better to paint the mobile's shapes. The choice of color is greater and the cost is considerably less.

One other cardboard which should be mentioned is matt board, which is generally used for matting pictures. It is of high quality, strong, durable, and comes in two surfaces, deckled and smooth. Available in different weights, matt board also comes in single and double thicknesses as well as in several colors — sometimes with a different color on each side, which can add interest to a mobile's twirling parts.

METAL

Although there are many types of tins readily available for mobiles, there is usually a variety of tin on hand. A large coffee can, flattened out and cut into shapes, works well; as do flat pieces such as the lids and bottoms of ham tins or sardine cans.

Metal in the form of a thin sheet of galvanized iron (tagger's tin) is available at hardware stores. The best gauges to use for mobiles are 0.006 and 0.012. These are lightweight and can be as easily cut by metal shears as paper is cut with a scissors. The same metal is also available in heavier

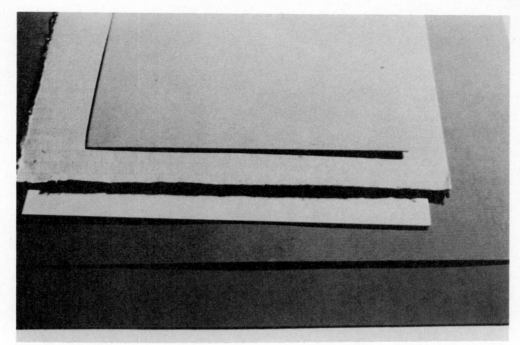

Figure 4. Various types of cardboard (above) are suitable for the construction of mobiles. Illustration board and poster board are among the best for beginners.

Figure 5. Shown is a colorful assemblage of painted cardboard. For the widest range of colors, paint the shapes yourself, instead of using colored railroad board.

gauges, which can be used in making very large mobiles or floor stabiles.

PLASTIC

Plastic, which is available in a variety of sizes, shapes, and weights, may be fused together and molded. Tubular plastic can be bent into any shape; plastic sheets can be sawed into desired shapes and then decorated for special effects.

One of the first types of plastic to experiment with is dipping plastic. This plastic, which is available in a variety of colors, adheres to the wires and stretches across the area in between. With this technique, one can construct many different shapes which are easy to manipulate. When finished, this type of mobile can be placed in an area where it can be moved by the wind. Being very light in weight, the mobile will revolve endlessly, throwing sparkling, colored shadows on wall surfaces.

PLASTER OF PARIS

Plaster of Paris may be used in mobiles to achieve more sculptured effects. It can be used alone in a mobile made solely of small flat or three-dimensional decorative shapes; or, it may be combined with other hanging objects to add weight. Plaster is often used as the focal point in a mobile made from a variety of materials. Because plaster can be a weight problem in counterbalancing, it is often used specifically for this physical characteristic.

A word of caution about plaster: always mix it in a rubber bucket. Then, when any leftover plaster dries, it can be easily removed by twisting and bending the bucket. Also, never pour liquid plaster down any type of drain. It will harden in the drain and, needless to say, cause irreparable damage because nothing will remove it. It is best to leave any remaining plaster in the bucket, then break it out when it is dry. Or, pour it into an empty wax carton and use it later to make small hand sculptures.

Figure 6. Immerse bent wire into dipping plastic, which is available in a variety of colors (above). Place the completed lightweight mobile so that the wind will cause it to move (below).

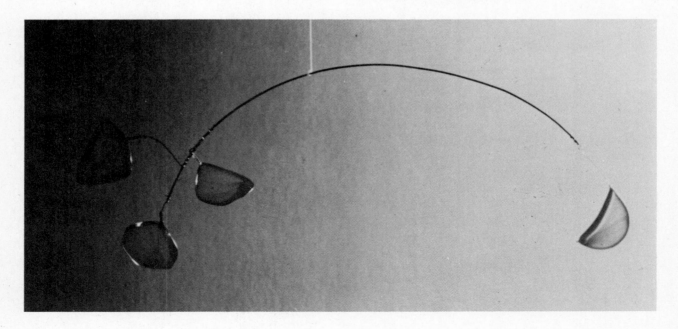

Plaster Molds

When added to water, plaster becomes a thick paste which may be used in two ways. It is generally poured into molds and allowed to "set" — that is, to go through hardening stages. The plaster first becomes very warm, then very cool, and finally bone dry. Because it will set very quickly, the plaster should be poured almost immediately after being mixed. It can be put into a variety of molds made especially for plaster; or, it can be poured into cut down, empty waxed milk cartons. After the plaster has set, the carton can be stripped away. The block or blocks may then be shaped and carved with small knives and files, and finally sanded into the desired shapes. (To start with a cylindrical shape, use a waxed paper cup.)

Figure 7. When plaster is mixed with water, a thick paste forms which can be poured into molds (below). The resulting blocks can be carved and sanded into desired shapes (right).

Dipping in Plaster

The second method of using plaster, although not the easiest, is dipping. Bend several pipe cleaners into the shapes to be used, such as letters to spell a name. Do not make up too much plaster because it will only harden and be wasted. Place the letters on an "S" hook; quickly dip each letter or shape into the plaster, coating it well, and then hang up the "S" hook to allow the letter to dry. The shapes may be dipped repeatedly, but it is advisable to let them dry fairly well before redipping. When dry, the shapes may be sanded and then spray painted, painted with a brush, or simply left plaster white.

GLASS

Glass is one of the most widely used materials for mobiles. The luminous qualities of glass are a delight when used alone or when combined with other materials — it adds sparkle and tinkling transparency to any mobile. Generally, glass is not used by the beginning mobile craftsman. This is not because glass is difficult to work with, but because a beginning craftsman must first learn balance and proportion, which are more easily attained with cardboard or paper. Once one is able to judge weight and its relationship to balance, glass becomes a highly desirable medium with which to experiment.

Glass has characteristics not found in plastic. Unfortunately, however, cutting glass is usually a problem until the technique is mastered. Glass must be cut with a glass cutter. This is a small diamond-tipped wheel which produces a "scratch" across the surface of the pane. While holding the edge of the pane with one hand, make a line on the glass. Tap along the line on the opposite side of the glass with the other end of the glass cutter. The pane should then crack along the inscribed line. Often, until one becomes experienced in glass cutting, the glass crack will deviate from the original line. Although there are also cutters made especially for circles, it is advisable to use only straight-line geometric shapes until an agility with glass is developed.

Glass is available at both glass outlets and craft centers and may be obtained in a variety of colors. Colored glass is generally thicker and often has a decorative surface. Moreover, parts of the glass may be slightly marbleized because of impurities. Although each of these features helps to create natural and decorative additions for a mobile, they are also the same features that cause glass to fracture and make it difficult to cut.

In some craft stores, glass is available in precut shapes. One may wish to experiment with these before creating original pieces. The precut shapes are those commonly made up for Tiffany lamps and other types of shades.

One other special characteristic of glass is that it is difficult to drill. This can cause problems in hanging glass pieces on a mobile. To circumvent this, merely wrap the piece of glass securely with thin wire as shown in the illustrations. Use the loose end of wire for hanging and for attaching the piece onto the mobile.

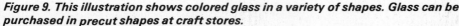

Figure 9. This illustration shows colored glass in a variety of shapes. Glass can be purchased in precut shapes at craft stores.

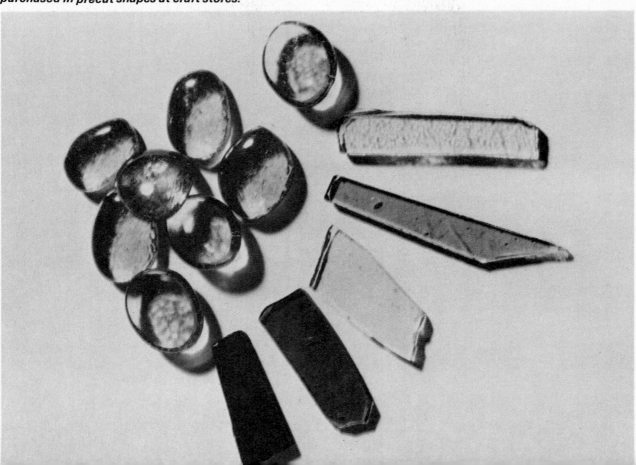

Figure 11. Experienced woodworkers can experiment with original designs. This piece was cut from two kinds of wood, glued together and varnished.

Figure 10. Inexperienced woodworkers should use a lightweight balsa wood, which is available in craft stores or hobby shops.

Figure 12. Veneers, sometimes used to make mobiles, are easily twisted and can be glued together or glued to some other surface to provide a wood texture.

WOOD

Because there are many types of wood available, wood should be dealt with in two distinct ways. For those with little experience in working with wood, the best is balsa wood, which is easily obtainable at any craft store or hobby shop. Balsa comes in thin sheets, which can be cut in various shapes with a razor blade or an X-acto knife and painted, varnished, or glazed. Because it is extremely light, balsa wood can be used to make small three-dimensional constructions or large, flat shapes. This wood also comes in a variety of block-type shapes, which can be used as is; painted and decorated; or, carved into small statues, figures, or animals.

For those experienced with woods, a wooden mobile should be easy to construct. In addition to designing and building an original one of different types of wood, experiment with various shapes. Consider contrasts of wood: try gluing two or more kinds of wood together; cut out a shape and put a clear or honey maple varnish on it.

Veneers are also used in mobiles. Available at lumber yards and sometimes through mail-order catalogs, veneers bend extremely easily and may be twisted and glued together. They should be held in place until the piece dries. Veneers can also be used as decoration by gluing them onto other surfaces, such as cardboard or plain, inexpensive woods.

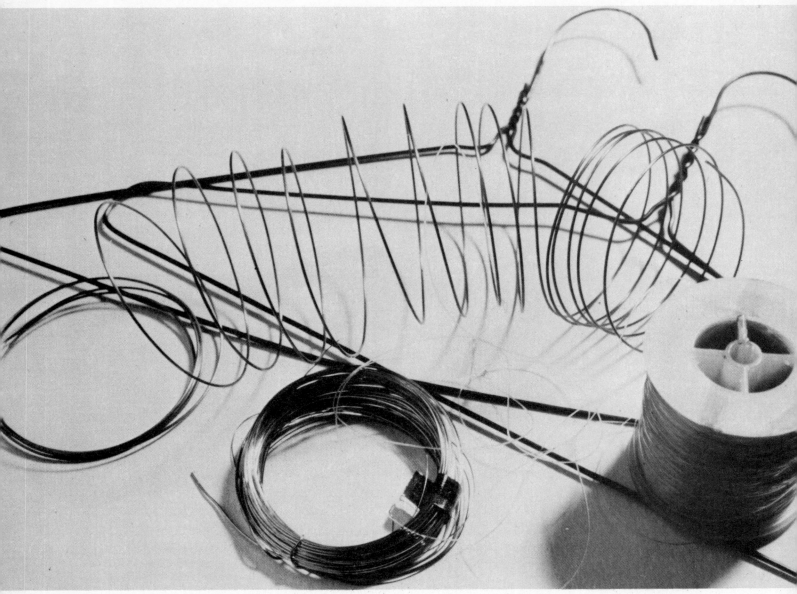

Figure 13. Of the various types of wire available (above), galvanized iron wire is best for holding the hanging pieces of a mobile. This wire can be purchased or can be appropriated from household coat hangers. Finer wire is used for attaching mobile pieces to the iron structure.

WIRE

The best wire for holding the hanging pieces in a mobile is galvanized iron wire. Although this wire will hold just about anything, one should always test first to see if it is strong enough. Obtainable at practically any hardware store, the best gauge to work with is the 12, 14, 16, or 18, depending on the weight of the materials. (The gauges refer to how thick or thin the wire is — the lower the number, the thicker the wire.) Sometimes this kind of wire is called "fencing wire" because this is its usual use. Other types of wires are also avail-

able. Brass or copper wires are usually too soft and too easy to break when bending, and they are more expensive than iron wire.

THREADS

The parts of a mobile should be suspended by some sort of thread. Many people use nylon thread, but thin nylon fishing line is better. Neither of these is overbearing in appearance and will not detract from the mobile. Try to avoid using heavy sewing thread because it breaks easily and wears out quickly.

PAINT

To decorate cardboard or paper mobiles, poster paint or an acrylic water-based paint is appropriate. Experiment with watercolors and try out various types of designs on scrap paper before painting a mobile. Needless to say, paint can add a great deal to its appearance.

For metal, an oil-based paint is necessary. Although acrylics or any water-based paint will adhere to metal at first, eventually it will chip off. Oil-based paint can produce either a flat or a shiny surface. Turpentine is used as a thinner for oil-based paint and also for cleaning brushes.

Whatever type of paint is used, buy only a small quantity. Large quantities are unnecessary because the area covered in a mobile of average size is minimal. To make a mobile more durable, spray water-based paints with clear acrylic spray and oil-based paints with spray varnish. Do not confuse these — they are not compatible. Also, spray where there is adequate ventilation at all times — spraying outdoors is most desirable.

TOOLS

The following is a list of basic tools used in constructing mobiles: (1) brushes — two or three soft hair brushes; (2) a center punch for making small holes with which to band pieces; (3) a compass for drawing circles or partial arcs; (4) a matt knife for cutting through heavy cardboard; (5) metal shears for cutting tin shapes; (6) needle-nosed pliers; (7) ruler; (8) scissors; and (9) tape measure.

Figure 14. Shown are basic tools needed for making mobiles. They include center punch, compass, ruler, mat knife, tape measure, pliers, brushes, scissors, and metal shears.

Basic Procedures

There are no set rules for building mobiles. Rather, mobiles should be a composition of parts which move within themselves and share a spatial relationship with each other. Also, there is no limit to the kinds of materials which are used for mobiles. However, some materials are more easily manipulated at first. Others may give the desired visual effect, but may not be heavy enough to work efficiently. In such cases, the materials must be weighted with small pieces of metal.

BALANCE

Balance is the mainstem of a mobile. It creates the "give" of the mobile which allows it the freedom to spin and twirl endlessly in the air. In other words, balance gives a mobile the bounce that it needs — it allows the members of the mobile to circulate within themselves freely and without obstruction.

Symmetrical Balance

There are two types of balance: one is symmetrical, the other is asymmetrical. Symmetrical balance produces very little play and is rather static. While a symmetrically balanced mobile will swing around in a circle when suspended from a point, it does not "give" enough to allow the smaller members to move easily. Symmetrical mobiles generally move as a whole rather than as individual moving parts.

Asymmetrical Balance

Asymmetrical balance allows more play within the structure. It generally consists of a counterbalance construction, such as one large ball counterbalancing two small balls. In such a construction, however, one end of the mobile will have a tendency to hang slightly lower than the other end. If the mobile hangs too low at one end, it can be balanced by moving the wires holding the objects either closer together or farther apart. One of the most important points to remember is that the play in a mobile is what gives it life and movement. This should be an important factor when designing and planning mobiles.

Figure 15. Symmetrical mobiles (left) are static and swing in a circle. Asymmetrical mobiles (right) show a great deal of movement within the counterbalanced structure.

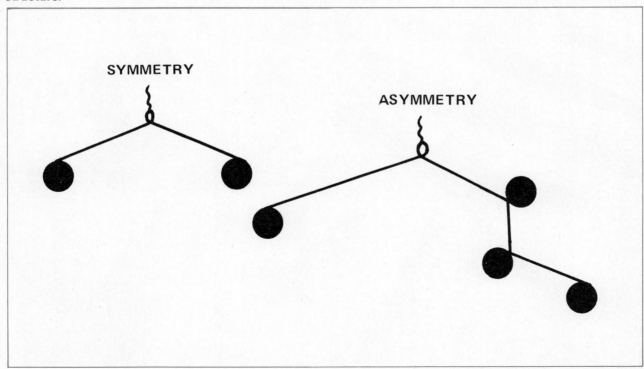

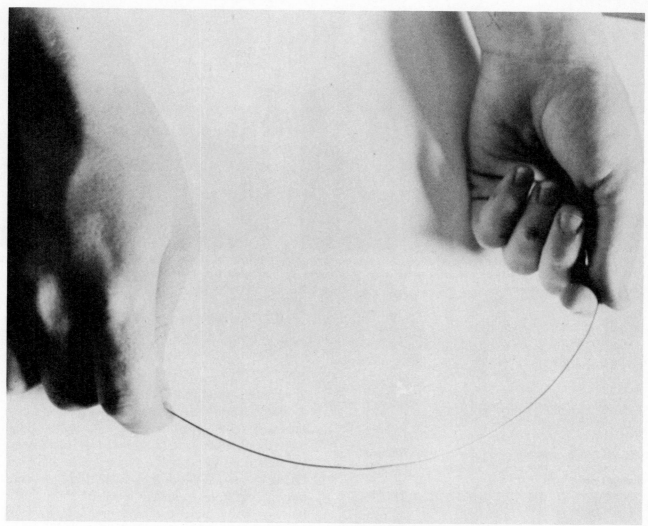

Figure 16. Most major structural arms of a mobile are curved downward, making them conducive to movement when the mobile is hung.

CONSTRUCTION

Although it is undoubtedly easier to follow instructions for a specific mobile than it is to simply read about how to make a mobile, the following general tips on making mobiles will be helpful. When ready to construct a mobile, consult the first project at the end of this article for step-by-step procedures.

Essentially, all mobiles are constructed in the same manner. Success depends upon the design and the ability to create a good balance. As mentioned previously, there are two types of mobiles: the kind which is suspended from the ceiling and the kind which is suspended independently from a small platform on a table or on the floor.

It is best to begin with two-dimensional mobiles rather than large three-dimensional shapes. The former tend to show more of a sense of movement by turning from a broad to a thin side and by having a flat surface for the wind to play against. It is also wise to start by making a completely geometric mobile: it will be much easier to grasp how to work with balance and with floating shapes.

Wire Arms

Generally the large, major structural arms which hold the mobile's parts away from each other are not straight. A gentle curve which slopes slightly down at each end gives the mobile more of a sense of play when it is hung. The hanging or the general tendency to slope down adds to the overall movement of a mobile.

Figure 17. To attach a mobile piece to the arm, punch two holes in the piece and run the end of a wire through the outer hole (above).

Figure 18. Wire is attached to another piece of a different shape (above) by the same method.

Piece Attachment

There are three ways to attach a piece of the mobile to the arm:

1. Attachment at end of arm (vertical). From the end of the curved arm bend 1/2" back toward the curve. Punch two holes in the piece to be at-

Figure 19. To attach a glass piece, wrap flexible, fine wire around it, then twist and secure at top with a small ring.

tached. Run the end of wire through the outer hole and push the bent end up through the inner hole. Bend the end flatly over onto the piece to hold it in place.

2. Attachment at end of arm (horizontal). Bend a 2" length of wire in half. Bend one piece up into a right angle 1/4" from the bent end. On the other piece, at the open end, also bend 1/4" up. Punch a balance hole through the piece to be attached. Punch a second hole 1/2" away. Slip the ends through the holes, with the long end through the balance hole. Bend the long end into a hook. Bend the short end back towards the hook.

3. Attachment for glass. Wrap flexible, fine wire around the piece of glass, twisting and securing it at the top with a small ring. This may be done at the bottom of the glass as well. An attachment for plastic is the same as for glass, except that small holes may be drilled into the plastic and connected with rings.

Hanging Mobiles

One way of hanging mobiles from the ceiling is from a light fixture. If this does not work, drill a hole in the ceiling and insert a lead or plastic plug which will expand to hold a screw. There is a flange or wing-type plug that works even better. Drill a hole about the size of the plug and insert the outside casing into the hole. Then screw the inner bolt into the plug to extend the flanges or wings. Do not tape or nail the mobile to the ceiling because it will eventually fall.

Projects You Can Do

The following are simple and varied projects. Read through them first, noting the step-by-step procedures and the illustrations accompanying them.

GEOMETRIC MOBILE

Out of cardboard, cut two 6" circles, two 4" circles, one 7" circle, and one 5" square. Paint each circle or pair of circles the same color. Paint the square the opposite color. Also needed is 16 or 18 gauge wire: two lengths of 12" each, two lengths of 16" each, and one length of 18". Remember that mobiles are always started from the bottom.

1. Take one length of 16" wire and smooth it into an arc by running the hand over the length of it several times until it is slightly arched (it is best to add 2" to the desired length of an arm to allow for the curvature). Connect one 2" circle at one end with a vertical connection and one 7" circle at the

Figure 20. Free-hanging geometric mobiles are especially attractive when they use a variety of shapes and brilliant primary colors.

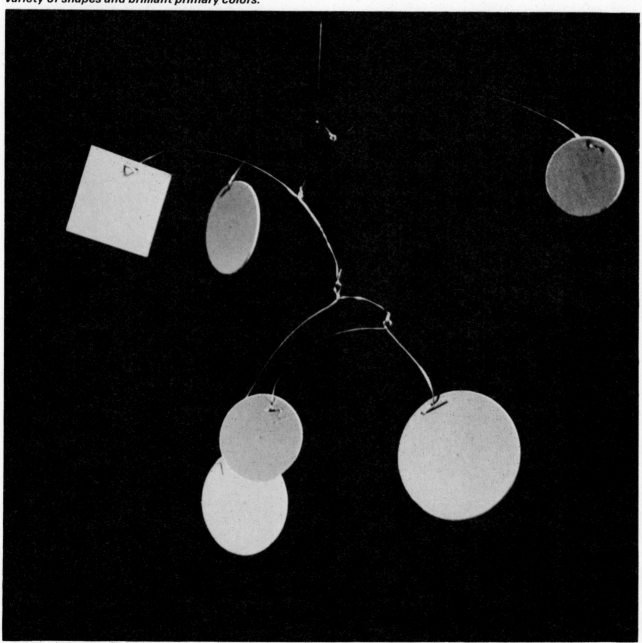

Figure 21. Children are delighted by the freedom and movement of mobiles. Because the mobiles shown on these pages use simple shapes and principles, they can be used as models for mobiles made at home.

Figure 22. *Many items collected while on a vacation will serve as eye-catching parts for a mobile. Shown is such a group of objects, including snapshots and various stones.*

other end, also with a vertical connection. Find the balance point by holding the wire arm with pliers until it is level. Construct a balance loop at that point.

2. Smooth the 18″ wire arm into an arc and loop it from the end to the balance loop just made. Vertically connect one 4″ circle to the other end. Find the balance points and loop.

3. Smooth a 12″ arm to an arc and connect it at the last balance point with a loop. At the other end, connect the 5″ square with the horizontal connection method. Find the new balance point and loop.

4. Smooth the other 16″ length of wire to an arc and connect it to the last balance point. Connect the 2″ circle to the other end, find the balance point, and loop.

5. Using the second 12″ arm, smooth it to an arc, loop, and connect to the last balance point. Add the 4″ circle at the other end, find the balance point, and loop. Run fine fishing line from the ceiling to the loop and connect the two with rings. Let the mobile hang.

VACATION MOBILE

While on vacation, people often collect small cards, sea shells, souvenirs, road maps, and snapshots. Then, when they arrive home, they have nothing to do with them except put them in a drawer and eventually throw them out. These items can be made into a very attractive mobile. One may glue snapshots to metal if other objects are heavy, or use cardboard and place one picture on each side. The same can obviously be done with sections of a road map, table napkins, or small items which need backing. Sometimes an agate or special stone can be attached by the method used for glass.

The best way to organize this kind of mobile is to first lay the materials on a table and arrange them as desired. Then determine the distance of the arcs so that each piece will have room to move after it is hung. Connect each item either vertically or horizontally or hang from fishing line, as in step 5 of the previous project. Remember, start at the bottom and work up. Continue to balance the mobile as work proceeds.

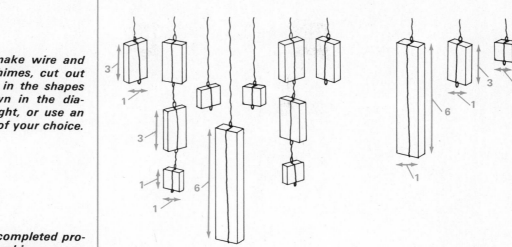

Figure 23. To make wire and glass mobile chimes, cut out pieces of glass in the shapes and sizes shown in the diagram on the right, or use an original design of your choice.

Figure 24. The completed project (below) combines movement, a variety of shimmering shapes, and a lovely, musical sound.

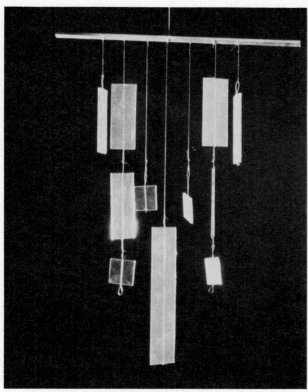

WIRE AND GLASS MOBILE CHIMES

There are several ways of approaching this type of mobile. First become familiar with the colors and shapes of available precut glass.

Using the design in the diagram or an original design, set out the pieces of glass that will be needed. Arrange a 16-gauge wire frame for the glass. Wrap thin wire around each glass and connect all units with rings, as shown in the diagram. Connect the glass chains to the proper wire. Suspend wire construction A from wire construction B. Hang the chimes on a porch or near a window.

For Additional Reading

Arnason, H. H., **Calder,** Van Nostrand.

Bland, William, **Mobiles,** Museum Press Limited, London.

Lynch, John, **How to Make Mobiles,** Viking.

Lynch, John, **Mobile Design,** Crowell.

Schegger, T. M., **Make Your Own Mobiles,** Oak Tree Press and Sterling Publishing Co.

Mosaics

The art of creating a decorative surface by placing together small pieces of various materials is as old as time and as new as tomorrow.

Mosaics, one of the oldest and most enduring of art forms, began more than 5000 years ago. It was not confined to a single area or period, but was used by many ancient peoples as a means of artistic expression.

The Sumerians of Babylonia adorned their buildings with cones of fired clay. Later they decorated various objects with silhouetted figures, cut from conch shells, set against a mosaic background of semiprecious stones. The Egyptians, Greeks, and Romans used mosaic primarily for architectural decoration, paving walks, walls, and ceilings with small stones and tiny cubes, or tesserae, of variously colored marble.

It was during the Byzantine Period in the Middle East — paralleled by the Early Christian period in Southern Italy — that mosaic art reached its height. This period is often referred to as the Golden Age of Mosaic. With Emperor Constantine's conversion to Christianity, mosaic emerged as one of the church's great mediums of expression. Artists were sent out from Constantinople to decorate the walls of great cathedrals. These artists both designed and executed their own work. Using the direct method, they worked "on location," embedding individual tesserae (cubes) of marble, precious and semiprecious stones and metals, and brilliantly colored glass into a bonding base of cement, mortar, or plaster. Their mosaic decorations, which caught reflected light, were especially appropriate for dimly lighted church interiors and for surfaces with curves, such as the curves of an apse. A radiance of vibrant, broken color seemed to emanate from the uneven surface. This new monumental style, with its religious themes, was in marked contrast to earlier symbolic art.

Through the fourth, fifth, and sixth centuries, Constantinople, Ravenna, Venice, and Rome became centers of great mosaic art. San Vitale, the Tomb of Galla Placidia at Ravenna, and the Hagia Sophia at Constantinople were built during this period. During the Middle Ages a more rigid, formalized mosaic style evolved out of strictly enforced rules designed to inspire reverence and

Figure 1. This detail is from the magnificent mosaic "Empress Theodora and Retinue," a sixth-century Byzantine work located in the basilica of San Vitale, at Ravenna, Italy. (Hirmer Fotoarchiv.)

meditation. This tendency towards abstraction and broad, simple treatment of subject matter was well suited to the technique of mosaic.

With the dawning of the Italian Renaissance in the fourteenth century, mosaic art began a decline that was to last for centuries. The indirect method, in which a "cartoon" or sketch was enlarged from the artist's drawing and copied on paper, was first used during this period. Students or assistants then glued tesserae onto the paper and transported the paper sections to the work site where they were pressed into place. The result of the indirect method was a flat, perfectly even mosaic surface; missing was all the sensitivity, directness, and originality of the old direct method.

During this period, the independent art of mosaic was gradually submerged by the dominating in-

Figure 2. This section of an intricate Roman mosaic pavement dates back to the second century A.D. (Courtesy, The Metropolitan Museum of Art, Anonymous Gift, 1945.)

fluence of painting. Mosaicists strove to imitate the methods and appearance of painting. Thus, whereas only a few strong colors were used in the best early mosaics work, color gradations increased to the point where the Vatican Studio boasted of over 28,000 different shades and tones. Moreover, the tesserae were fitted together more closely and polished smooth, eliminating the texture that is the very essence of mosaic. The art eventually deteriorated to the actual copying of well-known paintings, particularly portraits, in order to preserve them.

As economic conditions changed, less expensive frescoes replaced mosaics in architectural decoration. Mosaic art continued, but mainly in the form known as "comesso," or Florentine mosaic, fostered by the Medici family in Florence. This technique used ground and polished surfaces of natural, precious and semiprecious stones which were cut and so closely set that no spaces were evident between the tesserae. This style enjoyed wide popularity into the eighteenth century. It was not until after World War II, when mosaicists joined other twentieth-century artists in breaking with tradition, that mosaic art was again envi-

sioned as an independent and vital medium for truly creative expression. Outstanding mosaicists, such as Gino Severini and Juan O'Gorman, were keenly aware of the inherent qualities of their special medium and thought and expressed themselves in that medium. Not only did mosaic art become an integral part of architecture, but it was now viewed with interest as secular decoration and applied to such movable objects as sculpture, decorative accessories, and portable wall panels.

The mosaic artist today is no longer confined to specific materials used in rigidly prescribed methods. There is, at times, an almost indistinguishable line between mosaic, collage, construction, and assemblage. The concern of the contemporary mosaicist is not with labels, but with creative expression and the quality of that expression. Almost anything can be used to create mosaics: pebbles, sea shells, tiles, nails, glass, wood, and even the scrap of today's technological society The mosaic artist's choice of materials is as limitless as his imagination.

Common Terms Used In Mosaics

Buttering: the process of applying adhesive to the back of a tile or tessera before setting it in place.

Direct Method: the method in which individual tesserae are buttered and set by hand onto a base; or, set into a setting bed of adhesive, mortar, or cement in order to create a surface design. A sketch or color plan may be followed, but an experienced craftsman often works from spontaneous ideas.

Grout: the mortar-like material that is used to fill the spaces between the tesserae after they are set into place.

Grouting: the technique used in filling the spaces between mosaic tesserae with a mortar, cement, or other substance after setting is completed.

Indirect Method: the method in which a design is first drawn on paper onto which the tesserae are temporarily glued facedown into position. The paper, with tesserae attached, is then lowered paper side up and pressed into place on a prepared setting bed. After the mastic or mortar of the bed has hardened somewhat, the paper is moistened and peeled off. This method results in a design that is in reverse of the original drawing, unless the original drawing was sketched in reverse.

Marme: small cubes of marble; one of the oldest of mosaic materials.

Mastic: a thick, putty-like, waterproof adhesive used for setting mosaic materials.

Mosaic: the term given to a finished piece of work created by placing together small pieces of various materials which form a decorative surface or design.

Setting Bed: the layer of adhesive (*i.e.,* "white glue" or mastic), cement, plaster, or mortar into which tesserae are embedded by the direct or indirect method; also called bonding base.

Smalti: tiles cut by hand from slabs of opaque glass. Their irregular surfaces produce a highly reflective and varied mosaic surface. Also known as Byzantine tiles, Smalti are regarded as the "King of Mosaics."

Tessera: a tile or little cube of variously colored marble, glass, enamel, and ceramic used to make a mosaic. Because contemporary mosaics incorporate almost any material that can be adhered, the "little cube" definition is no longer adequate. To cover the great variety of both natural and manmade materials used by the mosaic artist today, a tessera should be defined as a fragment or piece of material used to create a mosaic.

Basic Equipment And Supplies

Most mosaic equipment and supplies can be obtained at craft and hobby departments of stores or at some art supply shops. Wood, hardware, and certain other materials can be found at lumber

Figure 3. "Moses and the Daughters of the Pharoah" is a centuries-old mosaic from the famous church of Santa Maria Maggiore in Rome, Italy. (Scala—New York/Florence.)

yards, building supply or hardware stores. Starter kits, containing everything necessary to make simple mosaic projects, are available at craft and hobby shops or at some art supply stores.

Work should be done in a well-lighted area and on a sturdy work surface. There should be adequate storage space for materials and tools. The use and limitations of the materials selected must be considered when planning a mosaic. For instance, some porous or fragile materials are not suitable for an outdoor project.

For the beginner, a great deal of elaborate equipment is not needed, but there are a few necessary basic items. These are described below.

Figure 4. The three most commonly used types of tesserae are glazed ceramic tile (left), Byzantine or Smalti title (center), and Venetian or glass tile (right).

TESSERAE

A mosaic can be made by using almost any material that can be cut and/or formed into a design and then applied or embedded onto a base. Tile has been the traditional mosaic material for thousands of years. Tiles are sold in various forms: mounted on paper with the back of the tiles covered; on a web-mesh backing that can be soaked off or glued (with the tiles still on) to a base; or loose in bulk packages. Tiles on the web-mesh backing can be cut with scissors into desired pieces or shapes; glue is then applied to the backing; and the entire area is pressed into place on a base. There are several different types of tiles available.

Ceramic Tiles

Ceramic tiles are most popular with beginners. They are the least expensive and the most easily

obtained. They come in a wide range of colors in 3/4″ squares, with either a glossy or matte (dull) finish. They are relatively easy to cut and lend themselves to a variety of projects. Porous ceramic tiles should be soaked in water and dried before use or they may absorb moisture from the embedding material and come loose.

Glass or Venetian Tiles

These tiles are economical (as well as beautiful), all-purpose materials suitable for floors, walls, panels, and small art objects. They come in 3/4″ squares with beveled edges that catch and reflect light.

Smalti or Byzantine Tiles

These are the most beautiful and the most expensive mosaic materials, and are preferred by professional traditional mosaicists. They are rectangular in shape, hand-cut from slabs of jewel-toned opaque glass, and have irregular sizes and surfaces.

Marme or Marble Tesserae

These are expensive, subtly colored cubes of marble — one of the oldest of mosaic materials.

Other Tesserae Materials

Depending on its form (sheets, cullet or nuggets, dalles or thick slabs, fragments of bottles, etc.), stained, colored, or clear glass may be cut and adhered as tile. It may also be embedded or cast. Furthermore, materials found in nature (i.e., beach pebbles, shells, driftwood, wood, dried seeds, other foodstuffs, etc.) and man-made objects selected for their interesting shape, texture, or pattern make exciting mosaic tesserae.

TOOLS FOR CUTTING AND SHAPING TESSERAE

Only a few tools are necessary for mosaic work.

Tile Cutters or Nippers

These are the basic and most widely used tools for cutting and shaping commercially prepared tiles. They are mechanically similar to a pair of pliers, with a working end consisting of two vertically aligned blades that open and close. They are

Figure 5. Basic supplies for the mosaics craftsman include tesserae materials, tile clippers, and grout. Other supplies include such common household items as sponges and toothpicks.

available at craft, hobby, and art supply stores that carry mosaic supplies and at some hardware stores. The best quality cutters are those with carbide or carboloid-tipped cutting edges, long cushioned handles, and a spring return which automatically reopens the cutting jaws.

Glass Cutter

A good ball-end glass cutter can be useful for cutting glass and thinner tiles. (It is a good idea to wear thick gloves when cutting stained glass.)

Hammer

Where size and shape of the pieces of tesserae are not important, the tesserae can be placed between several sheets of newspaper and then broken with an ordinary hammer.

ADHESIVE OR SETTING MATERIALS

In choosing an adhesive, consider the type of materials used (i.e., porous or nonporous, transparent or opaque): the function of the piece (i.e., table or tray top, purely decorative wall panel); and whether the piece will come in contact with the elements or with liquids.

Casein-Based Glues

These so-called "white glues" are versatile adhesives that set up quickly, are transparent when dry, easy to apply, and popular with beginners. They are water resistant but not waterproof.

Polyvinyl Glues

These are another type of the "white glues." They are similar to the casein-based glues and work best on porous materials. "Elmer's Glue-All" is a polyvinyl glue.

Mastic

When a strong, waterproof bond is desired, rubber-based mastic is recommended. It can be used in both direct and indirect methods. Putty-like in consistency, mastic spreads easily. It can be applied directly to the base and materials pressed into it, or each separate piece of material can be buttered on the back and then pressed firmly in place. There are two additional advantages of mastic: (1) because it does not dry as quickly as "white glue," changes are easier to make; and (2) because of its "tackiness," it can be used effectively on vertical or curved surfaces as well as on horizontal surfaces without "running." Mastic is available in beige, brown, and black tones as well as white.

Modeling Paste

A relatively expensive acrylic adhesive, modeling paste is useful for specific problems, such as small projects or adhering heavy or irregularly shaped materials. It resembles thick white putty; is easily spread with a spatula, palette knife, or tongue depressor; sets up quickly; and will adhere to practically all materials. It also works equally well on horizontal, vertical, or curved surfaces. Modeling paste may be colored by the addition of water-soluble paint. Sand, gravel, or crushed stone can be sprinkled over and pressed into the top layer for surface texture. It is conveniently water soluble in paste form but is water proof when dry.

Cement

Ready-mixed cements are best for the beginner because they are readily available at building supply and hardware stores and need only the addition of water.

Magnesite Cement

This versatile, but expensive, cement is the one preferred by many professional mosaicists. It can be used in both the direct and indirect methods. A variety of "unlike" materials can be embedded in it. And, it can be applied in thick or thin layers.

Temporary Water-Soluble Adhesives

For adhering tesserae to paper in the indirect method, it is important to use a temporary glue or paste that is strong enough to hold the tesserae in place but also easily soluble in water. A satisfactory flour-and-water paste can be made from one part flour mixed with eight parts water, boiled for five minutes, and strained.

New and Improved Adhesives

New and improved adhesives, such as latex cements, epoxy, and polyester resins, have made possible many new mosaic techniques, particularly involving the processes of casting, fusing, and laminating.

A BASE OR SUPPORT

Almost any rigid, durable surface can be used as a base for a mosaic if it is properly prepared beforehand. The surface should be dry, firm, and smooth with all bumps, lumps, grease, and dust removed.

Bases, with and without framing or edging, can be purchased at hobby, craft, or art supply stores. If making the base, consider using plywood or masonite; pottery, plates, pans; or three-dimensional sculptured forms. It is advisable to make or select a base before purchasing tesserae, adhesive, etc. After transferring the design onto the base, or onto paper the size and shape of the base, the proper amount of materials needed can be more accurately determined.

GROUT

Grout is the mortar-like substance which is worked into the spaces between tesserae after setting is completed. It is necessary for smooth functional surfaces, such as table tops and trays, and is added protection for outdoor projects.

A ready-mixed grout, which may be purchased in craft and hobby shops and some art supply and hardware stores, is good for beginners. Grout may be left white or it can be colored with dry colors available at the same stores where grout is sold.

FINISHING MATERIALS

To clean a mosaic, the following are necessary: soft rags, sponges, clear water (never use a detergent), steel wool or copper pads, sandpaper, plastic scraper, and tweezers for the stubborn bits of dried grout. Most mosaics require little or no "finishing" other than cleaning or, possibly, polishing, which enhances the natural qualities of the material. The grouted surface can be made stainproof or waterproof by coating it with a silicone polish or sealer. For pieces that are exposed to the elements or come in contact with liquids, the sealer should be renewed periodically.

FRAMING MATERIALS

Most mosaic designs, particularly wall panels, look best when left unframed. However, a frame or edging may be required for functional pieces, such as counter or table tops, or desired on a wall panel. Several ready-made frames are available in hobby and craft stores. When any framing or edging is attached it should be protected with masking tape before adhesives or cement and mosaic material are applied.

RELATED EQUIPMENT AND SUPPLIES

1. Eye goggles for protection against flying pieces of materials when cutting.

2. Spatula, palette knife or putty knife to spread mastic or cement, butter tiles, apply grout, scrape away dried grout and cement, and do many other jobs.

3. Plastic scraper, similar to a windshield ice scraper, for scraping excess dried grout or cement without scratching tiles.

4. Trowel for applying and smoothing large areas of cement or mortar.

5. Tongue depressor or "popsicle" stick for mixing and spreading.

6. Tweezers for holding and placing small tesserae.

7. Toothpicks for getting out tiny, hard-to-finish areas.

8. Screwdriver or penknife for removing any mistakes after glue, mastic, or cement has dried.

9. Buckets and plastic bowls for mixing.

10. Containers and boxes for storing loose materials.

11. Rolling pin for rolling and pressing when using the indirect method.

12. Drawing, "kraft," and tracing papers for planning and transferring designs when using the direct or indirect method.

13. Brushes for such odd jobs as grouting, sealing, weatherproofing, toning, and finishing.

14. Waxed paper, wax, grease, or oil for easy removal of cement or mortar bed.

15. Nails for nailing edging or framing.

16. Hardware cloth (also called metal builder's cloth) for reinforcing cement or mortar.

Basic Procedures

There are two traditional methods of working with mosaic materials: the direct method and the indirect — or reverse — method. For both of these methods, one must first create or adapt a design (to be transferred to a base or to a piece of heavy paper); prepare a base, support, or setting bed; cut and shape selected tesserae to carry out the design; and grout, clean, and seal the completed mosaic surface. In planning a design, simplicity should be the primary consideration. Initially, it is a good idea to stay away from complicated details and any design with rounded areas, such as a

Figure 6. These three basic designs all make use of the square. A checkerboard effect (left) is a popular favorite. Rows of squares are staggered for another design (center). For another basic design, four small squares form a larger square, which is then duplicated in rows (right).

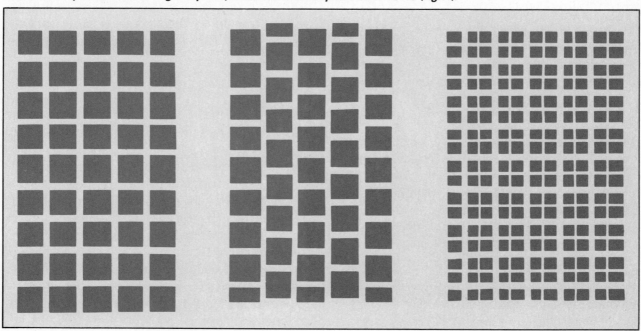

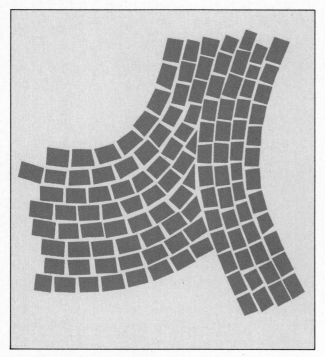

Figure 7. This is one of the basic designs for mosaic work. Note the gentle curve; it is prudent to avoid circular shapes or rounded areas when working with tiles.

Figure 8. Another basic design for mosaics resembles an abstract painting. Again, the rectangle is the geometric shape that is chosen. Several colors can be used in this design.

flower petal or the human form. Mosaic designs may be realistic representations. They can also be completely abstract or nonobjective designs developed from interwoven geometric or free-form lines and shapes. They are most successful when conceived as two-dimensional patterns, without an attempt to create illusions of depth.

The basic skills required for these procedures should not be difficult for the beginner to develop. With a little practice and experience, they can be performed with ease and confidence.

THE DIRECT METHOD

The direct method is basically the simplest mosaic method and is easier and faster than the indirect for beginners. In this method, mosaic tesserae are (1) either buttered with adhesive and set individually onto a base or support, or (2) they are embedded individually onto a base spread with adhesive or into a setting bed of cement or mortar. If desired, grout can then be used to fill in any spaces between the tesserae.

Although a rough sketch and/or color plan may be followed, the direct method is most effective

for working spontaneously from an original idea. The tesserae are placed right side up, which permits the artist to see the design immediately. Moreover, mosaic tesserae of varying thicknesses, weights, shapes, and textures may be used to create a more interesting surface. An uneven surface quality and control of light reflection, resulting in a more vibrant piece, is easily obtained by the depth and angle of placement of the tesserae.

THE INDIRECT METHOD

The indirect method is also called the reverse method because a design is first drawn or painted on heavy paper (such as "kraft" paper) onto which tesserae are then temporarily pasted or glued face down. An advantage of the indirect method is that mistakes in design are easily corrected on the paper before the tesserae are embedded or adhered. The paper with the tiles attached is then lowered, paper side up, onto a prepared base of adhesive or a setting bed of mortar. Thus the design is reversed from the original drawing. The paper is then rolled or pressed to embed the mosaic tesserae securely and evenly into the ad-

Figure 9. *A variety of geometric shapes are utilized in this basic design (above), which resembles a stained-glass window. Note that the spaces between the tiles are very irregular.*

hesive or mortar bed. After the mortar or adhesive has begun to harden, the paper backing is removed by wetting it thoroughly with a cloth or sponge and peeling it away from the tesserae.

A characteristic of the indirect method is that the mosaic surface that is revealed is level and flat, which is desirable for such utilitarian surfaces as table tops and trays. The indirect method is also used extensively in making large surface mosaics, such as murals and walls, where tesserae are put on in sections.

There are certain important things to remember when working indirectly. First, the paper on which the design has been drawn and to which the tesserae are to be pasted must be the same size as the base or setting bed to which the design will be transferred and embedded. Second, the adhesive should not only be strong enough to hold the

Figure 10. *The indirect method (below) makes use of heavy paper. Glue the tiles to the marked paper; then place the paper, tile side down, onto the adhesive base or mortar bed.*

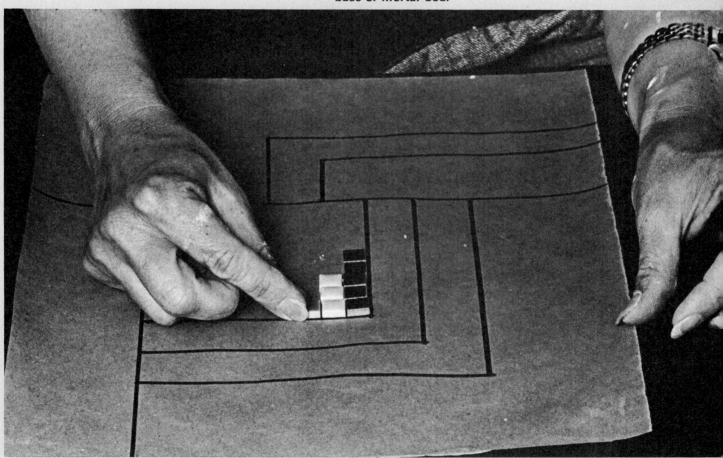

tesserae in place but easily soluble in water. Finally, if tesserae are of uneven thicknesses, the mastic, cement, or mortar should be thick enough for the thickest tile to be deeply embedded.

TRANSFERRING A DESIGN

When using the direct method, designs may be outlined directly on a base or drawn with a sharp tool or stick in a setting bed. To trace a design of the same size as the final mosaic design onto a base surface, use carbon paper or coat the underside of the sketch with heavy pencil or chalk. Then, place paper — right side up — onto the base. Tape the paper at the corners to prevent it from sliding out of position. Go over the entire design with a sharp pencil, ballpoint pen, or stylus. Remove paper, study the transferred design carefully, and select colors. Color the transferred design or mark the areas of color on the design, in order to easily follow the color plan. If freehand sketching is difficult and a design needs to be enlarged, rule off squares on the design. Mark off an equal number of larger squares on the project surface, and enlarge the design by drawing in one square at a time.

When using the indirect method, the design should be outlined on heavy paper (such as "kraft" paper) to which tesserae will be adhered. Be sure that this paper is the same size as the base to which the design will be transferred and embedded. If the design is not to be reversed when embedded, it must be drawn in reverse on the paper.

PREPARING A BASE

The surface of a mosaic base should be clean, dry, and smooth. (The one exception to a smooth surface is an especially "slick" one, such as plastic, which needs to be "roughed up" in order to provide a better adhering surface.) If the base is porous, a coat of shellac or waterproof silicone sealer should be applied to both sides of the base and let dry. This reduces the chance of warpage and also prevents moisture in the adhesive from being absorbed by the porous surface. (Loss of moisture causes the adhesive to crack and fall off.)

Hardware for hanging or installation should be attached to the base before applying adhesive and mosaic material. All edging or framing should be protected with masking tape before adhesive is applied.

PREPARING A SETTING BED OF CEMENT OR MORTAR

A setting bed of cement or mortar serves as an adhesive and as a base at the same time. For a setting bed, a box or wood form and a work surface should be prepared into which the cement or mortar will be poured. A form is a bottomless box or frame that may be loosely nailed together, or one corner may be hinged and another fastened with a hook-type latch for easy removal. About 3 to 4 inches is a good depth for a form.

If this framing-in is temporary, the box or form should be rubbed with a separating film of wax, grease, or oil. Thus, when the form is taken apart, the hardened cement or mortar slab will easily separate from it. The form should be placed on a work surface, such as a piece of plywood, covered with heavy waxed paper so that the mortar also does not adhere to it. To keep the form from sliding out of position, nails can be hammered a short distance into the work surface.

Mix the cement or mortar with water until it is the consistency of thick batter. Cement color may be added at this time to color the mixture. It is advisable to use a disposable container, such as a cleaned, cut-off plastic bleach bottle that can be thrown away afterwards. (Leftover plaster or mortar should never be poured down the sink drain.) Pour the cement mixture into the form or box to half the depth desired for the finished slab. Tap the sides of the box or form to level the mixture and to force air bubbles to the surface, where they can be broken.

To reinforce the cement slab, cut metal hardware or builder's cloth about 1 inch smaller than the base and press it into the wet mortar. Pour the second (and final) layer of mortar over the hardware cloth, tapping the sides again to level. Smooth the surface with a trowel or spatula and proceed with setting tesserae directly or indirectly into the mortar. (A design to be followed can be traced into the mortar with a sharp tool or stick, if desired.) After the cement or mortar has hardened and dried for a few days, the box or frame may be dismantled.

CUTTING AND SHAPING TESSERAE

The basic technique of cutting and shaping is the same for all types of tesserae. Hold the tessera to be cut between thumb and side of forefinger, with thumb on top for a firm grip. In the other hand, hold tile cutter or nipper far back on the handles. Hook thumb around the top handle; manipulate the bottom handle with other fingers. Open cutter and place cutting edges 1/16" to 1/8" over the edge of the tessera, away from the hand holding the tessera. The cutter edges will be at a right angle to the tessera edge and directly in its middle. Grip the tessera firmly within the cutter edges by squeezing the handles of the cutter. Give a sharp snip and the tessera will break, leaving the two pieces still held firmly between thumb and forefinger. These two pieces can then be cut to form smaller pieces.

Tesserae can be cut in any size and shape. When the cutter is used correctly, a fracture line is formed in the exact direction in which the cutter

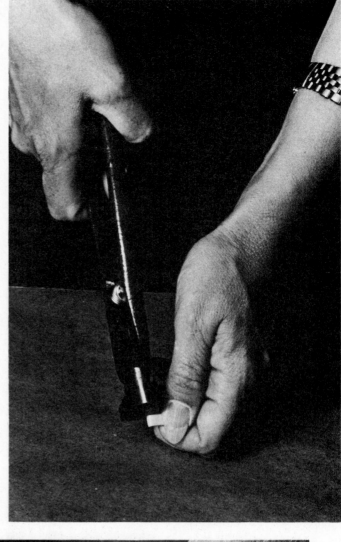

Figure 11. The basic cutting procedure is the same for all kinds of tesserae. Grip the tesserae firmly between the thumb and forefinger, as shown (above). Hold the cutter at the end of the handles.

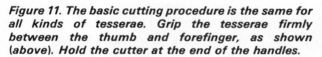

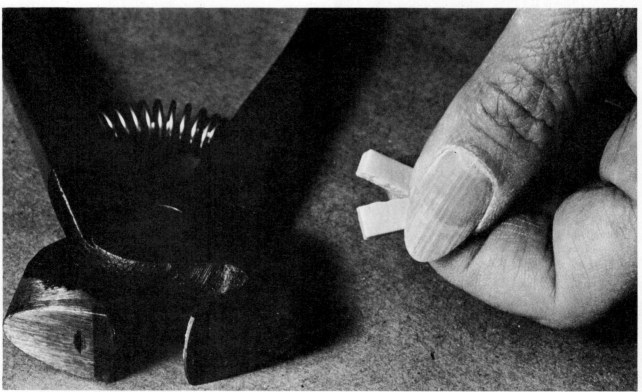

edge is aimed. For instance, placing the cutters diagonally will produce triangular cuts. Keep in mind that some tiles are easier to cut than others (e.g., ceramic tiles are easier to cut than glass tiles) and that smaller bits are more difficult to shape and handle. Therefore, small tiles are best avoided by the beginner.

GROUTING

Some artists prefer not to grout at all, feeling that the spaces between the tesserae have an interest of their own. Actually, grouting is undesirable in designs where a variety of unlike materials has been used. These are usually set in mastic or cement-type adhesives, which work their way up slightly between the tesserae.

Applying Grout

Cover all exposed wood or metal trim with masking tape. Gradually add dry grout powder to water and mix in a clean, grease-free container until the mixture reaches the consistency of heavy cream or thin batter. If colored grout is desired, add grout coloring until grout is a shade darker than desired because it will dry to a lighter color. Spread grout over the tesserae with the hand, rubber spatula, or palette knife. Make sure to

Figure 12. A soft cloth or sponge can be used (below) for cleaning grout. Steel wool is used for problem spots (lower left). Oil paint and turpentine are used to tone down grout (lower right).

Figure 13. Grout and water should be measured carefully (above left) to insure the correct proportions. Mix the grout and water (above right) until the mixture has the consistency of batter (right).

work it into all cracks and spaces. (When all cracks are filled, "tap" the project by raising it up 1 or 2 inches and gently dropping it down, thereby forcing out all air bubbles.)

Cleaning

Scrape excess grout off with hands, spatula, or dampened cloth or sponge. (Always use clear water; never add a detergent.) Set project aside to dry for about a half hour. Then wipe mosaic surface carefully with a damp sponge or cloth — this will leave a fine film of grout — and allow to set again for about 1 hour. With a soft, wet rag or moist hand, go over tesserae again with a circular motion and smooth grout between tesserae with wet fingertips. Let set another hour and then polish with a dry, soft cloth. (The drying process should never be rushed because grout that sets too quickly will become brittle and crack.) Steel wool or a copper pad, plastic scraper, and tweezers are useful for removing stubborn bits of dried grout. Dried grout can be "toned down" by brushing on and wiping off an oil stain made by adding oil paint to turpentine.

Sealing

The grout between tesserae or the entire grouted surface can be made stainproof or waterproof by coating it with a silicone or another waterproof sealer. Pieces that are used or displayed outdoors or that come in contact with liquids should be recoated with sealer periodically. The sealer can be applied with a dry, lint-free cloth or brush or simply poured onto a finished project. Let stand for a few seconds and pour off any excess. Allow to dry for about 2 hours and finally buff with a soft, dry cloth.

Projects You Can Do

Starting with a small project, such as an ashtray, trivet, or wall plaque, gives the beginner an opportunity — with a minimum investment in equipment and supplies — to become familiar with mosaic materials, to explore possibilities of basic techniques, and, to produce an interesting and satisfying mosaic piece in a relatively short time.

This simple project, using the direct method, may also be used as a coaster, paperweight, or decorative wall plaque.

Equipment and Supplies

For this project, the following items are needed: (1) one metal trivet frame 4¼" square, or four pieces of angle-shaped wood picture molding, mitered at the ends; (2) a square of 1/8" thick masonite or pressed board, cut to fit the frame; (3) 100 ceramic tiles (for example, 50 white and 50 black ceramic tiles); (4) mosaic adhesive such as white glue or mastic (approximately 2 ounces); (5) spatula, palette knife, putty knife, or tongue depressor for spreading adhesive and grout; (6) 1/2 pound of grout; (7) silicone polish or sealer; (8) 4 strips of sheet cork or felt backing if necessary; (9) masking tape 1" wide; (10) soft cloth or sponge; (11) steel wool or copper scouring pad; and (12) mixing bowl and newspaper.

Procedures

Spread newspaper on work area. If using picture molding, glue the pieces together with white glue or some other carpenter's adhesive and allow several hours to dry. (This is best done the day before doing the mosaic project.) Apply a coat of silicone sealer to both sides of the masonite square and let dry.

Put masking tape around edges of the frame to protect it from adhesive or grout stains. Then apply a ribbon of mosaic adhesive around the inside bottom of the frame. Place the masonite square into the frame, smooth side up.

If necessary, soak tesserae loose from paper backing. Soak in warm water and wipe dry.

Apply a ribbon of mosaic adhesive onto the ma-

Figure 14. To make a hot plate or trivet, the first steps are applying silicone sealer to the masonite square (top), and then placing masking tape around the four edges of the frame (bottom).

sonite along the left edge, working down from the top left corner. For example, place a black tile, ridged side down, into the adhesive at upper left corner. Next to it, along the left edge, place a white tile; then black, white, black, etc. Space the tiles in the first row by moving gently with forefinger or a toothpick.

Apply a ribbon of adhesive into the next row. Place tiles, starting with a white one at the top. Space as above. Repeat process until all 100 tiles are glued into place.

Figure 15. The next steps, shown above, are to soak the tesserae off the backing and dry the tiles. Next place a ribbon of mosaic adhesive on the masonite. The right-hand column of pictures shows the procedure for placing individual tiles, row by row, adding a ribbon of adhesive when a new row is begun. The tiles must be spaced carefully for a neat final result using the forefingers or a toothpick as shown.

Figure 16. After the tiles have been allowed to dry properly, mix and apply grout (top row). Be sure to spread the grout thoroughly to reach all areas. Follow proper steps for cleaning grout and the result is a handsome, finished hot plate (bottom row).

Wait 8 to 20 hours (depending upon humidity or dampness) until the adhesive is dry and firmly holding the tiles. Test by trying to move the tiles with the finger. When adhesive is dry, prepare grout. Put it in a mixing bowl and add water, by pouring it down the side of the bowl, a little at a time, while stirring slowly with a spoon or by hand. Mix until grout is smooth and the consistency of heavy batter. With the hand or a rubber spatula, rub the grout over the mosaic, working it into the spaces between the tiles. Clean the grout off the surface of the tiles with a damp cloth. Be careful not to scoop out any of the grout from between the tiles. Let dry for about 30 minutes.

Then wipe again with a damp cloth and, if necessary, smooth grout between tesserae with a wet fingertip. Leave to set for about 1 hour. Then polish with a dry, soft cloth.

With a sponge or cloth, clean the trivet top and edges. If necessary, scrub top with steel wool or a copper scouring pad and scrape any excess grout from the top of the mosaic with a plastic scraper, penknife, or palette knife. To waterproof the grout, rub mosaic with silicone polish or sealer. If trivet frame does not have feet, glue four thin strips of sheet cork or felt backing to the bottom of the trivet or at the four corners.

SMALL TABLE

This is a simple project, using the indirect method, that results in an attractive and useful table.

Equipment and Supplies

To make this table, you will need the following: (1) a 12″ square of 1/2″ to 3/4″ plywood; (2) a square foot of ceramic tesserae, pasted face down on paper; (3) adhesive such as white glue or mastic; (4) 3/4 to 1 pound of grout or mosaic cement; (5) spatula, putty knife, palette knife, or tongue depressor for spreading adhesive, grout, or cement; (6) mixing bowl; (7) masking tape, 1″ wide; (8) sponge, cloth, and newspaper; (9) shellac and brush; (10) silicone polish or sealer; (11) lighter fluid for clean-up, if necessary; and (12) 4 screw-on legs.

Procedures

Spread newspapers on floor beneath table frame. Shellac plywood square on both sides and let dry. Nail metal edging to plywood. Then screw legs into plywood base. Place masking tape around metal edging to protect it while working.

Check the sheet of tesserae to see that all pieces are attached to the paper and are facedown. If any have come loose, glue them back in place with a water-soluble glue or a water solvent flour paste. With the paper side down (bottom side of the tesserae up), wet tesserae with a sponge until they are thoroughly dampened.

Put grout or cement in a bowl. Add water, pouring it down side of bowl, a little at a time, while stirring slowly with a spoon or by hand. Mix until grout is smooth and is the consistency of heavy pancake batter. Pour three-fourths of the grout or cement evenly over the entire surface of the plywood.

Redampen bottom side of the tesserae. Place the entire sheet, paper side up (bottom side of the tesserae down) into the wet grout or cement. Push the paper and tesserae around until the paper is evenly spaced on the base. Push down firmly with the hand until the paper surface is level with the table top edge. Starting in the center, and using the flat of the hand, rub out to the edges of the

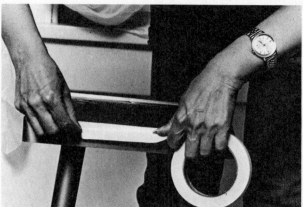

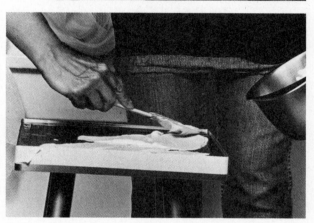

Figure 17. To prepare the table frame for this project, first shellac the wood (top). Mask the edges of the table (center) to protect them from grout; then apply grout, as shown (bottom).

paper sheet. Squeeze any excess grout or cement out over the edges. Continue until the top is perfectly level. (A flat board or rolling pin can be used for pressing and leveling.)

Let the cement or grout set for a few minutes. With a wet cloth or sponge, thoroughly dampen the paper holding the tesserae together. Let paper soak for a few minutes. Then, holding one edge of the paper between thumb and forefinger, pull it up and remove it in one piece, if possible, or in long strips. If paper continues to adhere to the tesserae, sponge it again. But, do not dilute the grout or cement with too much water, as this may weaken its consistency. If individual pieces pull up with the paper, push them down into place after removing the paper.

Straighten any pieces that are out of line. Equalize surface around any that are pushed down too far by gently rubbing hand over area around tesserae. If this does not level the surface, pry up the piece, place a bit more grout or cement into the area, and replace. Fill in any areas between tesserae with more grout or cement, redampening it if necessary, until cracks between are filled level with tesserae. Place a matting of dampened newspaper over the entire top and let the grout or cement dry gradually, usually 8 to 10 hours. The matting prevents the cement from drying too quickly and becoming brittle or powdery.

When the cement is dry, wipe off the chalky film surface with a damp cloth or sponge. If cement or grout spots remain on the tesserae, dampen surface thoroughly and rub with fine steel wool. Clean off and wipe dry. Waterproof the cement or grout between tesserae with silicone polish or sealer. Remove masking tape from the edging. Clean off any adhesive or foreign matter with lighter fluid.

Note: If desired, a mosaic of original design can be applied indirectly to the top of the table. The top can be made from personally selected tesserae rather than a square foot of ceramic tesserae.

In this case, soak tesserae in warm water for 10 to 20 minutes to loosen backing paper. Peel off paper, and dry tesserae with cloth or towel. Separate into piles by color shades. When shellac on plywood square has dried, place a sheet of heavy paper (kraft paper) on the surface. Trace outline of top and cut it out. (Cut-out shape should fit exactly the table top and barely miss touching edging.) Draw the design on the paper (backwards, if it is not to be reversed on the table top). Spread water-soluble glue (*e.g.,* Duco cement) or a flour/water paste mixture on small areas of the design and apply individual tesserae face down on the paper. Depending upon the design, it may be necessary to shape and cut the tesserae with a mosaic cutter or tile nipper before pasting them down. After all tesserae are pasted onto the paper and dry, proceed as above.

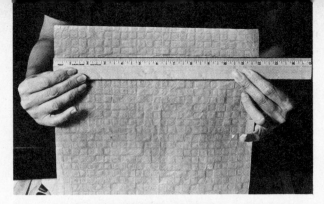

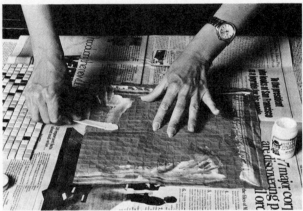

Figure 18. For a small table project, begin by (from top) measuring a 12" square on a sheet of tesserae, pasting down any loose tesserae, checking the firmness of the sheet of tesserae, and wetting the backing of the tesserae with a sponge.

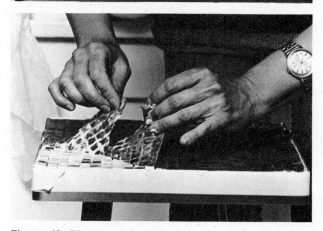

Figure 19. The next steps (from top) are to place the sheet of tesserae carefully on the table frame. Push down firmly with the fingers; then press and level with a rolling pin. Use a sponge to wet the paper backing of the tesserae sheet and then carefully remove the backing.

Figure 20. In the final stages of the table project (from top) press down tiles if needed. Also, apply additional grout if needed. The finished table has been carefully cleaned.

For Additional Reading

Aller, Doris and Diane, **Mosaics,** Lane (Sunset Craft Books), 1959.

Hendrickson, Edwin, **Mosaics: Hobby and Arts**, Hill and Wang, 1957.

Lovoos, Janice, and Paramore, Felice, **Modern Mosaic Techniques,** Waston-Guptill.

Timmons, Virginia Gayheart, **Designing and Making Mosaics,** Davis, 1971.

Williamson, Robert, **Mosaics: Design, Construction and Assembly**, Hearthside Press, 1963.

Young, Joseph, **Mosaics: Principles and Practices**, Reinhold, 1963.

Weaving

One of man's earliest discoveries and occupations, weaving is also an interesting and creative craft.

Historians write varied accounts of the origin of weaving, but it is impossible to pinpoint a date for its discovery. Since weaving materials — whether wool, cotton, or linen — are not long lasting, the examples of early woven textiles discussed here are those preserved under unusual circumstances. Studies have been made from carbonized remains of fibers, and from remains preserved by being embedded in bronze by patina and oxidation processes.

For centuries, weavers all over the world have produced woven fibers of exquisite quality and superb designs. These woven fibers have been used for personal adornment, for home decorations, or in religious sanctuaries. Carpets of Iran, Turkey, and China have long furnished color, warmth, and beauty in European palaces. The silk and brocaded fabrics of China and the Muslim world of Spain and India found their place in the attire of the European nobleman. In the past few centuries, these items have been placed in historical museums as collectors' items. It is, however, only in the recent past that fiber arts have been housed in art museums and galleries.

Artist-producers, like Anni Albers, Lenor Tawny and Clair Zeisler of America; Magdelina Abakanowicz of Poland; Yagoda Buic of Yugoslavia; and Olga de Amaral of Colombia have given a new vision to the weaving of fibers. They have enlarged it from the mere realm of usefulness to a major art form which takes on dynamic two-dimensional and three-dimensional forms. This renaissance has popularized weaving in school curricula, and adults are forming organizations to learn to weave as a leisure time activity. Museums and collectors are hunting for colonial quilts, studies are being made of ancient and past weaves, and new interpretations and uses are being found for weaving. In fact, the term weaving has expanded to such dimensions that writers are seeking a substitute word that will be more comprehensive to encompass the expanding field. The new terms "fiber form" or "the art fabric" refer to woven articles that may be woven on a loom or put together by hand, most often out of fibers. Sometimes, however, even metal and other substances are occasionally used.

Figure 1. This woven silk fabric in the Hispano-Moresque style (opposite) is an example of early 15th-century Spanish textile work. (Courtesy, The Metropolitan Museum of Art, Fletcher Fund, 1929.)

Figure 2. Weaving was one of man's first occupations. This Egyptian funerary model depicts a weaving shop scene from the Middle Kingdom. (Courtesy, The Metropolitan Museum of Art, Anonymous Gift, 1930.)

Figure 3. These sculptured pillows were designed and made by Cathy Heavans. Weaving is not only a functional craft, but it has also become a major art form.

Common Terms Used In Weaving

Apron: the material attached to the warp beam and the cloth beam and to which the warp ends are tied.

Basket Weave: the weave in which the weft weave is under and over two or more warps and then reversed in the next row.

Beam: the horizontal bars in the main structure of the loom.

Beaming: the process of putting the warp on the beam.

Beater: the frame that holds the reed and pounds the weft back into place.

Boat Shuttle: a shuttle that looks like a boat and holds a bobbin.

Bobbin: the spool, the quill, or the tube on which the weft thread is wound.

Breast Beam: the front beam over which the finished cloth passes on its way to the cloth beam.

Cloth Beam: the reel in front of the loom on which the finished cloth is wound.

Count: number of ends of thread per inch in a width of material.

Cross: the crossing of the threads of the warp on one or both ends of the warp.

Dent: an opening in the reed. Reed size is determined by the number of dents per inch.

Draft: the graphic directions for weaving.

Drawing In or Entering: the process of bringing the warp threads through the heddle eye.

Draw Down: graphic representation of a weave on paper.

Dressing: the process of beaming, entering, and sleying.

Entering Hook: a hook used to draw the warp threads through the heddle.

Eye: the opening in the middle of the heddle.

Filling: the weft threads.

Harness: a frame which holds the heddles and is an integral part of the loom.

Heddle: made of wire, strip metal, or cord, it has an eye in the middle through which each warp thread is entered.

Heddle Hook: a pliable hook used to draw the warp ends through the heddles.

Lamm: the horizontal bars or levers extending between the harnesses and the treadles to which they are attached by cords or chains.

Lease Sticks: long sticks with holes at each end; used to hold the cross in place while the loom is being threaded; also called shed sticks.

Lease Peg: the pegs in a warping board between which the cross is made.

Overshot: any thread, warp, or weft which skips or floats over two or more threads and which creates the pattern in the cloth.

Plain Weave: often referred to as tabby weave, the weft weaves over and under one warp.

Ply: the number of strands wound together to form a thread or yarn.

Reddle: a wooden bar with nails or pegs every 1½ inches used to spread the warp threads to the correct width and to direct them in a smooth line onto the beam; needed for warping from back to front.

Reed: the comb-like part of the beater which holds the threads an equal distance apart, determines the fineness of the cloth, and helps to beat the weft into place; size of the reed may range from 20 to 4 dents per inch.

Reed Hook: a hook to draw the threads through the reed.

Reeding: the process of drawing each warp thread through its respective dent in the reed.

Repeat: a term to denote a unit of the pattern in the warp or the weft which is used several times to make a whole design.

Selvage: the edge of the cloth covered by the weft ends so there are no raw edges; there are usually more threads per inch to the selvage than the rest of the cloth.

Shed: the opening in the warp threads between which the shuttle and the weft are passed.

Shuttle: used to wind the weft on and to carry the weft back and forth through the shed. Kinds of shuttles: stick — flat stick on which weft threads are wound; boat — boat-shaped shuttle with a bobbin that holds the weft thread; and rug shuttle — that which holds heavy and longer lengths of yarn for rug weaving.

Figure 4. This intricately detailed Medallion rug dates back to 16th-century Persia. (Courtesy, The Art Institute of Chicago, Gift of Mr. Joseph V. McMullan.)

Figure 5. This charming garden carpet is an example of early 20th-century Caucasian rug weaving. (Courtesy, The Art Institute of Chicago.)

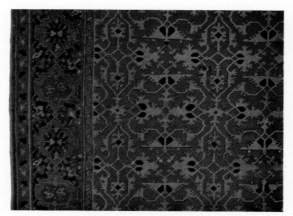

Figure 6. This detail of a 16th-century Lotto rug, probably from Usak, Turkey, illustrates the traditional Lotto design of yellow arabesques on a deep-red background. (Courtesy, The Art Institute of Chicago.)

Skein: a hank or a loosely coiled length of yarn.

Sleying: the process of placing the warp through the reed.

Spool Rack: a rack or frame which holds spools of yarn.

Tabby: a plain weave.

Tapestry Weave: a weave in which the warp set is not dense, so that the weft packs and covers the warp threads.

Tension: the tightness or stretch of the thread during the process of weaving.

Tie-Up: that part of the draft which shows combinations of harnesses used; also refers to the tying of the lamms to the treadles in setting up a loom.

Treadle: the peddles at the bottom of the loom which operate the harnesses.

Twill Weave: diagonal pattern on the surface of a fabric made of either two threads up and two down, or three down and one up.

Warp: the vertical or lengthwise threads.

Warp Beam: the beam at the back of the loom on which the warp is wound.

Warp Chain: the looped or chained warp that has been taken off the frame or warp reel; it is made like a crocheted chain stitch and prevents the warp from tangling.

Warping: the process of putting the warp on the beam.

Warp Ends: refers to numbers of threads in warp.

Warping Frame: a wooden frame with pegs evenly spaced on which small warps can be wound.

Weft: the yarn or thread interweaving with the warp to make a fabric; also known as the "woof."

Basic Equipment And Supplies

Early man wove with very basic equipment. In African, Mexican and Navajo societies, the equipment for weaving is still very basic, consisting of a simple device to stretch a warp and another device to weave the weft into the warp. In fact, the very expensive carpets of Turkey and Pakistan are woven on very simple structures.

LOOMS

There are many different types of looms. For the convenience of the modern home and schools, a floor loom — especially a rising shed or Jack loom — or a table loom is recommended. The projects listed in these pages may be woven on either of these, or on a self-structured back strap loom or a stretcher frame.

For most kinds of fabric a four-harness Jack loom is most suitable. Floor looms come in varied widths and a 36-inch floor loom is adequate for a home weaver. Table looms take less space and can be folded away. A 15- to 20-inch table loom can weave 15- to 20-inch fabric in lengths from 8 to 10 yards. Table looms cost approximately $100 and floor looms $300-$500. The *Shuttle Spindle and Dye Pot* magazine of the Handweaver's Guild of America will provide addresses for information on purchasing looms and other weaving equipment.

Back Strap Loom

These earliest and most primitive looms consist of two wooden beams between which the warp threads are stretched. One beam may be attached to a tree, a door knob, or any kind of a hook. The other one is strapped to the waist of the weaver with the help of a belt. This type of loom is used for small widths such as belts and bands.

Floor Looms With 4, 6, 8, 10 or 12 Harnesses

These looms can weave more than one layer of cloth and very wide fabrics. The warp runs horizontal and the sheds are opened by treadles attached to the harnesses through the lamms. The beam that takes up the warp may be straight or sectional. The latter is easier to warp on. There are two main types of floor looms. (1) Jack Loom — the harnesses on this kind of loom function independently and are supported by lamms which are tied to treadles. When these treadles are pressed, they raise the lamms which in turn raise the harnesses. This is also called the rising shed loom. (2) Counter Balance Loom — the harnesses on this type of loom operate in balance with each other, hanging from a bar on top of the loom. When one harness is raised, the connecting harness is lowered. With this type of loom, it is easier to weave with the patterned side of the fabric developing

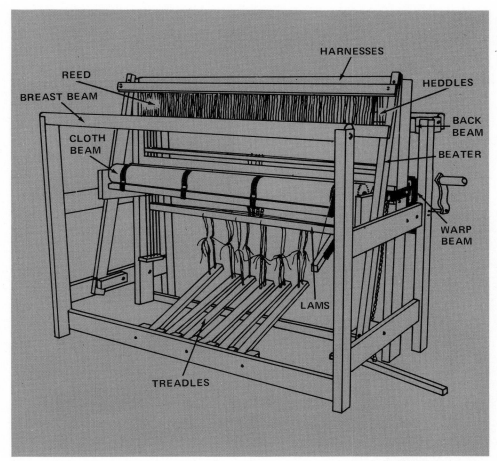

Figure 7. Each harness of a Jack loom can operate independently. This allows for production of both balanced and unbalanced weaves. This type of loom is also referred to as the rising shed loom.

on the bottom side of the warp. The shed opens by the sinking of the harnesses instead of rising as in the Jack loom. This action is controlled by the treadles and the lamms.

Table Looms

The width of this loom runs from 8 to 20 inches and it is available in two, four, or six harnesses. The sheds are controlled by levers. The four-harness table loom will produce practically any type of weave.

Other Equipment Used With the Loom

In addition to lease sticks, a bobbin winder, a reed hook, a heddle hook, and heddles, other materials that you will need when using a loom are:

1. Loom Bench. When using a floor loom, it is advisable, although not necessary, to have a loom bench on which to sit straight up and be able to take a good grip of the beater.

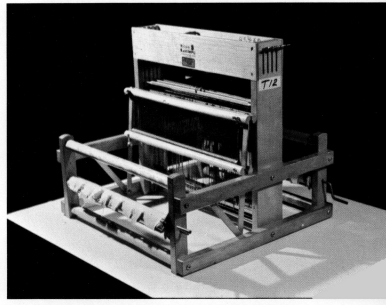

Figure 8. Several factors should be considered before purchasing a loom. This table loom has four harnesses and will weave most types of weave. It is moderately priced and can be easily stored.

2. Warp Board. This is a frame with sturdy pegs on which a length of warp is prepared.

3. Shuttles. Used to wind the weft on, shuttles are available in various types.

4. Warp Sticks. For looms without a sectional warp beam, warp sticks, made of light wood, are needed to keep the surface of the warp smooth and the tension even. Strips of paper may be substituted for these.

5. Reeds. A loom usually comes with one reed. Reeds are of different sizes: 15, 12, 10, or 8, referring to the number of dents per inch. The higher the number, the finer the reed. A 15-dent reed will allow for more threads per inch, indicating the use of finer yarns. A reed may be sleyed (threaded) single, double, triple, or alternately double to accommodate a particular number of threads per inch and the weight of the yarn.

Figure 9. Equipment needed for weaving (above) includes warp sticks, lease sticks or shed sticks, a bobbin winder, and a variety of shuttles. A warp board (left) is used to prepare the lengthwise threads, which are wound around spaced pegs. Reeds (below left) come in a number of sizes, allowing for varying numbers of threads per inch. The heddle hook (below right), generally made from pliable metal, has a wooden handle. The flat reed hook can be metal or plastic.

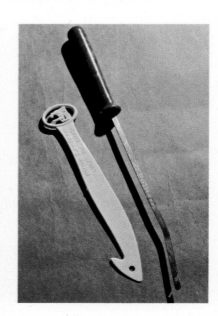

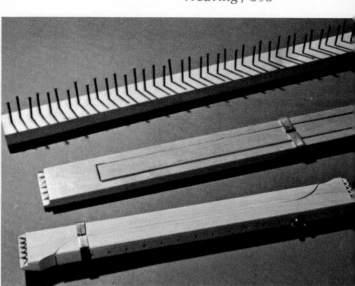

Figure 10. The reddle or spreader (above right) is a wooden bar with nails inserted, used for spreading and directing warp threads. The spool rack, ball winder, and skein holder (above left) all facilitate handling the yarn. Basic supplies probably already in the home (left) include scissors, straight pins, a tape measure, a crochet hook, and a comb. A variety of fleece and fibers, natural and artificial, are available to the weaver (below).

ADDITIONAL EQUIPMENT

The above listed items are adequate equipment for a beginning weaver. Additional equipment to facilitate weaving would include a skein holder, spool rack, ball winder, a spreader or reddle, and a stretcher. Additional small equipment that is always necessary includes: tape measure, a sharp pair of scissors, straight pins, large-eyed needle such as used in knitting, and a comb to comb out tangled yarns. These are implements that should always be kept handy. For the advanced weaver, a sketch book and graph paper with 1/8-inch squares will be needed for designing and pattern drafting.

Other weaving materials include yarns, made either of such natural fibers as cotton, silk, wool, jute, sisal, and hemp; such man-made fibers as nylon, rayon, or acetate; and a combination of natural and synthetic fibers. Furthermore, contemporary weavers are using almost anything (e.g., grass, hair, metal wires) and present technology produces unlimited textures and colors of yarns.

Although generally any kind of fiber may be used for the weft, the warp needs to be more controlled. For a beginning weaver, it is helpful if the warp fibers are strong and smooth. Suggested warp materials are carpet warp, pearl cotton, linen warp, weaving worsted, and knitting yarn.

The materials for the weft depend a great deal on the purpose for which the woven object is being used. For example, wearing apparel cannot be too coarse unless worn over other garments; scratchy materials will cause marks on wood and glass. Smooth yarns woven with the warp materials mentioned above will produce smooth fabrics, but the quality of the weaving can be changed considerably with textured weft yarns.

Color in the woven fabric is determined by the weft and the warp colors, except in a warp-faced fabric. The weft thread plays the most important part in determining the color effect. Texture, also, is decided by the selection of the weft material. Suggested weft materials are knitting wool, rug yarns, animal hair, and novelty yarns.

The material listed under warp materials can also be used as weft or as alternating wefts with other weft yarns. When used with the same warp they will produce an even woven fabric.

Figure 11. The beginning weaver should select strong, smooth warp fibers (left), such as knitting yarn, carpet warp, linen warp, and pearl cotton. Selection of the weft materials (above) depends partly on the function of the finished woven object. Novelty textured yarns (below) add interesting effects.

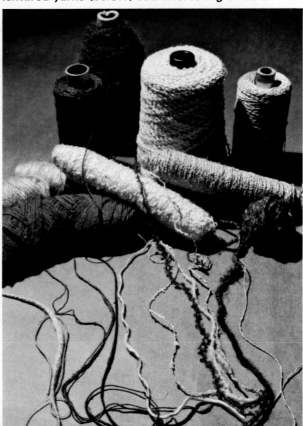

Basic Procedures

Weaving begins with two sets of yarns: the warp and the weft. The warp is a set of threads which is stretched taut; the weft thread is woven into these to form patterns on the surface of the cloth. The interlocking of the two sets of threads forms the cloth. Although an experienced weaver finds short cuts for dressing the loom, a beginner, after selecting warp and weft materials, will do well to follow the step-by-step procedures described here.

CALCULATING THE WIDTH AND LENGTH OF WARP

The first step is to determine the width and length of a given woven piece. There is usually a 1-yard wastage of warp length on a floor loom; some of this length is taken in tying the ends and some cannot be woven. There is further allowance to be made for weaving take up and shrinkage. This will depend upon the weight of the yarn, the density of the warp, and the weaver's hand. At least 2 extra inches must be allowed for a 1-yard width and 3 inches take up for every yard of length. This can be calculated as follows:

Desired finished width = 30".

Desired finished length = 3 yards.

Calculated width of warp = 30 plus 2 = 32 inches.

Calculated length of warp = 3 yards plus 1 yard (loom wastage) plus 9 inches (take up) = 4¼ yards.

To facilitate warping and to be safe, one would increase this length to 4½ yards. If desired, add another 1/2 yard for experimentation.

Calculating the Total Quantity of Warp and Weft

To calculate the above, it is first necessary to determine the type of fabric to be woven (light or heavy weight) and then to choose the appropriate materials for warp and weft. Next, determine the length and width of material to be woven, which depends on the size of loom available. Example: Jacket material woven on a floor loom 36 inches wide. Weight desired - medium weight. Width of fabric needed - 30 inches. Length of fabric needed - 3½ yards. Warp material - 2 ply linen, cotton, wool, or mix. Weft material - homespun or craft spun with cotton or linen for tabby. Width 30 inches plus 3 inches (weaving take up and shrinkage) = 33 inches.

The total yardage is then calculated as follows:

33"	(width of warp)
× 15	(number of ends per inch)
495	(number of ends in the width)
+8	(selvage reinforcement)
503	(total number of ends)
× 5 yds.	(3½ yards length + 1 yard loom wastage + 1/2 yard weaving take up and allowance for experimentation)
2515	(total yardage)

There are about 2000 yards to a pound of 5/2 cotton: approximately 1½ pounds of cotton will be needed for the warp. The chosen weft is a heavier yarn and comes 700 to 1000 yards to a pound: the amount needed will be approximately 3 pounds.

PREPARING OR WINDING THE WARP

The next step is to wind off the warp to prepare for putting it on the loom. Using the previous example, the amount of warp needed is 5 yards with a total of 503 ends. This will be prepared on a warping board or a warping reel. The distance between each peg on a warping board is 1 yard. Hence, for a 5-yard warp start at peg A, go over

Figure 12. Before putting it on the loom, wind off the warp on a warping board or a warping reel.

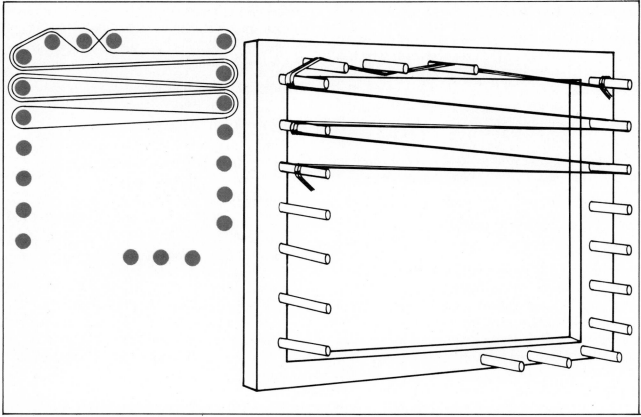

Figure 13. To prepare the warp yarn, start at peg A and follow the lettered sequence (right). Then, wind the yarn back around the pegs to A as shown (left). Continue this process for the desired number of lengths.

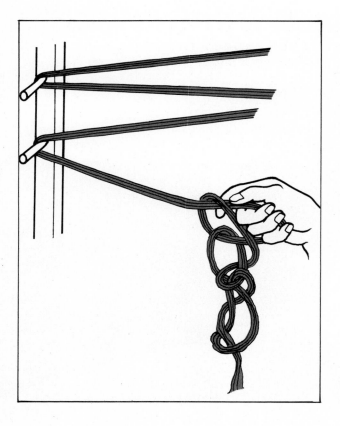

peg B, under peg C, then around pegs D, E, F, G, H, and I. Return the strand of yarn to A, going around pegs I, H, G, F, E, and D but this time *over* peg C and *under* peg B to peg A. By doing this, a cross is formed between two ends of threads in the middle of pegs B and C. Continue this procedure until 25 such groups have been built up. There will now be 500 ends. Add another 3 ends for a total of 503. Insert two lease sticks on the two sides of the cross and tie their ends about 1/4 inch apart. Take off warp from warp board by making a chain. For security insert the lease stick ends into the last chain.

Figure 14. After the warp lengths have been wound on the warping board, they are removed by the chaining method. The yarn is looped upon itself to form continuous links.

DRESSING THE LOOM

A loom can be dressed front to back, back to front, or by sectional warping. Only the first method will be described here.

Reeding the Warp

Since it was determined to use 15 warp ends per inch, choose a 15-dent reed which is 36 inches long (this information is noted on the end of the reed, as 15-36). Find the center of the reed and mark it with a string; measure 16½ inches to the right of this tie and mark similarly. Place the reed on the edge of a table and tape it so it juts out about 2 inches from the table. Pull off the looped end of the chained warp from the lease stick, lay the prepared warp with the short end to the front, and tape in place. Cut through the looped end facing the front and start drawing the warp ends through the reed where it was marked with a reed hook. Remember 4 selvage ends were doubled

Figure 15. In dressing the loom as instructed, use a 15-dent reed that is 36" in length. Tape the reed to the table, overlapping the edge, and work the chained warp from the lease stick.

Figure 16. It is important to thread the reed correctly to prevent the warp yarns from becoming tangled. Use a reed hook to draw the yarns through the sections of the reed (insert, lower right). The schematic drawing of the loom shows how the warp yarns travel through the different parts when warping from front to back.

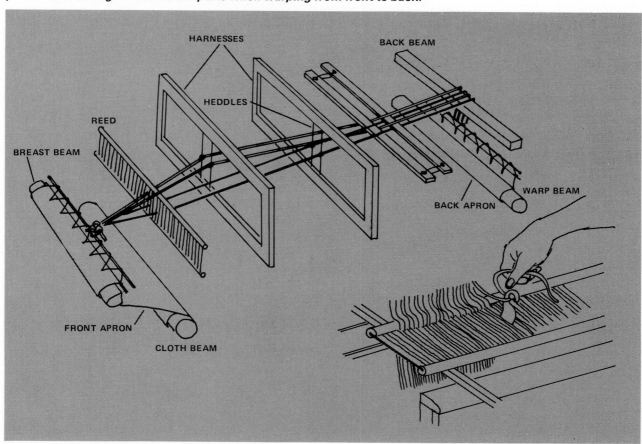

on each end. Therefore, the first eight ends will be reeded double through four dents. The rest of the ends will be drawn one at a time through the reed until the last eight threads are reached. These will again be doubled through the dents. The crosses are now useful as the weaver can pick up each thread of the warp in a consecutive manner from the lease stick, and the yarns will therefore remain in order. This is an important step so be sure that the warp ends picked up come to the reed, one from above the lease stick and one from below in consecutive order. Every 1 to 1½ inches, check on the order of the threads and tie the ends with a slip knot. The ends of the warps pulled through must be of equal length. This will make the next step easier.

Threading the Heddles

Once the reed is threaded correctly, the warp will not get tangled. Pick up the warp and the reed from the table and using both hands, transfer them to the loom. Rest the reed in the beater with the short ends of the warp to the rear and towards the heddles. Bolt the top bar of the beater in place. Pull the lease sticks to the breast beam and tie the second lease stick to the beam on each end. If the loom allows the removal of the back beam, take it off in order to facilitate heddling. Move the bench to the back of the loom and start pulling each

Figure 17. Place the reed in the beater, making certain that the short ends of the warp are at the back toward the heddles. Then bolt the top bar of the beater.

warp thread through the prescribed heddles (determined by the pattern draft, which will be explained later). It is important to check on the order and regularity of the warp on every repeat of the pattern or about every inch of warp and to tie the bunches in slip knots.

Figure 18. The manner in which the yarns are threaded through the heddles is determined by the weaving pattern. While holding the yarns through the fingers, draw each warp yarn through a heddle eye with a sley hook (left). After threading one pattern unit, tie the yarn ends together in a slip knot (right).

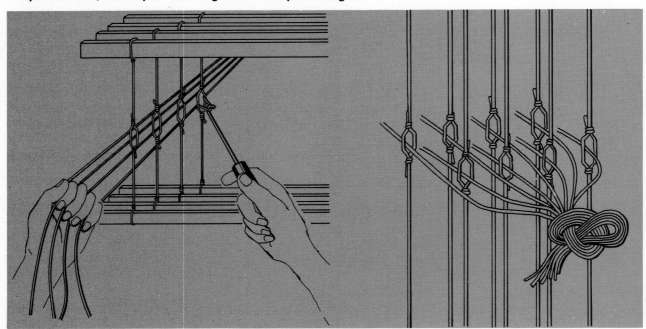

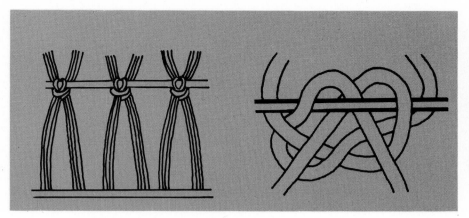

Figure 19. After the warp ends have been drawn through the heddles, they are tied in bunches to the apron bar. Split the bunches in half and tie the warp to the bar with a weaver's knot (right). Begin in the center and alternate the knots to each side until all the warp ends are tied (left).

Tying the Warp

After all the warp ends have been drawn through the heddles, replace the back beam. Bring the apron bar over the back beam and tie the warp to this apron bar in small bunches, using a weaver's knot. It is advisable to begin by tying in the center of the warp and alternately working towards the selvage. This is done by taking 1 to 1½ inches of the warp from the center, undoing the slip knot, making sure the ends are even, and then tying it in a weaver's knot to the apron bar.

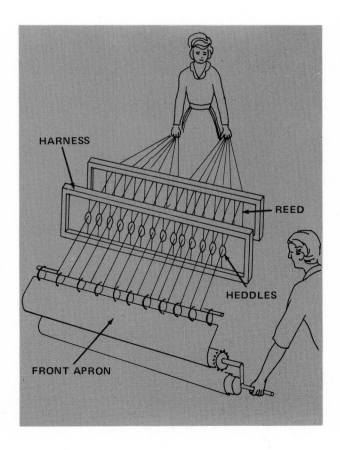

Beaming the Warp

When the entire warp is tied to the warp apron, move to the front of the loom, push the beater towards the harnesses, and start easing the warp tension. This is done by picking up six to eight 1-inch bunches of warp and pulling the ends taut by finger combing or with a comb. Do this for the entire width. When the entire warp is an even tension, start winding it onto the warp beam by cranking the warp onto the warp beam as far as it will easily slide. Continue to comb the warp and to wind it on until only enough length is left in the front of the loom for tying to the cloth apron. Cut the folded ends and bring the cloth apron over the breast beam as with the back apron. Tie these ends to the cloth apron, with a very taut tension. Test for even tension by moving the hand back and forth over the warp — any slack areas can be corrected at this time.

(Note: The above tying method is for a sectional warp beam. On the straight beam or the table loom, folded paper must be inserted between each round of the warp on the warp beam; on a floor loom that has a straight warp beam, warp sticks are better than paper.)

PREPARING FOR WEAVING

Filling the Shuttle or Bobbin

The first step in preparing to weave is to wind the weft threads on a shuttle. If the weft thread is

Figure 20. It is helpful to have a person stand in front of the loom to hold the warp yarns. While the yarns are being held tautly in two bunches, the warp beam is being cranked to wind the warp yarns.

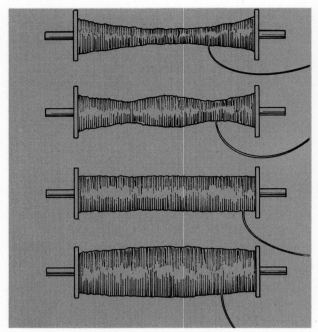

Figure 21. As the spindle of the bobbin winder turns, the weft thread is wound onto the bobbin. The weft yarn should be guided by hand as it is being wound.

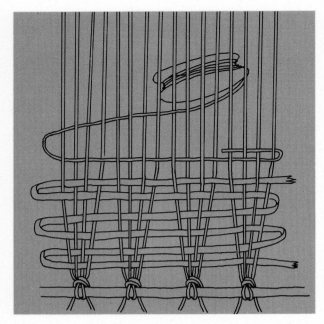

Figure 22. A strip of coarse material is run under and over each warp thread before starting the actual weaving of the weft threads. This will spread the warp threads evenly across the loom.

heavy, use a flat shuttle; for a thin yarn, wind it on a bobbin for the boat shuttle.

One usually needs a thin yarn equivalent to the warp for the tabby weft and a heavier thread for the pattern weft. So it is a good idea to have shuttles filled with both kinds of yarns. Bobbins are not expensive and are available in wood, plastic, or paper quills.

The Tie Up for Opening a Shed to Weave

Once the warp is evenly stretched from the cloth beam through the reed and heddles to the warp beam, the alternate threads of the warp need to be raised and lowered and the weft thread woven into them.

This is done by raising one set of alternate harnesses which opens a shed for the weft to pass through and to be beaten in place by the beater. Then this action is reversed by bringing up the lower threads and locking another weft thread in place in the next shed. Normally for a tabby weave, harnesses 1 and 3 will be raised first and are called tabby a; harnesses 2 and 4, raised in alternate succession, are called tabby b.

The harnesses are controlled by levers on a table loom and by treadles on a floor loom. Usually a four-harness loom has six treadles which are tied

(technically referred to as the "tie up") to the harnesses in arrangements that will conveniently weave certain patterns. For a beginner it will be well to tie the treadles and harnesses in the following sequence, starting from the right tie: treadle 1 to harness 1 and 3 (tabby a); treadle 2 to harness 1; treadle 3 to harness 2; treadle 4 to harness 3; treadle 5 to harness 4; treadle 6 to harness 2 and 4 (tabby b).

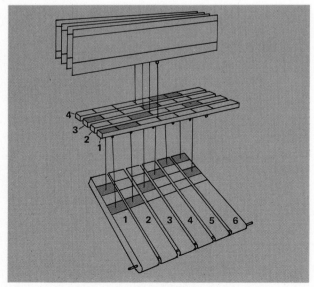

Figure 23. There are usually six treadles and four harnesses on a floor loom. These are tied in arrangements to weave a certain pattern. This tie up is used for a tabby weave.

Now the two basic treadles are to the right and left and there are single controls for the four harnesses.

Checking the Threading Order and Correcting Errors

Now the loom is ready for weaving, but first it is necessary to check for threading errors such as a missing dent; having more threads in a dent than required; missing a heddle in the pattern sequence; repeating a heddle threading in the pattern sequence not needed; having threads crossing between heddles or behind the reed.

These errors occur even with professional weavers and are all correctable. To check for any of these, treadle on the tabby treadles in alternate sequence and see whether the threads so raised lift in a regular sequence; look behind the beater or from the side of the loom through the shed to see if the shed is clear — if not, there may be a crossed thread; try weaving a tabby pick to see if a mistake shows up. Sometimes a threading mistake may be in the threading schedule, which will only show up in the pattern weave.

Correct these mistakes by rethreading the particular ends or if necessary by taking some threads out or adding a new warp thread or heddle. New heddles may be tied to the correct harness by making a string heddle or using a repair heddle which may be bought from a loom supply company.

Following a Pattern or Threading Draft

A drafting system is a way of noting the order in which each end of a warp thread or a group of warp ends will be threaded through the heddles. It shows how many harnesses a pattern will need, in what order they should be raised to produce a certain pattern, and the general outline of the weave pattern. The writing of these drafts may vary because they do not follow a universal pattern.

The draft used here will be written from right to left. The Xs on the graph will mean harnesses and the combination of harnesses, the / mark means treadles, and the darkened areas warp threads (assuming the weaver is working on a Jack loom. If a counter balance loom is being used, the dark-

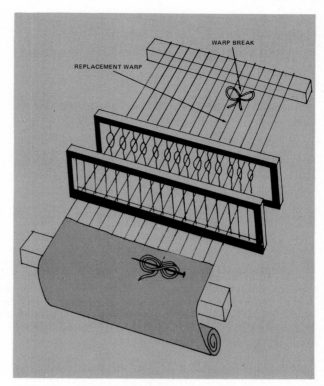

Figure 24. When a warp yarn breaks on the loom, it can be spliced with a new yarn length. Remove the old yarn from the heddle and reed and attach a new piece by tying the ends at the back of the loom.

ened areas in the draw down will signify weft threads).

The drafts explained are for very basic weaves: the plain weave or tabby weave, the basket weave, the twill weave and its simple variations.

Instructions for Reading a Draft

The first four horizontal lines on the draft indicate the harnesses. The threading draft is read right to

Figure 25. A heddle can be replaced or a new one added to correct a threading error. A heddle jig, consisting of four pegs spaced on a board, is used to wind and knot a piece of string for the new heddle.

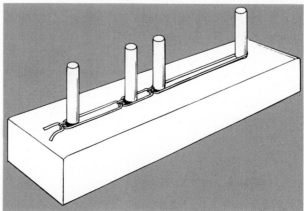

left and from bottom to top. Harness No. 1 on the bottom of the four lines is the harness in front of the loom. Harness No. 4 on the top is the harness on the back of the loom.

The threading draft for the first four weaves — (1) plain or tabby weave; (2) basket weave; (3) 2/2 twill; and (4) 3/1 twill — is a straight draw, meaning that the first warp thread enters through the heddle on harness No. 1, the second warp thread enters the heddle on harness No. 2, the third warp thread enters the heddle on harness

No. 3, and the fourth enters the heddle on harness No. 4. These are indicated on the draft by blocked squares, reading from right to left and bottom to top.

Check marks on the right of the draft mean the combination of harnesses needed to weave a pattern. These are read from top to bottom. In the draft for tabby it will read first harnesses 1 and 3, then harnesses 2 and 4. This is commonly called the "tie up," i.e., the order in which the harnesses are connected with the treadles. However, for a table loom this will only indicate the combination

Figure 26. A draft must be prepared before a weaving project is begun. The harnesses are represented horizontally across the top. The check marks indicate the number of harnesses needed to weave a certain pattern. The marks should be read from top to bottom, harness number four is located at the back of the loom. The threading draft shows how the heddles are to be threaded. It is read from right to left and from the bottom to the top. The treadling order is marked to show the way in which the harnesses are tied and the order in which the treadles are used. The drawn down or weave draft is a system of blocking the graph to show how the weaving pattern will look.

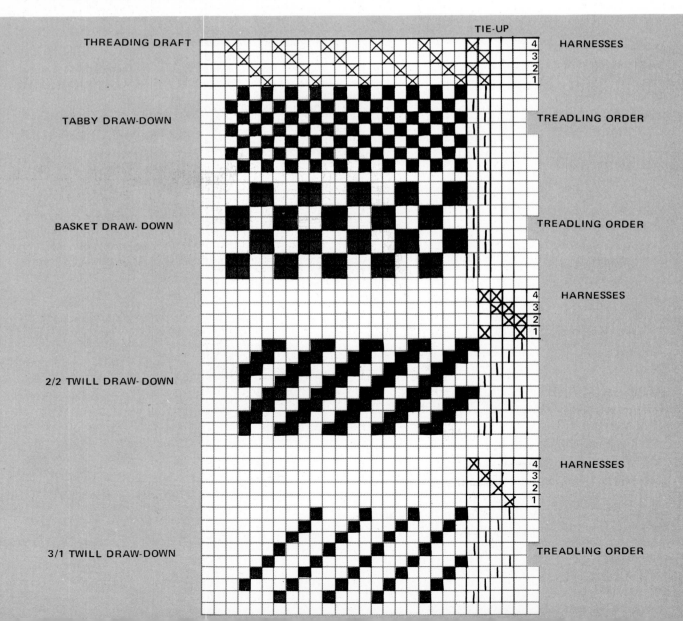

of harnesses to be raised with the help of the levers.

The marks below this indicate the treadles to which these harnesses are tied and the sequence of their use. These are also read from top to bottom.

The blocking system below the threading draft shows how a certain weave will look — this is called the weave draft or draw down.

Explanation of the Drafts

For a tabby or plain weave (draft I), the threading order is a repeat of 1, 2, 3, 4. The treadling order is a repeat of harnesses 1 and 3 followed by 2 and 4. The weave draft or the draw down shows four repeats of the above treadlings which makes the even tabby surface, *i.e.*, one thread up, one thread down.

The basket weave (draft II) is a development of the tabby weave but more difficult to show on a draft. In this weave the treadling order takes up the opposite harnesses rather than alternate harness as in the tabby. Harnesses 1 and 2 are raised first then harnesses 3 and 4. Each of these is repeated twice to balance or square the weave. The weave draft shows four repeats of the weave system.

The 2/2 twill (draft III) means two warps up and two warps down as in the basket weave. However, the sequence in which the harnesses are raised is 1 and 2 one time; 2 and 3 one time; 3 and 4 one time; and 4 and 1 one time. If this treadling is repeated the surface of the fabric will show a diagonal line effect as shown in the weave draft.

The 3/1 twill (draft IV) means one warp is up and three warps are down, so that the weft passes over or under three warps. In this case only one harness is raised at a time (on a Jack loom).

Other Twill Treadlings

The twill is a very basic weave on which many other weave systems are based. One can also make an original arrangement of the twill draft. Following are some examples of treadlings to produce variations in the twill draw:

1. Zigzag twill: 1-2, 2-3, 3-4, 4-1, 4-3, 3-2, repeat.

2. Vertical point twill: 4, 3, 2, 1, 2, 3.

3. Plain twill: 1-3, 2-4, 1, 4, 3, 2, repeat.

Figure 27. The plain or tabby weave is one of the four basic weaves. The tabby weave is shown on the loom (above) and close-up on a finished fabric (below).

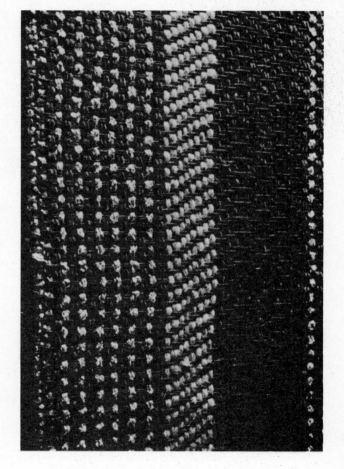

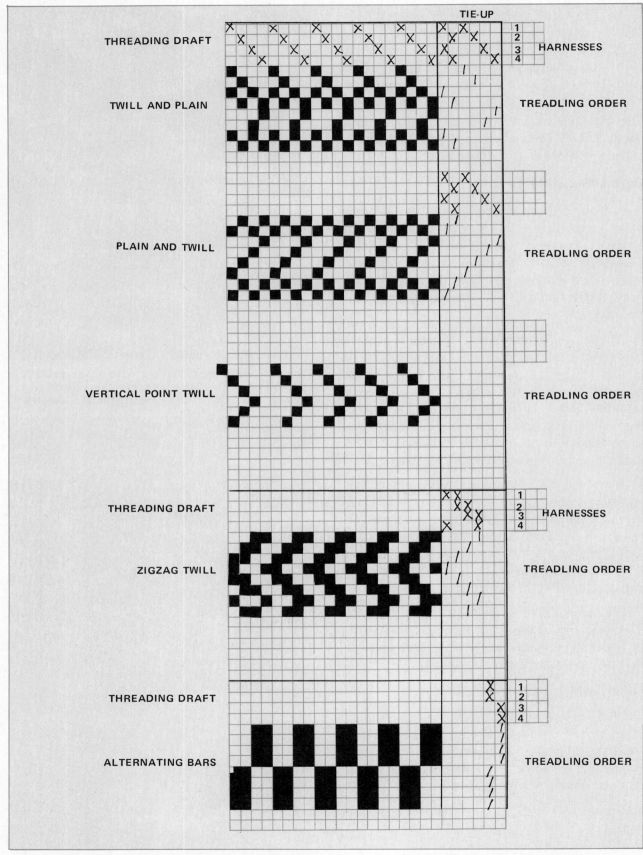

TIE-UP

THREADING DRAFT

TWILL AND PLAIN

PLAIN AND TWILL

VERTICAL POINT TWILL

THREADING DRAFT

ZIGZAG TWILL

THREADING DRAFT

ALTERNATING BARS

HARNESSES

1
2
3
4

TREADLING ORDER

TREADLING ORDER

TREADLING ORDER

HARNESSES

1
2
3
4

TREADLING ORDER

1
2
3
4

TREADLING ORDER

Figure 28. Variations of the twill weave can be made by following the instructions on the draw downs. The harness tie up, treadling order, threading draft, and weave draft are shown for each variation.

4. Twill and plain: 4-3, 2-4, 1-3, 2-1, 2-4, 1-3.

5. Alternating bars: 1 and 2 four times, 3 and 4 four times. (This may be decreased to one time or repeated more times, which will elongate the bars.)

WEAVING SYSTEMS

In addition to the threading order, the treadling, and the materials, the chosen system of weaving the weft also affects the fabric surface. There are two basic ways of weaving.

One Shuttle Weave

A pattern draw can be woven either with one weft thread or with more weft threads. When woven with one shuttle, the shuttle usually carries the same kind of thread as the warp. One shuttle weave is commonly used for the grouped warp and weft type weaves such as the basket weave.

Two Shuttle Weaves

A twill weave variation may be woven with two weft yarns: the pattern weft which may be the same as the warp or heavier than the warp thread, and the binder thread which is woven as tabby weave alternating with the pattern weft. The latter is usually done with a thinner and softer yarn or yarn the same as the warp thread and is wound on a second shuttle. Most overshot patterns are woven with an alternating tabby.

REMOVING THE FABRIC FROM THE LOOM

When a warp is woven as far as it can allow the shed to open, it is time to take the work off the loom. To do this, first cut the ties on the back apron or wind the knots in sections, occasionally bringing four warps through the heddles and tying them in a bow knot. This prevents the weft from slipping. Then pull the warp out through the heddles and reed to the front of the loom. Roll the fabric on a dowel or a rolled newspaper and release it from the cloth beam. Untie or cut the warp from the front apron in the same manner as the back. Finishing of the top and bottom of the woven piece or ends of a fabric will depend on individual preference. Overhand knots or double half hitch knots are two common ways of finishing ends.

Figure 29. As the fabric is removed from the loom, roll it on a dowel or rolling pin. Cut the warp from the front apron and finish off the ends with the desired type of knot.

Projects You Can Do

TWO PILLOWS ON A STRAIGHT TWILL DRAW

Necessary equipment for this project includes a loom 15 inches wide; reed, 15 dents to the reed; loom accessories; tape measure; scissors; comb; threading hooks; 4 flat shuttles 8 to 12 inches long. Yarn supplies include 8 ounces of carpet warp (800 yards to one spool) for the warp; approximately 1 pound of yarn for the weft in assorted textures and colors (e.g., smooth texture yarns, slub — thick and thin — yarns, heavy textured yarns, bulky yarn, ratine and rickrack yarns, natural hair yarns). The color scheme is, of course, up to the weaver.

Warping Instructions

To calculate the warp, do an estimate for a warp 3 yards long and 14 inches wide as follows:

$$
\begin{array}{rl}
14'' & \text{(width)} \\
\times 15 & \text{(number of ends per inch)} \\
\hline
210 & \\
+8 & \text{(selvage reinforcement)} \\
\hline
218 & \text{(total number of ends)} \\
\times 3\text{yds.} & \text{(length of warp)} \\
\hline
654 & \text{(total yardage)}
\end{array}
$$

With medium weight weft yarns, this will weave a fabric about 2 yards long and 13 inches wide. If woven on a floor loom, use the following dimensions: width, 20 inches; length, 3½ yards.

Figure 30. Woven fabric may be used to cover pillows, with variations in fringes and tassels. Note that many weaves and many color combinations are possible and pleasing.

To warp, use a warping board or warping mill. Wind off 218 ends each 3 yards long. To count efficiently and to keep the ends of the warp in order, make a cross about 1/2 yard away from one end of the warp. Each cross is two ends; therefore, 10 crosses are 20 ends. With a different color yarn, tie in groups of 20 until 218 ends are warped off. Pick up the warp on a lease stick and chain the warp. Reed the warp single through the reed except for the four selvage ends on each side, which should be sleyed double through the reed. Sley the warp through the heddles in a straight twill draw, i.e., 1, 2, 3, 4. Tie and beam the loom as described in "Basic Procedures."

To weave the pillows make a color and texture sample by wrapping selected weft yarns on a cardboard 2" x 5". Weave 1 inch of heading in plain weave — i.e., 1-3, 2-4 — with rug yarn. Using rug yarns or combination of yarn comparable in thickness to a rug yarn, weave as follows:

weave 2 inches in tabby weave (1-3, 2-4 repeat); weave 1 inch in twill weave (1-2, 2-3, 3-4, 4-1 repeat); weave 2 inches in reverse twill (1-2, 2-3, 3-4, 4-1, 3-4, 2-3, 2-1 repeat). Continue to weave, changing treadles and yarns every 1 to 3 inches. Alternate each section by a basket weave (1-2, 3-4) in alternate colors or 1/4 inch of tabby weave alternately in the two adjoining colors. Continue to weave for 30 inches ending with an inch of tabby.

Start the other pillow weave in selected yarns and treadles, creating a different mood through color, texture, and weave. Keep an inch by inch record of steps taken.

Then, take the pillows off the loom as explained earlier. Cut in two 30-inch lengths and sew seams. Stuff the pillows with foam rubber, Kapok, or polyester batting. Finish edges or corners with decorative fringe.

Figure 31. This scarf was fashioned from a woven fabric. Since ancient times, weavers have experimented with articles of clothing and personal adornment.

SCARF BASED ON COLOR SEQUENCE WARP

The warp may be made in six sections, each with a different color arrangement: the first in all light color, the second with one end light alternating with one end dark, the third with two ends light and two ends dark, the fourth with three ends light and three ends dark, the fifth with four ends light and four ends dark, the last section all dark. Cotton or a medium weight 2- to 4-ply knitting wool in two contrasting colors works best. The same quality and colors of yarn are used for the weft.

The threading draft is a straight twill — 1, 2, 3, 4 (see diagram). Remember that there is the same number of ends for each of the five even sections. The uneven section (3/3) will be two threads less. The variations in pattern will come from the placement of the dark and light ends; each color end is placed through the harnesses in a twill threading that is 1, 2, 3, 4; this is repeated until all the warp ends are threaded.

Weaving Instructions

A single repeat of each weave is illustrated here with color squares representing the warp ends showing on the surface of cloth. If a counterbalanced loom is used, the white squares will represent the warp ends. It is important to balance the number of ends and picks, *i.e.*, to use the same number of weft picks for squaring each section as the number of ends in the warp of each section.

The effect of the color and weave combination depends on an even weave. Consult the accompanying color key for the weft.

For Additional Reading

Albers, Anni, **On Weaving,** Wesleyan Univ. Press, 1965.

Beutlich, Tadek, **The Techniques of Woven Tapestry,** Watson-Guptill, 1971.

Black, Mary E., **New Key to Weaving,** Bruce, 1965.

Davison, Marguerite Porter, **A Hand Weavers Pattern Book,** M. P. Davison, 1963.

Forbes, R. J., **Studies in Ancient Technology,** Vol. 4, E. J. Brill, 1964.

Held, E. Shirley, **Weaving: A Handbook for Fiber Craftsmen,** Holt, 1973.

Shuttle Spindle and Dyepot (Quarterly), Handweaver's Guild of America, Inc., West Hartford, Connecticut.

Zeilinski, S. A., **Encyclopedia of Hand Weaving,** Rycroon Press, 1959.

Design
In Crafts

Design is the underlying groundwork and foundation for organizing all crafts and their materials.

Design is order, and to find pleasure in design is a universal human response to the language of art and to the order that is in nature. Design is also, in arts and crafts, the cornerstone of the creative process.

The design of a work is an arrangement of space, forms, and colors in a pattern that is both aesthetically pleasing and, when necessary, functional. Today, for example, we tend to think of the Parthenon only as a work of art, as an architectural form that pleases the eye.

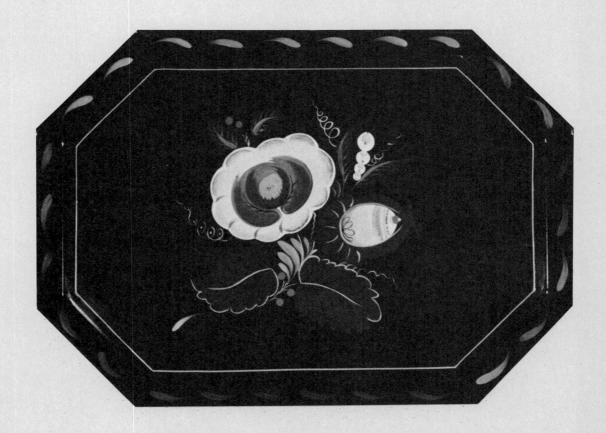

Figure 2. The classical beauty of the Acropolis in Athens, which reaches its height in the Parthenon, exemplifies symmetrical design and harmony.

The ancient Greeks who built it, however, thought of the Parthenon not only as an aesthetically pleasing and satisfying architectural form but also, and perhaps first and foremost, as a functional building. They *used* it. In it they worshipped their gods. The Parthenon was not only beautiful, but useful. This was so because of its design — a *good* architectural design, since it incorporated both the aesthetically pleasing and the functional.

Figure 1. In every area of crafts, the artist must combine the principles of good design and composition with his own creative imagination and his skill in working with materials.

In the visual arts and crafts — which include architecture, painting, and sculpture, or combinations of all three — it is chiefly in architecture and in crafts that design is called upon to furnish aesthetic pleasure and at the same time serve a human purpose. From his study of architectural forms from ancient times, Louis Sullivan, the renowned Chicago architect of the late nineteenth and early twentieth century, gave his profession the concept that a building's design should express its use, often stated in the dictum "form follows function." Of course, in painting and in sculpture, as opposed to architecture, the chief and sometimes only function of the completed work is to please the senses.

The English work "design" comes from the Latin *designare*, which means "to mark out." Used as a verb, the English word means to make a plan or pattern for a unified and coherent whole. Used as a noun, the word means the manifestation of that plan or pattern in the completed whole.

All design begins in nature. Every snowflake, for example, has its own unique pattern. And when the basic elements of human design are investigated, it is found that all of them originate in models from nature such as a snowflake, or a leaf, or an egg, or even the stripes of a zebra. Why this is so is not known, but it is generally agreed that derivations from natural models are intrinsically satisfying to humans. They are both aesthetically pleasing and, when they must be functional.

Thus, there is no proper history of human design. There are and have been many different "schools" of design, but all of them throughout history have relied upon one or more aspects of elemental, natural design. What we today label as Egyptian, Greek, Etruscan, or Roman art, or as the Byzantine or Romanesque or Italian Renaissance or Flemish schools of painting, sculpture, or architecture, or as Impressionism or Cubism or any one of a score of more recent movements in the arts, all have their basis in elemental, natural design.

It does happen, however, that for a time some specific school or movement will achieve prominence and exert a strong influence on artists and craftsmen. One of these in fairly recent times was Art Nouveau, which flourished at the end of the last century and the beginning of this one. Its principles enjoyed a wide revival in the United States and Europe in the 1960s, this more recent influence extending to advertising, fabric design, illustration, and interior decorating.

Figure 3. Natural design is found everywhere, waiting for the careful observer who can see the patterns of dandelion seeds or the veining of a leaf. (Courtesy, The Volume Library.)

Figure 4. Sand sculptured by the wind creates a panorama of curved, three-dimensional forms and patterns. (Courtesy, The Volume Library.)

Preceded by and influenced by the Pre-Raphaelites (one of whose artistic principles was "to study nature attentively"), Art Nouveau emphasized flowing linear patterns related to natural forms together with flat color patterns. The lamps designed by Louis Tiffany are Art Nouveau, for example, as are the architecture of the Spaniard Gaudí and the exotic, sensual illustrations of the Englishman Aubrey Beardsley. Traces of the movement's influence can be found in the works of such artists as Pierre Bonnard, Paul Gauguin, Edvard Munch, and Henri de Toulouse-Lautrec, to name only a few. Its influence can also be seen in the intricately embellished decorative work done by Louis Sullivan for the buildings he designed.

The turn of the twentieth century, in fact, was a period of great excitement in design and crafts. Closely related to Art Nouveau and to the Pre-Raphaelites, William Morris's "arts and crafts movement" flourished in England. It was both a social and an aesthetic movement, emphasizing handwork in opposition to the late-Victorian ugliness of mass-produced factory items. Morris's work had a tremendous impact throughout Europe. It led to the establishment of the Wiener Werkstätten, an influential organization of craftsmen and designers, at Vienna in 1903. The ideas of the movement were adapted by the Bauhaus and, still later, by contemporary Scandinavian designers.

The Bauhaus was a more recent but extremely influential school of design. It was an actual school — that is, students attended classes there — founded by Walter Gropius at Weimar, Germany, in 1919. The Bauhaus attempted to do away with distinctions between "fine" art and "applied" art and to combine in its instruction both the accepted

Figure 5. The intricate designs and flowing lines of Art Nouveau style are shown perfectly in Beardsley's pen drawing for an edition of "Le Morte d'Arthur."

THE LADY OF THE LAKE
TELLETH ARTHVR OF THE
SWORD EXCALIBVR

principles of art through the ages and the concepts introduced by twentieth-century technology. One of these concepts was that the twentieth-century artist is actually a craftsman who must satisfy a specific need — a principle that would surely have been endorsed by pyramid makers, Gothic cathedral builders, Renaissance painters, and followers of Morris as well. Another principle of the Bauhaus was that the artist should have practical training in craftwork to acquaint himself with materials and processes. To this end the school offered courses in ceramics, weaving, and stained-glass design.

In 1925 the school moved from Weimar to Dessau, where its founder, Gropius, designed a building to house it, an asymmetrical structure whose dynamic composition exemplified another Bauhaus aim: the unification of all the arts and crafts in architecture. The building is, of course, both functional and aesthetically pleasing. Gropius himself, however, was wary of simplifying to the extent that Sullivan had; that is, he would not say that the function of an art object (or a technological product) must necessarily determine its appearance, or form.

Figure 6. Picasso's 1910 "Nude" (left) shows the abstract design so prominent in Cubist painting.

Figure 7. Perfect symmetry of design is found in the unique crystal structure of each snowflake.

The Bauhaus closed when Hitler came to power in Germany in the early 1930s, but many of its teachers came to the United States and taught and designed here, including Gropius and Ludwig Mies van der Rohe. Their influence on contemporary urban architecture and design has been tremendous — it can be seen not only in stark glass and steel buildings throughout the country, but also in such diverse fields as typography and tableware design, and, in general, the contemporary approach to art education.

The basic, elemental aspects of all good design are symmetry, or the lack of it (asymmetry), balance, line, rhythm, and repetition — in sum, the arrangement of form and mass and colors in space. The human eye perceives design in mountains and in shorelines, and in grains of sand and snowflakes. The artist understands these perceptions and utilizes them in his creations. The two wings of a butterfly, for example, which duplicate each other in reverse and balance each other more or less perfectly, have the quality known as symmetry, a quality that is thought to give humans a feeling of security. The eye follows the flow of the wings' pattern and returns to its beginning reassured by it. In their works, creative artists and craftsmen often utilize this element of design to enhance the impression their finished work will make upon the viewer.

The blossoms on the stem of a flower, on the other hand, are usually asymmetrically balanced. That is, they may not duplicate each other in reverse but overall they *will* balance, perhaps with two small blossoms on one side of the stem and a larger blossom on the other side. In the same manner, the leaves on a tree limb may be asymmetrically placed, but balanced overall. Moreover, they will repeat each other rhythmically around the limb. This is their natural design. In man-made designs, artists often try to convey this same quality.

In nature, of course, we see everything as lines — diagonal, horizontal, perpendicular, circular.

Figure 8. In his "organic" plan for houses like Fallingwater, architect Frank Lloyd Wright integrated architectural style with the natural forms of the setting. (*Courtesy, The Volume Library.*)

Figure 10. An aerial view reveals intricate geometric patterns on the landscape. (Courtesy, Canadian Government Travel Bureau.)

Whatever his medium, the artist must also use lines: horizontals for their quality of calmness, perhaps, diagonals for tension, and so forth, with different types of lines combined and opposed to achieve different effects. Combinations of lines — combinations that are usually repeated rhythmically, sometimes with slight variations to add interest — are used especially by designers in the decorative arts and crafts.

A final element of design is a harmonious relationship between parts, that is, an overall pattern. The bell tower of St. Mark's, Venice, for example, exhibits a harmonious relationship between all of its parts. So, too, do Michelangelo's *David*, da Vinci's *Mona Lisa*, Rembrandt's *The Night Watch*, and Picasso's *Les Demoiselles d'Avignon*. So, too, do a patchwork quilt, an Oriental rug, a windmill, a Grecian urn — as well as a stalk of corn, a snowflake, and the body of a butterfly. The bell tower of St. Mark's, incidentally, was begun in the ninth century but not finished until the sixteenth, when the belfry and spire were added. So harmonious is the relationship of the tower's parts, however, that even though it was built over a period of almost seven centuries, it still gives viewers the impression of a unified and coherent whole.

Design, then, is the ordering of space, forms, and colors so that human beings feel comfortable with the arrangement. Design is, however, only one element in a visual or craft object. Such objects have at their source not only the ordering of space so that humans feel at ease with the arrangement but also so that, in the finest art, they feel lifted out of themselves to a higher plane of feeling, just as they often are by what they discover in nature.

Figure 11. The tall bell tower that dominates St. Mark's Square in Venice is a perfect example of varying styles of design combined into a harmonious whole. (Courtesy, Italian Government Travel Office.)

Figure 12. An intricate four-layer woven design, shown in a natural setting, displays harmony in form and color.

Common Terms Used In Design in Crafts

Asymmetry: a form of composition that lacks symmetry because one side is generally different from the other; the design, however, is still usually balanced.

Balance: the harmonious relationship or arrangement of the elements in a design so that they are in proper proportion to each other.

Composition: the arrangement of elements in the design for an object that is being created.

Design Feasibility: the determination of whether an object can actually be made from the proposed design.

Dynamic: in design, a composition that appears to be moving, stimulating, and generally of a rather exciting nature.

Grid: the underlying pattern that provides the format or arrangement for a design.

Harmony: the rhythmic cohesiveness in a composition so that all parts form a unified whole without any element of discord.

Inversion: in symmetry, the 180° displacement of a unit.

Mirroring: in symmetry, the creation of a mirror image of a design element.

Modular System: in design, a system of organization comprised of identical units called modules.

Module: a unit in a design that is exactly the same as every other unit in that design.

Proportion: the balanced unity of all elements in a design.

Regularity: the repetitive aspect of a design in which proportions and modules are all the same.

Rotation: in symmetry, the moving of a design unit around a center point with the same part of the unit always facing toward the center.

Static: a design characterized by elements that appear to be fixed or stationary.

Symmetry: a form of composition in which all parts correspond in size, form, and arrangement on opposite sides of a plane, line, or point.

Translation: in symmetry, the repetition of the basic elements along a line of design so that they are all oriented in the same direction.

Basic Equipment And Supplies

The word "design," as used in history and in present-day arts and crafts, refers to the basic elements and principles of composition — the orderly plan that determines the aesthetic effectiveness of an artistic object. Design does not affect the physical properties of materials themselves, but the way in which materials are arranged, ordered, and combined to create a work of art. When working with clay, for instance, design affects the form of the pottery, not the clay itself.

The designer/artist/craftsman must, of course, consider his or her chosen material when thinking of the design. The material disciplines the artist's design concept. For instance, an artist would not choose to make a large table of clay, but would use a material more appropriate to the object's function, such as wood, metal, or plastic. Each material has certain possibilities and limitations. The inherent characteristics of a material — its strength or fragility, its rigidity or malleability, its durability or delicacy — define how far the designer can go in experimenting in terms of design.

This principle of *design feasibility* or practicability is based on determining the function of an object and then relating the design concept to an appropriate and suitable material. In making a wind chime, for instance, the choice of that particular object determines the function; then the design is conceived, and finally the construction materials are selected. If the design includes tubular shapes, such materials as hollow wood (bamboo), thrown clay forms, metal tubing, or all three could be used. If the design concept calls for flat or varied shapes,

materials that might be selected include plastic discs, sea shells, fired clay, or found objects such as juice-can lids.

To design an object efficiently, first work out the formal concept of what the object is and what it is to look like; then see which material best suits the design. The process of determining design feasibility begins with the design idea, which is sketched and then studied carefully. Next to the sketch, make notations indicating essential ideas: color, texture, how and where the object will be used. The attentive craftsman will then put the initial design aside and return to it later to restudy the concept and revise or add to his original idea.

When a composition has been conceived and the materials chosen, the design should be analyzed to discover what is good about it or what should be changed to improve it. Compositional sense — at least good compositional sense — is not something that is learned overnight. It is usually acquired by practice and experience. The craftsman discovers by trial and error which combinations will help him to achieve the effect he wants. It is best to begin by following known paths — the work of other designers, the principles established in great paintings and sculpture.

Follow known paths, too, in learning to work with a given material. Work and practice step by step until the correct sequence is mastered. Once the physical processes of handling the chosen materials have been mastered, it is time to be creative and try out original designs. Within the limitations of the material and his skill in working with it, the craftsman's aim is to achieve a design that is aesthetically pleasing. There are several ways of organizing materials to do this.

Figure 13. Choosing materials that are suitable for the design concept is an important step, whether the craft be pottery making or crewel work.

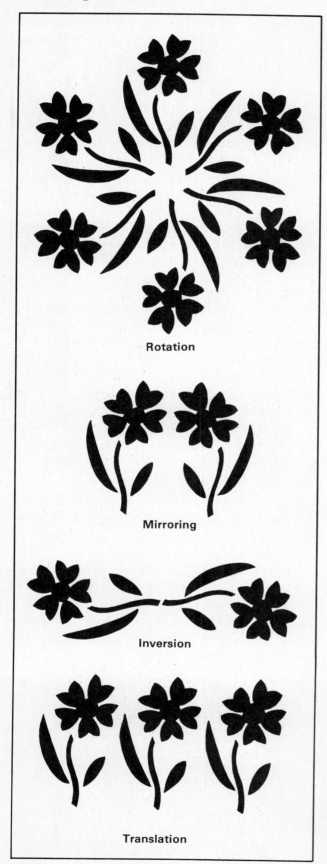

Rotation

Mirroring

Inversion

Translation

Figure 14. Symmetry Operations

SYMMETRY

The easiest, most common, and most obvious form of visual organization is *symmetry*. The principle of symmetry is easy to learn and to apply because it has its own set of rules. When these rules are followed, the composition will always work in a certain way. Symmetry is a sort of "fail-safe" system of composition, but it is useful both as a system of design and as a learning tool.

There are four "rules" of symmetry, called symmetry operations. They are mirroring, rotation, inversion, and translation. In each operation, the space relationships between the elements change to achieve a different effect, a different "feel." Each one results in a different basic pattern of organization. It is important to bear in mind, however, that although these operations are described as distinct processes, they are most effective and most frequently used in combination.

The first operation is mirroring. This operation is exactly what it says: the creation of a mirror image. To experiment with the simplest example of mirroring, take a sheet of paper and draw a line down the middle. Now, on one side of the median line, draw any simple pattern. Then hold a pocket mirror along the line so that it reflects the pattern. The pattern is, of course, exactly reversed — right becomes left and vice versa.

Rotation is another of the symmetry operations. As the name implies, it refers to moving an element of

Figure 15. Design elements are repeated along a line in this ancient frieze, a detail from the Treasury of Atreus at Mycenae, built about 1500 B.C. (Courtesy, The Metropolitan Museum of Art; original in the British Museum.)

design around in a circular motion. The same side of the shape or form must always face the inside of the imaginary circle that is the basis of this design. Rotation might typically be used for the center of a mosaic, for example, because it is an interest-drawing focal point. One can use partial rotation or complete the operation, whichever better suits the purpose of the design. Rotation can be the starting point for many intricate designs.

Inversion is the third symmetry operation: turning the basic design element upside down and backwards. It is just as controlled as any of the other operations. In fact, it can be expressed very precisely as a 180° displacement from the standard position. Inversion is unique in the symmetry operations, however, because the relationship between the initial position and the inverted one is quite unlike the others.

The last symmetry operation is translation. Translation is merely the theoretical term for repeating the basic elements in a line so that they are all oriented in the same direction.

Symmetrical organization appears in many natural forms. A tall stand of cattails growing for miles around a lake shore can be seen as an example of translation. Their reflection in the water creates a mirror image. Rotation appears, for instance, in the arrangement of flower petals around the center of a flower or in the arrangement of clover leaves around the stem.

In each case, note that the combining elements are all the same — a cattail stalk, a flower petal. This is also true when the symmetry operations are applied to many basic patterns in crafts. In a mosaic table top, for example, the simplest design element, a square, is used. Each tile is exactly the same. Even when the design is inverted, or mirrored, or otherwise altered, the basic element remains the same. And underlying each design using the basic square is a basic format — the checkerboard.

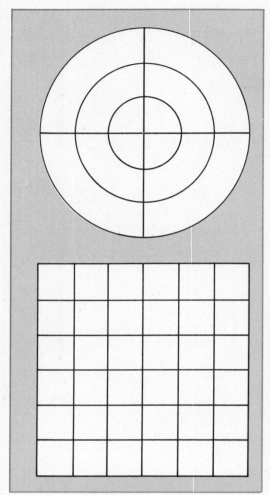

Figure 16. Grids (above) reveal the underlying format of a design. Each stitch in a needlepoint pattern (right) can be planned on a grid.

Grids

In the case of a pattern using edge-to-edge squares, the basic underlying format is the checkerboard grid. In all cases, a grid is the underlying format that relates similar design units. The designer chooses units that are the same in shape, size, and weight. The grid simply reinforces the basic arrangement. It demonstrates each element's relationship to other parts of the composition.

The checkerboard grid is a familiar one. It can be used as the underlying format in ways as varied as laying out the streets of a city, planning the design of a rug, or working out an intricate Scandinavian sweater pattern. It is, of course, not the only possible grid that the designer can use.

Modular Systems

In the symmetry operations and in using the grid, the design units consistently utilized are identical. Each unit is the same, and all are interchangeable within the design framework. The units are called *modules*. A module is a unit that is exactly the same as every other unit in its system.

Modular systems are not new, but they are peculiarly typical of contemporary design thinking. There are several reasons for this: modular units can be mass-produced, making them inexpensive. They are easy to use. And they are flexible in their application, which makes them appropriate in a mobile, changing society.

In furniture, modular units provide a choice of arrangements and a flexibility in the number and placement of the units. Modular systems are widely used in contemporary construction, notably in prefabricated housing units, in identical units put together in skyscrapers, and even in entire housing complexes such as Habitat. Bricklaying illustrates

Figure 17. Modular construction is the key concept in Habitat, the innovative, 158-unit housing complex built for Expo '67 in Montreal. (Courtesy, Wide World Photos.)

an ancient modular system; steel-beam construction involves modules also.

Fresh and creative design ideas within the modular concept are an important aspect of contemporary design. But the module is by no means the only design element with which the designer and craftsman can work.

Variations From Symmetry

A symmetrical organization, by its very nature, is regular. The proportions are all the same, the design units (or modules) all the same. This regularity sometimes may be too repetitive for the designer's taste, or it may not work in the piece being created. Before leaving symmetry altogether, try making some progressive changes within the established system.

For instance, if the grid that constitutes the basic format is made up of 2" squares, try using a few 4" squares as a variation. A 4" square will fit into the same modular system (taking the place of four smaller squares), but it will effectively break the monotony and add a pleasing variation to the design. One can use the larger squares in regular or irregular ways: they can be inserted in a regular pattern or interspersed more or less at random throughout the design.

Remember that when irregularity is introduced, it may be hard to control. Be careful where nonconforming elements are placed. Unless one adheres

to design judgments and basic principles already described, the nonconforming elements will not appear as pleasing variations, but as intruders in the design.

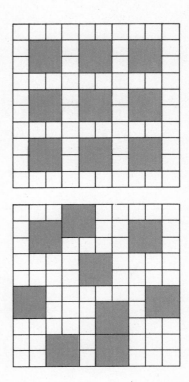

Figure 18. Although both these basketry designs are symmetrical, they also show the interesting spatial relationships that make a composition dynamic.

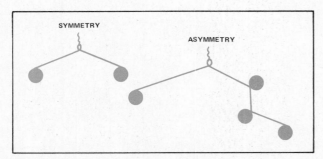

SYMMETRY

ASYMMETRY

Figure 19.

STATIC AND DYNAMIC COMPOSITION

One of the criticisms often made of compositions based on symmetry is that they are too static. In fact, symmetrical compositions may be quite dynamic. These two design factors do not have a one-to-one correspondence.

Simply, static compositions tend to sit in one place visually. There is little eye movement involved in looking at them. In a dynamic composition, on the other hand, the eye moves through the composition discovering spatial relationships between areas. If this latter type of composition is desired, then the eye plan should be fluid. It should not stop. There must always be a path for the eye to follow.

A dynamic composition is not necessarily "better" or "worse" than a static one; it is merely planned differently. The designer should decide which type of composition — static or dynamic — will best fulfill his expectations and wishes for the object he is creating and the effects he wants to achieve.

ASYMMETRY

In a symmetrical composition, one half of the composition matches the other in a predetermined way. Its obvious opposite is asymmetry.

Neither symmetry nor assymetry is necessarily static or dynamic, balanced or unbalanced. These are all separate factors that operate independently. Symmetrical compositions, as already mentioned, can be either static or dynamic, but they are always balanced within the harmonious nature of symmetry. Asymmetrical compositions are often dynamic, although they too may be static if the designer wants them to be. But an asymmetrical composition should also be balanced.

Harmony in Composition

Is an asymmetrical composition "harmonic"? Harmony in composition is the result of good proportions, of well-defined relationships between areas, and of balance. Some combinations create harmony; others create discord. Therefore, an asymmetrical composition can be harmonic or not, depending on how the basic relationships are handled.

To achieve harmonic compositions, consider the relationships between the parts. Such relationships can be definite and obvious, or subtle and ambiguous. Beginning designers and craftsmen may feel more comfortable if they begin working to-

Figure 20. These two crafts projects —
a string construction (right) and a
patchwork quilt (below) — utilize basic
principles of good design to produce
balanced and dynamic patterns.

ward clear and definite relationships, trying the ambiguous ones when they have had more practice.

First, look at the space relationships within the design. Are the elements of the composition so close together that the eye cannot appreciate each shape, or are they so far apart that they have no relationship at all? Does the design continue throughout the entire composition? Are the spatial relationships monotonous? Perhaps they should be varied.

JUDGING AN ORIGINAL DESIGN

At the beginning, try each concept one step at a time. First try symmetry. Then try changing to asymmetry. Strive for good spatial relationships; work on achieving balance and harmony.

Always draw out a plan first. Then decide on a material that is suitable and feasible for both the design and one's budget. Try to be imaginative and to put ingenuity to work in design concepts. The craftsman should apply his own sense of design and his own taste in design when planning a project.

Once a design is completed, put it away for a while before reviewing it critically. Then ask these questions:

Does the design have good proportion?

Is the composition too repetitive?

Is there too much going on?

Could the parts be better related to one another?

Are the spatial relationships well organized?

Does one side balance visually with the other? (To test this, imagine the work suspended from the center by a string. Does one side seem or feel as though it would hang lower than the other? If so, the composition is out of balance.)

Finally, is the design the best you can do?

Then begin your project and enjoy it. When it is finished, ask the same questions that were asked about the design. Planning and revising designs are only half the game. Making the piece is the other half.

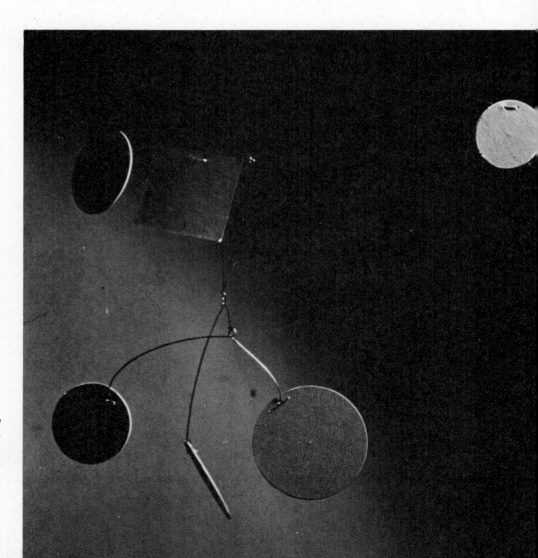

Figure 21. A well-designed mobile tests the craftsman's ability to combine asymmetrical design with good balanced composition.

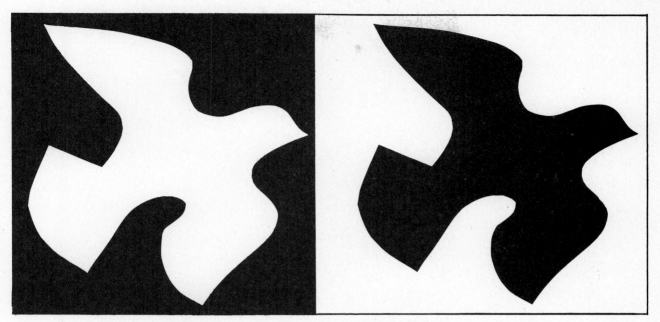

Figure 22. In this pattern, negative and positive areas can be arranged and experimented with for interesting visual effects.

Projects You Can Do

Each of the following projects should be considered as an exercise in applying the design principles discussed earlier. They will provide practice in creating and manipulating compositional forms, bridging the gap between theory and working with the materials chosen.

EXERCISE ONE

With a sheet of black construction paper, cut out a pattern similar to the one in the illustration. Use a knife to cut the patterns carefully, leaving the positive and negative sections intact. Then fasten each section with glue or tape to a light-colored (preferably white) board. Which seems stronger — the negative shape design or the positive one? What kind of result could be achieved by placing parts of the negative design in with the positive design? Do some of the shapes or areas lose their definition?

By working with two sets of the pattern, one can develop an awareness of shape definition. A white figure (positive) on a dark background (negative) is often more powerful than a dark figure on a light ground. In thinking about why this is so, consider another idea: in writing dark ink is used on white paper; the eye is also accustomed to reading dark type on light paper. The dark element is always the figure, the lighter color the ground. By reversing this pattern and placing the white figure on a dark background, the ordinary is changed into an unusual perceptual phenomenon.

Through such reversals of the ordinary and the expected, many unusual designs can be created. However, the aim is not just to be different, but to find out what effect an unusual compositional handling will have on a design that might otherwise be ordinary.

Color reversal is only one example of the factors that can give designs an unusual viewpoint. The more distinctly personal an artist makes his work — so that it is unique to his way of working — the closer he is to creating and developing his own style, one that sets his work apart from others in the same field. This personal style is the outstanding characteristic of a creative artist/craftsman.

Figure 23. An unusual and striking variation on the basic square has been achieved in these fabric-covered cubes designed by Mary Ellen Savage.

EXERCISE TWO

From magazine illustrations, cut out textures and colors that seem to be similar or related in some way. Look for large areas of solid colors or close-ups of textures such as woods, autumn leaves, snow, fabrics, and the like. Cut these areas into 1" squares.

On a piece of cardboard, draw a simple checkerboard grid of eight 1" squares by eight 1" squares. (Correctly sized graph paper can also be used.) Begin to place the cut-out squares on the grid, working them into patterns. Try several versions of this project. Vary the grid or the colors; use the symmetry operations (mirroring, inversion, etc.) to vary the pattern. For instance, perhaps the squares include many shades and textures of blue. Using only blue tones, from very pale to navy, will hold the composition together, no matter how sporadic the design. The color is the unifying factor. Then try a two-color design, perhaps yellow and brown. By patterning these colors in a definite order, all sorts of design and pattern relationships can be created.

Variations

How can this exercise be applied in original work? Consider a construction using squares of clear and smoked plastic, or a needlepoint design for a jacket, or stained wood squares glued together to make a cheese board or trivet.

As an alternative, vary the size. For instance, use tiny squares (say, ⅛") of silver and brass soldered or enameled together to make a medallion. Or, to go in the opposite direction, try huge squares of poured concrete alternating with bricks grouped in squares for an unusual patio floor.

Don't overlook any possibility for variations on this same theme. For example, combine large squares of cork with mirrored tiles to personalize a small wall at home; or cut and lead stained glass in alternating colors, then frame them to use as a window covering.

All these ideas were generated from one simple square grid. Use other grid patterns and try to devise some original ideas. While doing so, experiment with various shapes and with shapes grouped differently over the grid. Look for unusual patterns that are interesting and that seem to have a practical application in your craft.

Whatever the project, be meticulous. Ask yourself if all the possibilities have been explored. Can one or two particular designs be developed even further? Then return to the same questions that were asked earlier about the design. Each time the design is reviewed and revised, it will be reshaped and clarified. The better the artist becomes at clarifying his designs, the better the end product will be.

EXERCISE THREE

The last exercise involves exploring other variations on a basic theme to generate design possibilities from a basic compositional idea. This exercise concentrates on using imagination in terms of materials. Take a piece of jewelry as an example: a band necklace from which a small medallion is suspended. In the original concept, imagine that the band necklace is silver; the medallion is a silver crescent backed with rosewood and decorated with two small pearls. The piece, then, has four components and three different materials — silver, rosewood, and pearls.

The first variation could be in the band necklace itself: make it of copper or bronze or even leather. Or replace it with a gold or silver chain. The second piece, the silver crescent, could be made of bronze, copper, or wood. Next, the pearls could be replaced with agates or other semiprecious stones or even small beads. Finally, the rosewood could be replaced by any other decorative wood, by several kinds of metal, or even by clear or smoked plastic. From the same basic design, at least 20 different necklaces could be generated.

This imaginative way of thinking can be applied to nearly any kind of craft material. All one needs to do is draw the design on paper and then substitute materials that seem compatible with it. Thus, one compositional design can be the starting point for any number of creative, unusual works.

For Additional Reading

Kepes, Gyorgy, **The Language of Vision,** Theobald, 1945.

Moholy-Nagy, Laszlo, **Vision in Motion,** Theobald, 1947.

Naylor, Gillian, **The Bauhaus,** Dutton Studio Vista.

Neumann, Eckhard, **Bauhaus and Bauhaus People,** Van Nostrand Reinhold, 1970.

Papanek, Victor, **Design for the Real World,** Pantheon, 1971.

Pevsner, Nikolaus, **The Sources of Modern Architecture and Design,** Praeger, 1968.

Thomas, Richard K., **Three Dimensional Design,** Van Nostrand Reinhold, 1969.

Wong, Wucius, **Two Dimensional Design.**

Figure 24. These examples of the potter's and the weaver's crafts illustrate how the basic principles of good design can be applied in varied kinds of work.

Knitting

The ancient art of knitting has perpetuated itself because of the ever-increasing popularity of hand-crafted garments.

Examples of cotton knitting thought to be more than 6000 years old have been found in Egypt. Other objects discovered in Coptic tombs of the fourth and fifth centuries have proven that knitting was prevalent among these people. It appears that natives of those lands which border the southern and eastern part of the Mediterranean provided the knitting teachers for the rest of the world. The craft spread from these countries northward to Spain and Italy, and then to the rest of Europe and the British Isles.

Early knitted articles were for purposes other than clothing: the Arabs were experts in making knitted carpets and wall hangings. Learning from them, Spanish and Florentine knitters reached their peak with Arabic knitting during the Middle Ages. Furthermore, because of its elastic quality, fine knitting was used for undergarments, caps, and hosiery.

Figure 1. These early 19th-century tin knitting needles and their steel case (opposite) come from eastern U.S., probably Pennsylvania. (Courtesy, The Henry Francis du Pont Winterthur Museum.) Knitting was an established domestic art in the 14th century, too, as shown in Master Bertram's "Visit of the Angels to Mary" (above), found in a German abbey. (Courtesy, Art Gallery, Hamburg.)

Figure 2. This striking afghan (above) combines style with warmth.

As with other guilds of the Middle Ages, the "knytters" guild required a man to be apprenticed for six years before he became eligible for "journeyman." The requirements involved knitting a carpet, patterned with as many as 12 colors, as well as shirts and hose.

Italy soon became the center of the knitted silk hosiery industry. This was due to a combination of Arabic and Oriental influence which provided knowledge about silkworms and, consequently, silk manufacturing.

In 1589, Reverend William Lee invented a frame knitting machine much to the dismay of the hand-knitting industry. He was so ill-treated by the professional handknitters that he was denied protection by Elizabeth I. He emigrated to France and died there an embittered man. Nevertheless, he did pave the way for the development of a tremendous hosiery industry in France.

By the early 1700s, colored pattern knitting in silk, mainly for the wealthy, gained fame. Fine steel needles were used for making purses, garters for men, and dainty pincushions. The pincushion halves were joined and stuffed into a ball. Then the seaming was hidden by a fancy cord that ended in a loop so that the ball could hang on a belt at the waist.

When lighter weight imported fabrics from the Orient became fashionable, there was a decided trend toward fine white knitting. Using a fine white cotton thread to make gloves, mittens, doilies, hosiery, and, later, fine lace became a popular fashion. It also became fashionable to wear fingerless white gloves while knitting to prevent perspiration from soiling the cotton. Again, this was the fashion for the wealthy.

The American colonists knitted primarily those items essential to their physical well being. An excerpt from an eighteenth-century letter tells of a lady who managed, although ill, to knit 36 pairs of stockings in six months for her large family.

During the nineteenth and twentieth centuries, the craft of knitting became increasingly popular, mainly because so many garments and other items began to be fashioned from wool.

Figure 3. A beautiful chair covering (left) results when delicate embroidery is worked on a knit background.

Figure 4. The ski sweater with a matching hat (below) is a project popular with knitters.

Figure 5. A coat sweater, complete with belt, is popular for fall and winter wear. The garment should be blocked, using either steam or the "wet block" method.

Common Terms Used In Knitting

Bind Off: a term used to describe the completion of the entire knitting project or a section.

Cast On: the technique of putting the beginning stitches on the needle.

Decrease (dec): the deletion of any number of stitches in order to change the shape or direction of the knitting; knitting two stitches together and thereby decreasing one stitch.

Double Pointed (dp): a needle with two pointed ends.

Duplicate Stitch: a stitch worked over a knit stitch with a tapestry needle threaded with yarn of a contrasting color; this duplicates the knit stitch.

Even: to work (knit) the same number of stitches without increasing or decreasing.

Garter Stitch: one of the most basic knitting patterns. All stitches for each row are knitted, causing ridges to be formed on both sides by every two rows worked. This produces a flat piece.

Gauge: the number of knit stitches (horizontal and vertical) which equal 1 inch. For example: 6 stitches=1 inch, 6 rows=1 inch.

Increase (inc): to add a stitch or stitches to the number of stitches already on the needle.

Knit (K): the basic stitch which gives a flat appearance.

K 2 Tog: the technique of knitting two stitches together by inserting the needle into two stitches at a time rather than into only one, thus decreasing one stitch.

Multiple of ——: the number of stitches necessary to create one complete pattern. If a multiple of 6 plus 2 is required, the number of stitches on the needle must be divisible by 6 with 2 remaining, e.g., 26, 38, 44, 62, etc.

PSSO: an instruction to pass the slipped stitch over the stitch just worked.

Picking Up Stitches: to create additional stitches, as around the neck of a sweater.

Purl (P): the basic stitch which gives ridged rows on one side.

Round Needle: a circular needle with two pointed ends connected by a strong flexible cord; enables the knitter to work around and around to form a continuous knitted tube.

Selvedges: the side edges of the work.

Slip (sl): the transferring of a stitch from one needle to the other without knitting or purling.

Stockinette Stitch (st st): the pattern in which rows are alternately knitted and purled. This common knitting pattern stitch is also referred to as K1 row, P1 row.

Turn: to turn the work and needles around so that the yarn is at the opposite side.

Weight: a reference to either the weight of an individual skein of yarn or to the heft of yarn (lightweight, medium-weight, etc.).

Yarn Over (yo): to wrap the yarn around the needle so that a stitch is added in the next row; generally used to achieve a lacy effect.

Basic Equipment And Supplies

From a plain stockinette stitch pattern to very intricate work, the supply requirements for knitting are basically the same: needles and yarn. Other items mentioned will facilitate or safeguard the work but are not essential. All are available in yarn shops and in department stores with art/needlework sections.

NEEDLES

Needles may be single-pointed, double-pointed, or round. They may be made of aluminum, bone, plastic, nylon, steel, or wood.

Single-Pointed Needles

Single-pointed or straight needles are used to work a flat piece of knitting, one which will either be attached to another or used alone, such as a scarf or belt. The needles are sized from 0, the smallest, to 15, the largest. They are available in lengths from 10″ to 18″. English and Canadian needles are sized in the opposite manner, with the smallest needle #14 and the largest 0. The hollow, plastic needles that are referred to as jumbo needles are #19, #35, and #50.

Double-Pointed Needles

These are used in making tube-shaped pieces such as socks or parts of sweaters. Sized like straight needles, these are available in different lengths and a set is comprised of four rather than two. In steel needles, the largest number has the smallest diameter.

Round Needles

These act much as double-pointed needles but there is greater choice in lengths. The longest round needle is 36". One row is referred to as a round and the wrong side or purl side is always inside.

It is also possible to knit back and forth on a round needle and not join the work into a tube. This is the method used for working a large afghan in one piece — all the stitches fit on the round needle so that seaming strips or blocks is unnecessary.

YARNS

The available selection of different fibers is vast: cotton, linen, rayon, wool, mohair, raffia, acrylics, and various blends of these. Synthetics have proven extremely popular because knits made of these yarns are machine washable. Most yarns are color fast and mothproofed. Within the last few years, yarn companies have grouped yarns into weight groups, enabling the knitter to interchange yarns with those specified in a pattern: *Group A - lightweight*; suitable for fine baby garments, socks, and sweaters. *Group B - medium weight*; sport yarns for indoor weight garments. *Group C - knitting worsted weight*; a four-ply (four stranded) yarn commonly used for afghans and sweaters. *Group D - bulky weight*; used on needles #9 to #11, mainly for outdoor weight garments. *Group E - extra bulky*; the heaviest yarn manufactured, requiring use of the largest sized needles.

Figure 6. A good selection of knitting needles includes round needles for tube work or large pieces such as afghans and thick needles for work using very heavy yarns.

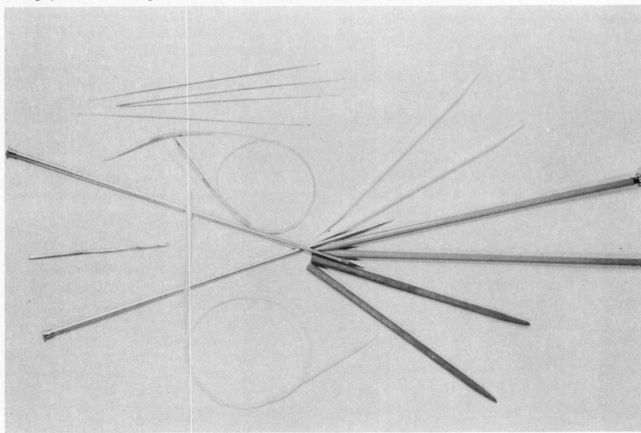

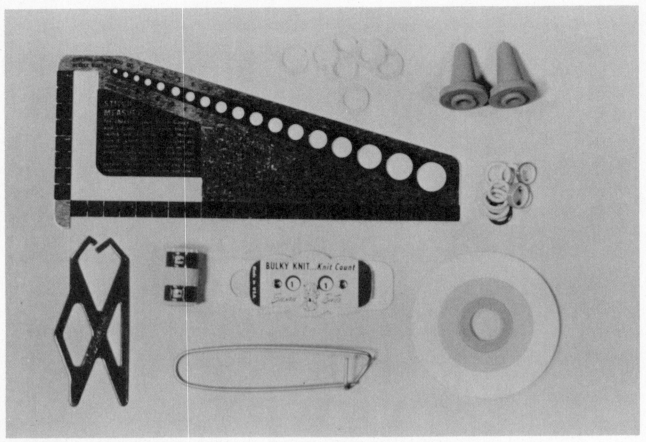

Figure 8. A number of knitting accessories can be purchased inexpensively. They include a stitch gauge, markers (small plastic rings), and point protectors for the tips of the needles.

KNITTING AIDS

These are inexpensive aids which tend to make knitting projects easier: (1) crochet hook — handy for tucking in ends; (2) cable hook — holds cable stitches for the twisting process; (3) markers — plastic or metal rings slipped onto the needle to act as dividers; (4) knitting directions; (5) point protectors — placed at the pointed ends of the needles to prevent stitches from slipping off when work is put aside; (6) ruler; (7) stitch holders — a device for reserving stitches; and (8) tapestry needle.

Basic Procedures

The basic procedures for learning to knit are quite simple. Keep in mind that the directions given are for right-handed persons — make adjustments where necessary. Occasionally, an asterisk (*) will appear at the beginning of a sentence or phrase; then, another asterisk will appear at the end of the sentence or phrase. The directions between the asterisks are repeated across the row for a specified number of times. This is an abbreviated method of giving directions that can be easily followed.

TESTING THE COLORS

It is always a good idea to test the fastness of dyes. Cut off a 2″ piece of each color; wet the pieces with lukewarm water; and place them on the corner of a paper napkin. Fold the opposite corner of the napkin over the pieces and let them dry. If the colors do not run, they will be colorfast when the piece is washed. (Remember to wash a handknit with mild soap and lukewarm water — never use a harsh detergent.)

CASTING ON

There are a few different methods of casting on, but the most widely used is done with the left thumb (right thumb if one is left-handed) and one knitting needle.

Figure 9. To cast on, begin by making a slip knot on the needle and pulling it tight (A). Use the index finger and thumb to make a square (B), and move the thumb to create a loop (C). Put the needle under the strand on the thumb (D) and then under the strand on the index finger (E). Move the needle back through the loop on the thumb (F), and pull the stitch tight (G).

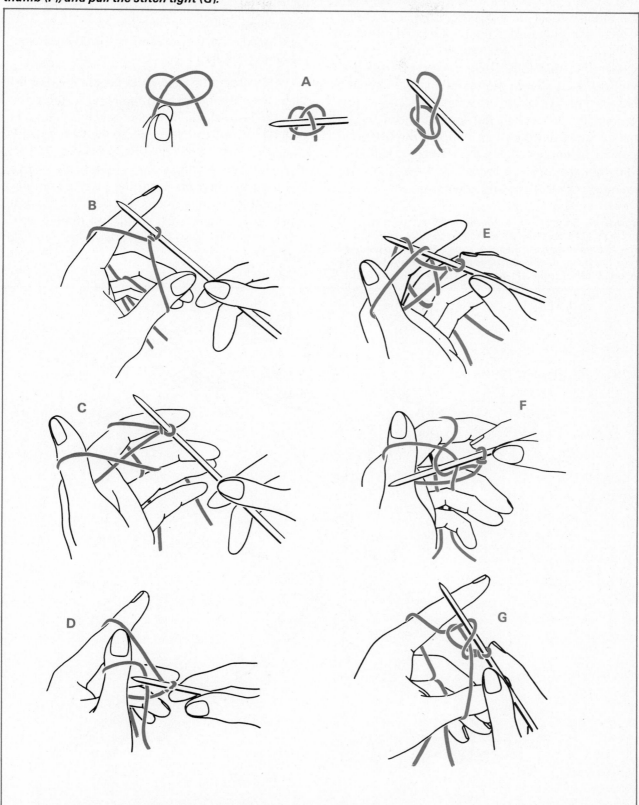

A long strand of yarn at the left is used to make the new stitches. In determining the length necessary for the yarn, allow about 1/2" for each stitch. The yarn to the right is used to knit the stitches from the thumb. Make a slip knot; slide it onto the needle; and pull to secure it on the needle. *Wrap the yarn around the left thumb once. Insert the needle into this loop from the bottom up and pointing away. Wrap the right-hand yarn around the needle counterclockwise and pull this through the loop. Pull the long strand. *Repeat this procedure from * to * until the required number of stitches are cast on. Make a half knot with the two yarns. If there is a long strand remaining, cut it to a length of approximately 6".

Figure 10. To knit, hold needle with cast-on yarn in left hand (A), and insert right needle into first stitch (B). Holding yarn as shown, move yarn under, then over the point of the right needle (C). Draw yarn back through stitch one (D) and slip stitch off needle (E).

TO KNIT

Place the needle with the stitches in the left hand, the empty needle in the right hand. The closer to the tips of the needles that one works, the faster the knitting will go. Furthermore, resting the right-hand needle on the forearm is extremely helpful in knitting rapidly.

To begin, insert the right-hand needle into the first stitch from the bottom up, pointing in the direction of 11 o'clock. The left needle should be pointed toward 1 o'clock. Wrap the yarn counterclockwise around the right-hand needle. Pull the loop through by tipping the right-hand needle. Slip the old stitch off. Until the yarn is held in a comfortable manner, there will be a tendency to yank the yarn after each stitch. Just remember to pull gently, otherwise the result will be very tight stitches.

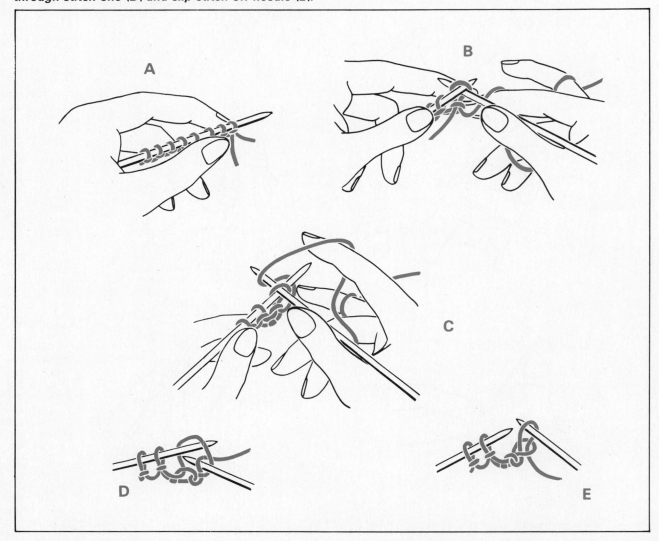

TO PURL

The empty needle is in the right hand pointing toward the knitter. * It is inserted into the stitch in the direction of 10 o'clock. The yarn is toward the knitter. Wrap the yarn counterclockwise and, with the left thumb, push the needle back and away. The loop is now on the right-hand needle, *behind* the left-hand needle. Slip the old stitch off the left-hand needle; repeat from *.

Figure 11. To purl, hold needle with row of knit stitches in left hand (A). Place right needle through loop of stitch one, from front to back (B). Wrap yarn under and then over right needle (C). Pull yarn through to back of stitch (D). The new stitch thus formed (E) is moved onto the right needle (F).

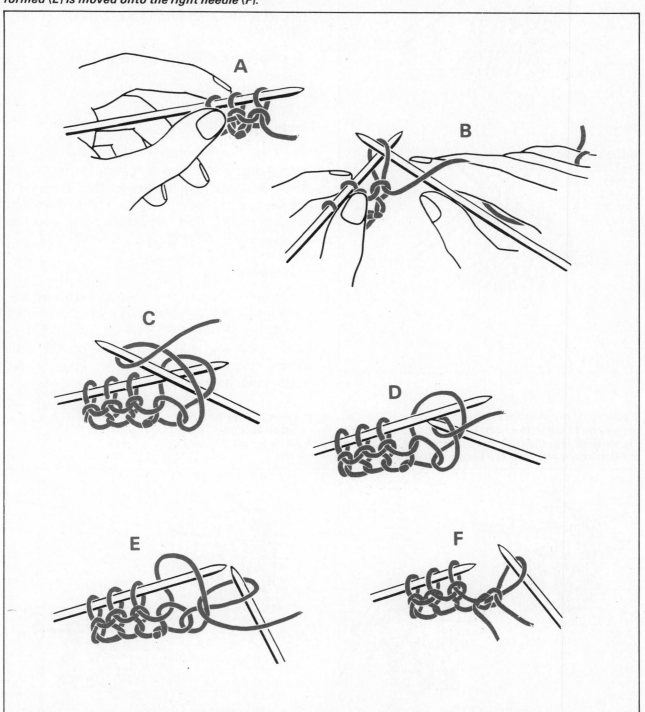

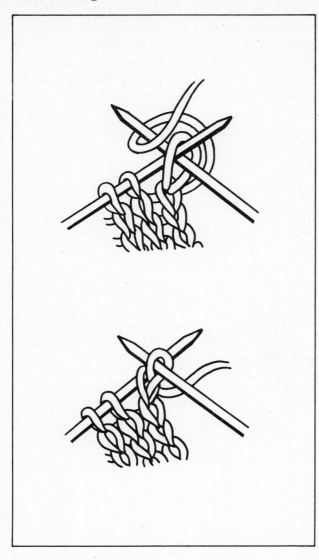

Figure 12. To increase a stitch (left), insert the right needle and knit (A), but, instead of removing the needle, insert it in the back loop of the stitch and knit again. This process will form a new stitch (B).

INCREASING AND DECREASING STITCHES

It is sometimes necessary to increase and decrease the number of stitches on the needle in order to shape pieces as they are being knitted.

Increasing

Insert right needle into front of first stitch and knit, but do not remove the stitch from the left needle. Then, insert the right needle into the *back* loop of the same stitch and knit again, forming two new stitches on the right needle. Now, remove the stitch from the left needle and continue to knit.

Decreasing

Insert needle into front of second stitch then into front of first stitch so that both stitches are on the needle at the same time. Knit the two stitches together, forming one new stitch on the right needle. Remove the two stitches from the left needle and continue knitting.

Figure 13. There are two methods for decreasing. To slant stitches to the right, put the needle through the front of the second stitch and then the first stitch (A); knit the stitches together (B). For a slant to the left, place the needle through the back of the first stitch and then the second (C); knit the two together (D).

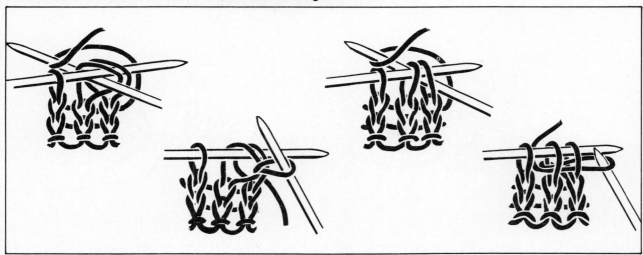

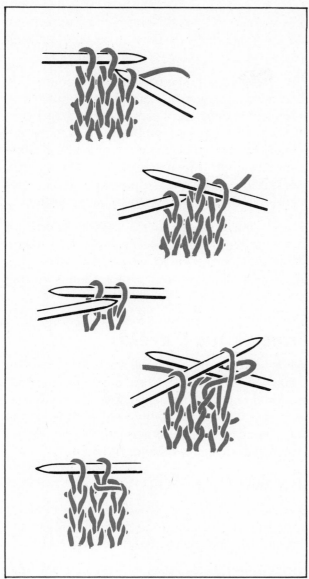

Figure 14. To bind off, first slip off stitch one (A). Knit or purl stitch two (B). Place needle through stitch one (C); draw the yarn over stitch two (D). Stitch one is bound; continue working two with three (E).

BINDING OFF

When binding off, the stitches are worked in pattern as they are removed from the needle. Begin by working two stitches loosely. Insert the tip of the left-hand needle into the first stitch worked; pull it over the second stitch and over the tip of the right-hand needle; let it drop. Work another stitch; then pull the stitch before it over it. Continue in this way until only one stitch remains; cut the yarn leaving about 10"; pull this yarn through the stitch. Take the needle out and pull the yarn tight.

TESTING THE GAUGE

The most important single aspect of knitting is attainment of the correct gauge — the gauge called for in directions. It is usually necessary to work a 3-inch swatch to compare gauges — the gauge of the knitted swatch to the gauge required in the directions.

As an example, consider that directions for a man's sweater call for a gauge of five stitches to 1" using #8 needles. This does not include ribbing at the bottom of the sweater, which is knitted on smaller needles. The directions call for 100 stitches; therefore, 20" (5 stitches divided into 100) is the correct measurement of this piece.

Onto the needle size required for the main portion of the sweater cast on 15 stitches. Work in the pattern stitch for 3"; bind off. Steam the wrong side of the swatch through a damp cloth. This releases the yarn as body heat would do. Now measure it. If it is more than 3" wide, a smaller needle will be necessary to draw the stitches closer together. If it is smaller, a larger needle is needed to spread them out. Remember that a deviation of even half a stitch per inch will affect the final results.

JOINING

When starting a new ball of yarn, begin at a new row. Leaving an end of about 6", simply loop the yarn onto the right needle after it has been inserted into the stitch. Complete the stitch. This stitch will be loose in the next row, but do not knot it until three or four rows have been worked. The ends can later be hidden in the back of the work with a crochet hook.

Joining or seaming two pieces of knitted work is done with yarn and a tapestry needle. The seams may be back stitched right sides together; this leaves a rather bulky seam. It is also possible to overcast the stitches on the edges with right sides facing; sometimes there is a tendency for loose seaming to result. Weaving is the preferred method.

Weaving the Seam

Lay the work flat on the lap or table, right sides up. Thread a tapestry needle with yarn; work from the bottom up along the side edge; use only the alternating loose stitches — these are easy to see.

Work from side to side, down through one loose stitch and up through the next one on the same side; down and up through the loose stitches on the other edge; back to the first side and down through the last stitch used and up through the next; * back to the other side and down through the last stitch used and up through the next. Repeat from *. The joining thread will look like a winding path. This method is used when the knitted pieces are parallel to each other.

The second weaving method is used when parts of the knitting are joined together, such as at the shoulder of a sweater or of a strip at the back of the neck. The track of the needle is the same as for duplicate stitching.

Consider a stitch to be a V. In order to join two sides of knitting heading into each other, weave under the point of the V as it is inverted and then under the point on the other piece as it is right side up. The joining yarn is *not* pulled tight. It affects a stitch and the knitting appears continuous.

MAKING CORRECTIONS

To correct a mistake, it is often necessary to rip out stitches. It is much easier to put the stitches back on the needle after ripping them if one uses a needle *at least* three sizes smaller than the needle used originally. This will not affect the gauge of the knitting because the needle is used merely to hold the stitches. Just pick up the ravelled stitches from the back or the front; make certain the stitches are properly positioned; then, resume knitting with the correct size needle.

A long needle gives better control when picking up the stitches. In fact, getting used to a longer (14″) needle for all straight work places less strain on the wrists. As mentioned earlier, resting the needle on the inner forearm actually speeds the knitting.

BLOCKING

Blocking is easier once a garment is joined, though some people prefer to block in pieces. If the latter is done, there is a tendency for the pins to distort the seam line; thus, added steaming is necessary to smooth them. However, in the case

of large pieces — coats, skirts worked in sections, afghans — it is easier to block in sections and then join.

Place the garment on a padded board or anything that steam cannot harm. Pin the garment to measurement and *lightly* steam it through a damp cloth. In the case of synthetic fabrics, be extremely careful not to apply too much heat or the yarn will melt. The garment can also be "wet blocked" by washing it and pinning it to measurement while damp; omit the steaming and let dry.

If fold lines appear, use a sleeve board for steaming the creases, again through a damp cloth. It is important to weave the seams and block carefully to insure a professional looking garment.

Projects You Can Do

When considering the projects below, keep in mind that each one teaches something the previous did not. Refer to the list of "Common Terms" for the meanings of abbreviations. Use of the latter increases from project to project to accustom the knitter to working with them.

HEADBAND OF SPORT YARN

Be sure to notice the two different methods of decreasing used here. One method pulls to the right (K2 tog); the other to the left (K1, sl 1, psso).

Because the headband is worked in stockinette stitch (st st), the edges curl. This is not only common to st st, but useful because the headband should cling when completed.

Materials: (1) one 2 oz. skein Brunswick Sport Yarn; (2) one pair #5 straight needles; (3) one card Bucilla Needlepoint and Crewel Wool in a contrasting color (cc); (4) tapestry needle; and (5) graph paper. The gauge is 6 sts = 1 inch.

With #5 needles, cast on 10 sts. P1 row. * Next row: K1; increase one stitch in the next stitch by inserting the needle into the stitch *below* the stitch on the needle; knit through it; and make a new stitch. Knit the stitch increased into, knit to within the last 2 sts, increase 1 st in the next st, K1. P1 row, K1 row, P1 row. Repeat from the * until there are 22 sts. Work even in st st until the entire piece is 17½″; end with a P row. Begin shaping on

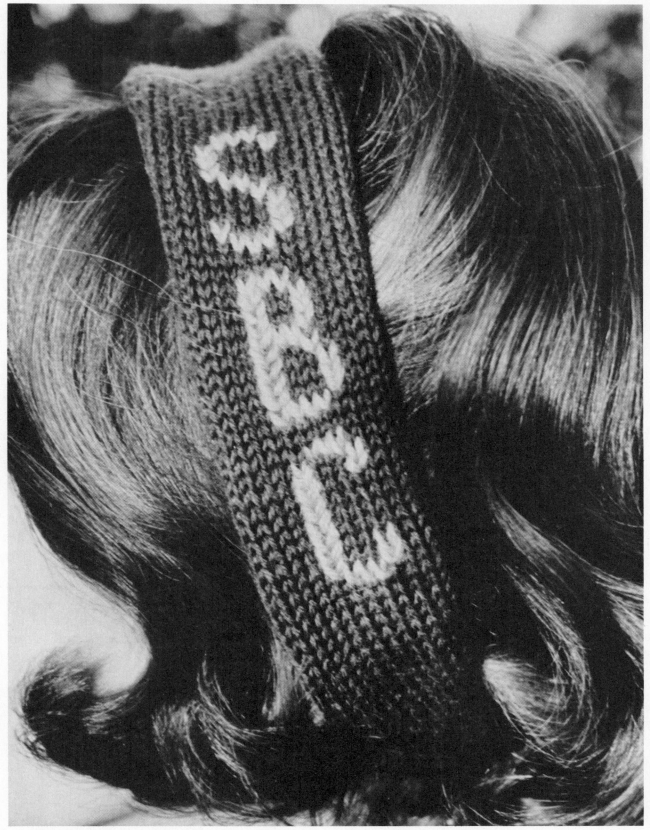

Figure 15. This attractive finished headband (above), complete with initials, makes a present that is both useful and totally individualized.

the next row: * K1, sl 1, K1, psso, K to last 3 sts, K2 tog, K1. P1 row, K1 row, P1 row. Repeat from * until 10 sts remain. Bind off, leaving an 8" end; pull end tightly through the last stitch. With the tapestry needle, join the cast on row to the bind off row; use the second weaving method described under "Basic Procedures."

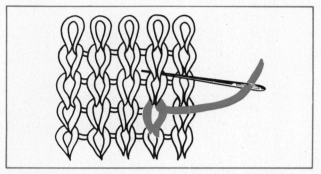

Figure 16. Shown above is the method for making the headband initials with duplicate stitches.

With the graph paper, plot out one or more initials. Use six squares for the width of each initial and ten for the height — each square represents one stitch. Create a pattern for working duplicate stitches over the knitting by placing a dot in the center of the squares chosen for the initial. Using only two strands of CC (Contrasting Color), thread the tapestry needle. Begin by coming up at the point of the V (stitch) on the right side. Refer to the diagram of duplicate stitch and do not pull too tightly.

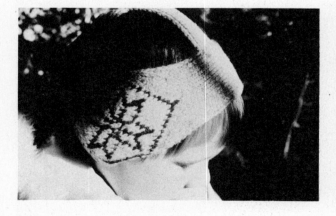

HEADBAND FOR WARMTH

Materials: (1) one 2 oz. skein knitting worsted; (2)

one #8 straight needles. The gauge is 5 sts = 1 inch.

Cast on 8 sts. P1 row, K1 row, P1 row. Next row: K1, inc 1 st in next st (this includes the increased stitch *and* the stitch increased into), K4, inc 1 st in next st, K1 (10 sts). Repeat these four rows until 20 sts are on needle. Work even until piece measures 16½"; end with a P row. Shape end: K1, sl 1, K1, psso, work to the last 3 sts, K2 tog, K1. Repeat this decrease row every fourth row until 8 sts remain. Bind off. Weave ends tog.

STRIPED HAT

Materials: (1) one 2 oz. skein knitting worsted main color (MC); (2) one 2 oz. skein contrasting color (CC); (3) one pair #10½ straight needles; and (4) one pair #4 straight needles. The gauge is 3½ sts = 1 inch.

With the larger needles and CC, cast on 80 sts. With smaller needles K in Garter Stitch for eight rows. With larger needles work an increase row as follows: * K7, inc in next st, repeat from * across row (90 sts). With MC P next row and work in st st (K1 row, P1 row), carrying the CC up the edge of the work by intertwining the two yarns every second row. Work until there are 14 rows of MC, 4 rows CC, 4 rows MC, 2 rows CC, 2 rows MC, 2 rows CC, 4 rows MC, finishing with CC only. With smaller needles K2 tog across the row. P1 row. K 2 tog across the next row. Break yarn leaving a 15" end. Thread through a tapestry needle. Gently remove the needle and, taking care not to ravel the work, thread the needle through the stitches. Draw tight and go through the stitches again so that there will not be too much stress on the single strand of yarn. Then, weave the seam by going from top to bottom using the first weaving method described under "Basic Procedures." Secure the end on the wrong side.

To make a pompon: Cut a piece of sturdy cardboard 2" x 4". Wind yarn approximately 100 times around the narrow portion. Thread the tapestry needle with yarn and slide it under the strands on the cardboard. Cut the other side of the wound yarn and quickly tie the strands *tightly* with the threaded yarn. Sew with this same yarn to the top of the hat. Even the pompon with scissors.

Figure 17. This boy's head is warm and cozy in his striped hat, topped off with a pompon.

Figure 18. The completed scarf (above), delicate in texture, is inexpensive and simple to make.

SCARF

This scarf can be worked as a short scarf using only two balls of yarn or as a baby's carriage throw. The yarn called for is particularly soft and fluffy; it is a synthetic yarn and machine washable. Fluffy yarns are more difficult to work with at first.

Materials for long scarf (58"): (1) 3 balls "Fluffy" yarn; (2) 1 pair #8 needles. Work a multiple of 2 sts for lacy pattern. The gauge is 3½ sts = 1 inch.

Cast on 42 sts. Work in Garter st for 8 rows placing markers on the needle 4 sts in from each end on last row. Lacy pattern. Row 1: K4, sl marker, * bring yarn to the front over the right needle, sl 1, K1 (a yo has been created), psso. Repeat from * to second marker, sl marker, K4.

Rows 2, 3, and 4: K4, sl marker, P to marker, sl marker, K4. The yo of row 1 is treated as a stitch. Repeat these four rows for pattern. When the piece measures 57" ending with row 2 of pattern, K 8 rows of Garter st. Bind off. Block.

For carriage throw, six balls of Fluffy are required. Cast on 126 sts and work as for scarf for 36".

Figure 19. Knitting a coat (above) is a major under-taking, even for the experienced craftsman. The purchased zipper has a special coat closing at the bottom and a pull ring at the top.

Figure 20. This charming baby blanket, the work of an accomplisher knitter, has a design that will delight mother and baby alike.

For Additional Reading

Hamilton-Hunt, Margaret, **Knitting Dictionary: 800 Stitches-Patterns,** Crown Publishers, 1963.

Phillips, Mary Walker, **Step by Step Knitting,** Golden Press., 1967.

Walker, Barbara G., **Sampler Knitting,** Scribner, 1973.

Knitting: A Golden Hands Pattern Book, Random House, 1973.

Crocheting

Crocheting enjoys widespread appeal because it is easy to do and lends itself to many delightful interpretations.

The history of crochet dates back to the sixteenth century, when French nuns used a hook for making lace. Indeed, the term "crochet" is derived from the French *croche,* meaning hook.

The art of crochet was inspired by sailors who came into port with macramé lace parasols and bags. These were made during long journeys and sold to wealthy ladies all over the world. In trying to copy these larger versions of lace, the nuns created crochet and all its intricate stitches.

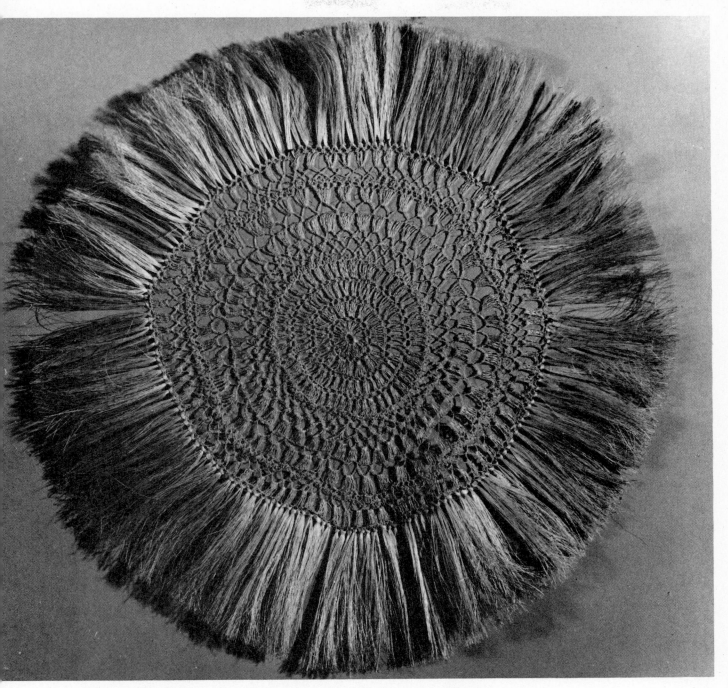

Figure 2. This crocheted sansevieria fiber doily is from Jamaica. (Courtesy, Smithsonian Institution.)

The great Irish famine of 1846 took crochet out of the convent and brought it into the social circles of Ireland. The nuns taught their pupils to crochet and used the money derived from the sale of these articles to purchase food and clothing for the

Figure 1. Ronald Goodman created the wool crochet sculpture, "Gemini, My Brother," opposite. (Courtesy, The Museum of Contemporary Crafts of the American Crafts Council. Photo by Bob Hanson.)

poor. During the famine, rare old patterns of lace were skillfully copied by the Irish girls. Eventually, crochet became one of the accomplishments of the well-born young lady.

Irish crochet, an outstanding example of this art, is a type of lace made with a very fine thread. It is composed of a series of shamrocks, roses, and little rings surrounded by a lacy background of chain stitches with small picots, or knots. Irish crochet, recognized by the whiteness of the linen thread, is used mainly for collars, trims, and doilies.

Until recent years, crochet was almost exclusively worked with crochet cotton for making tablecloths, doilies, bedspreads, and fine edgings for mats and handkerchiefs. Garments, except for fine blouses and baby outfits, were seldom crocheted. Knitting books used crochet only as an edging around the neck and cuffs of knitted garments. Many experienced knitters never attempted crochet at all and the two crafts were considered as different as the materials they required. This is not the case today. Crocheting with wool and other knitting yarns has become increasingly popular and fashionable. Patterns are now available for all types of garments, from men's sweaters to evening gowns and bikini bathing suits. Nor is there a restriction on using fine yarns. Many of today's fashions are designed for bulky yarns and double strands.

Common Terms Used In Crocheting

Afghan Hook: longer than the ordinary crochet hook with a round instead of a flattened grip, the afghan hook resembles a knitting needle with a hook on one end instead of a point.

Afghan Stitch: a stitch which forms squares.

Bind Off: the completion of a section of a crocheting project or the entire project; also, a technique used to decrease the number of stitches.

Blocking: the process of adjusting the finished project to the desired shape and size.

Chain Stitch: the stitch which begins all crochet work.

Crochet Hook: a narrow piece of metal, bone, wood, or plastic about 6 inches long with barblike hook on one end.

Figure 3. A delicate Irish crochet cape collar uses an intricate traditional design. (*Courtesy, Smithsonian Institution.*)

Cro-Hook: a double-ended afghan hook, with two barblike ends rather than one, which allows for the use of two yarn colors at one time and enables one to make reversible garments.

Double Crochet: a stitch twice as long as single crochet; creates a pattern of solid shapes and bars in an openwork pattern.

Filet: a type of crochet formed by blocks and spaces and often consisting of the double crochet stitch throughout.

Gauge: the number of rows and the number of stitches equivalent to 1 inch. When blocking the gauge, one can also learn approximately how much the yarn will stretch. Since many yarns may stretch when wet, a gauge measuring 4 inches before blocking may measure 4¼ inches after blocking. Therefore, hook size must be adjusted accordingly.

Hairpin Lace Fork: a fork or loom used in combination with a crochet hook to make delicate strips of lace.

Half Double Crochet: a stitch longer than a single crochet and shorter than a double crochet.

Motif: complete crochet designs used in creating such large items as linens, bedspreads, and afghans.

Single Crochet: the shortest of the basic crochet stitches which creates solid pattern shapes and bars in an openwork pattern.

Slip Stitch: a very small stitch used to fasten off the end of the work, to make a finished edge without adding an additional row, or to form a corded edging.

Swatch: a practice piece of approximately 2 square inches.

Treble Crochet: sometimes referred to as the triple crochet, this stitch is one step longer than a double crochet.

Yarn Over: a procedure necessary in most crochet stitches; the loose yarn is laid over the hook from back to front.

Common Abbreviations And Symbols Used In Most Pattern Books

Project directions in pattern books involve many small steps, each of which is set off by commas, semicolons, or periods. The following is a list of common crochet abbreviations (these are employed in the projects described at the end of this article): beg (beginning), CC (contrasting color), ch (chain), dc (double crochet), dec (decrease), hdc (half double crochet), inc (increase), lp (loop), MC (main color), pat (pattern), rep (repeat), rnd (round), sc (single crochet), sk (skip), sl st (slip stitch), sp (space), st (stitch), sts (stitches), tog (together), tr (treble or triple crochet), and yo (yarn or thread over). An asterisk (*), double asterisk (**), or dagger (†) indicates that the instructions immediately following the symbol are to be repeated the directed number of times in addition to the initial procedure. The * to * means to repeat the instructions between the asterisks the number of times indicated in the pattern.

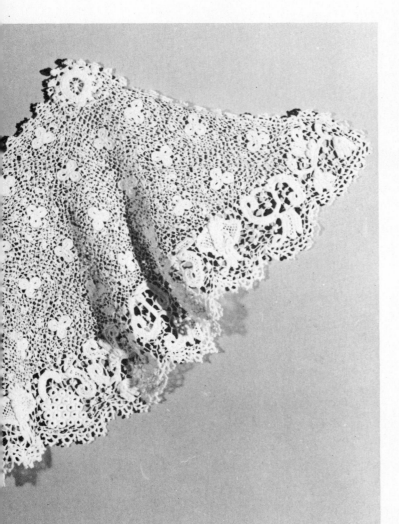

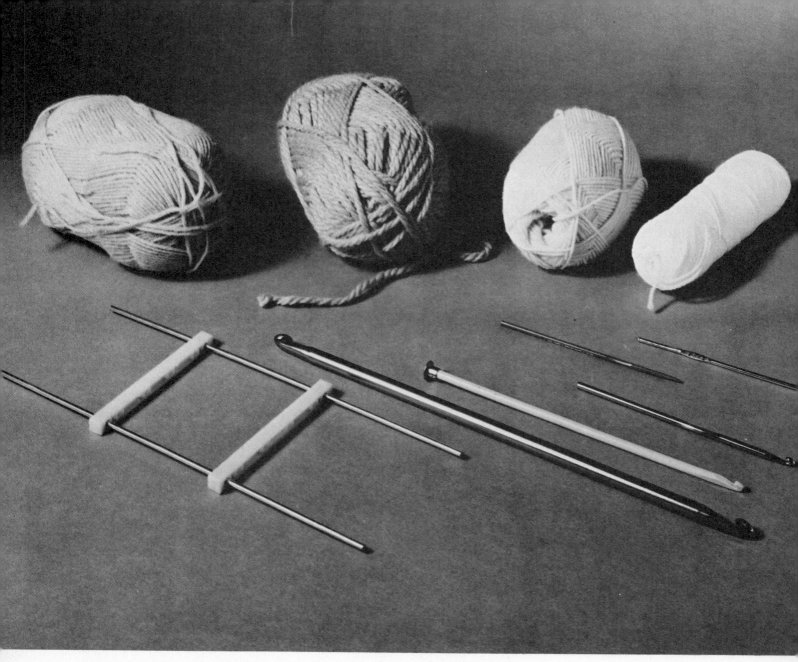

Figure 4. Among the supplies available for crocheting are yarns of various weights and several types of hooks.

Basic Equipment And Supplies

The basic equipment and supplies necessary for the art of crocheting can be found in nearly all art needlework stores or departments. These include scissors, a tapestry needle, and a tape measure in addition to the following hooks and yarns.

CROCHET HOOKS

There are several types of hooks, each especially adapted for use with a certain size thread or yarn. Crochet hooks are usually made of aluminum, plastic, or steel. It is important to use the number hook specified in the directions or the size hook that will yield the correct gauge.

Steel Hooks

Steel crochet hooks are 5 inches long and range from size 00 (the largest) to size 14 (the smallest). The largest hook is used for knitting worsted weight yarns or heavy cotton crochet threads. The second largest hooks (0-1) are excellent for sport yarns and medium-weight cotton crochet threads. Size 2-5 hooks are best for fingering yarns and lightweight cotton crochet threads. The smallest hooks, sizes 6-14, are used for fine and very fine cotton crochet threads.

Aluminum or Plastic Hooks

Sizes in aluminum hooks range from size B (the smallest) through size K (the largest). Plastic hooks range from size D through Q. Most of these hooks are 5½ or 6 inches long. The plastic size Q hook is 8 inches long. These hooks are used for varying weights of wool, cotton, or synthetic yarns.

Wood Hooks

The sizes of wood hooks are 10 (the smallest), 13, 14, and 15 (the largest). These are 9 inches long and are used for extra heavy yarns (or several strands of yarn) or for heavy cotton rug yarns.

Afghan Hooks

Afghan hooks are made of aluminum or plastic and are lettered the same way as regular aluminum or plastic hooks (from size B to N). They are available in 9-inch and 14-inch lengths. Afghan hooks do not have a finger grip depression (flattened section). They are used for the afghan stitch, which requires all of the loops in the row to be retained on the hook. This is why afghan hooks are uniform throughout the shank and longer than the regular crochet hook. Also available is a flexible afghan hook (18 inches long), which is useful for large projects.

Cro-Hook

A cro-hook, available in aluminum or plastic, is a double-ended afghan hook. It allows for the making of reversible garments, using two skeins of yarn at one time.

Hairpin Loom or Fork

A hairpin fork comes in various widths, beginning with 1/4 inch and ranging up to 4 inches. Also available is an adjustable hairpin fork which converts to various sizes.

YARNS

Anything which can be wrapped around a needle is suitable for crocheting. Unusual material will produce unique results — texture plays an interesting part in the beauty of crochet. With very fine

thread and a fine hook, delicate laces can be fashioned. Heavy threads and yarn give the bold effects often used in modern furnishings. Choose a tightly twisted thread for hard surface effects and long-wearing quality. Select a soft thread or yarn for softer textures. Crochet may be done with cotton, linen, silk, wool, manmade fibers, or combinations of any of these. The texture desired and the purpose of the article being made should determine the choice of thread.

Because sizes and dye lots vary and often cannot be matched, it is advisable to purchase enough thread or yarn to complete an item before beginning to work.

Yarns are generally classed in four groups by weight (thickness): (1) fingering or baby yarn is the lightest; (2) sport yarn is medium weight; (3) knitting worsted is a heavy weight; and (4) bulky yarn is the term applied to all yarns heavier than knitting worsted. All these weights of yarn are available in wool, orlon, or cotton.

Basic Procedures

The following directions are for the basic crochet stitches. It will be helpful to practice each stitch described. The right-handed person holds the hook in the right hand and the loose thread in the

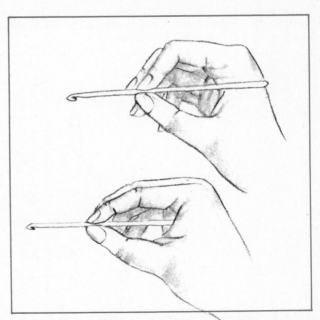

Figure 5. A crochet hook is held in the right hand with the loose thread in the left hand (the reverse for left-handed persons). Hold the hook on top or at the finger-grip depression.

left hand. The left-handed person does the opposite. Either of the two hand positions shown in the drawing may be used: the hook is held at the finger grip depression or on top. Most of the practice stitches are worked in rows of 21 stitches. It will be helpful to study the illustrations closely.

CHAIN STITCH (ch st)

The chain stitch (abbreviated ch st) is the stitch used to begin all crochet work. To start, make a slip knot approximately 4 inches from the end of the thread by making a loop and pulling another loop through it. Attach the slip knot loop to the hook as shown.

To work a long chain, hold the tag end of the thread between the thumb and third finger of the left hand and hold the thread coming from the ball of thread over the index finger. To cause a slight tension against the thread, wind it around the little finger before placing it over the index finger. With the hook in the right hand, lay it in front of the new thread and wrap this over the hook. Then, with the hook pointing down, pull a new loop through the loop on the hook.

To hold the chain close and to pull the new stitch through easily, one must keep raising the thumb and third finger. Before pulling each chain stitch,

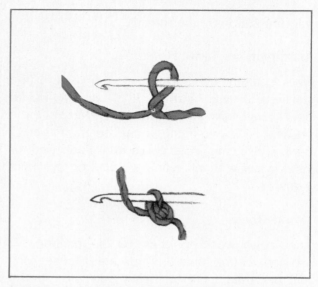

Figure 6. Begin chain stitch with slip knot about 4" from the end of the thread. Pull one loop through another and attach slip knot loop to hook, as illustrated.

slip the preceding stitch completely onto the shank part of the hook. This will make the stitches uniform in size. After forming the first chain stitch, continue in the same manner until the desired number of stitches have been made.

The chain should be flat. If it is not, check to be sure that the loose thread is being brought over the hook from behind.

Figure 7. As chain lengthens, hold the tag end securely between thumb and third finger. Raise the fingers while working the chain stitches to keep the tension even (left). The chain should be flat (right).

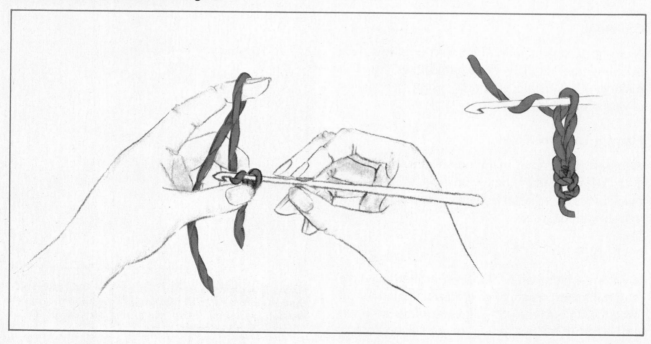

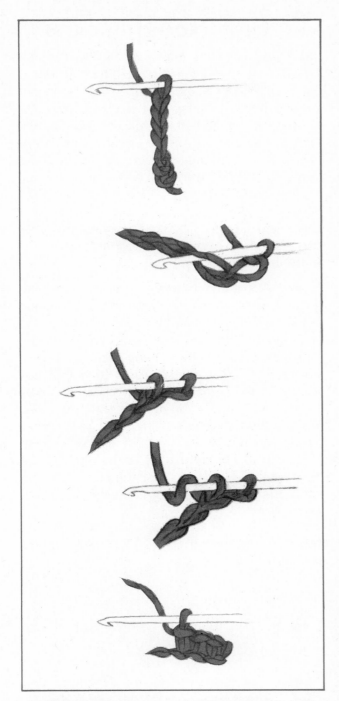

Figure 8. Use a chain as the foundation for the single crochet, as illustrated. Follow instructions in the text and be sure each loop is brought up onto the shank of the hook to keep stitches uniform.

SINGLE CROCHET STITCH (sc)

A single crochet stitch is worked by using chain stitches as a foundation. The row of single crochet stitches begins on the second chain stitch — the loop on the hook is not the first chain stitch. Insert the crochet hook into the chain, placing the hook

between the loops in the second chain. Two threads should lie on top of the hook and one thread below the hook. Pull a loop through this hole. There are now two loops on the hook. Next, lay the hook in front of the thread, bring the yarn over the hook, and pull a loop through the two loops already on the hook. One single crochet stitch has been made. Continue to work single crochet stitches in each of the chain stitches of the foundation row. When the row is completed, there should be one less single crochet stitch than there are chain stitches — remember that the first single crochet stitch was done on the second chain stitch.

Be sure that each loop is brought up onto the shank part of the crochet hook; this makes for uniform stitches that are loose enough to work easily.

Now work a second row of single crochet stitches, proceeding as follows: make one chain stitch, turn the work around, and work one single crochet stitch in each stitch of the row just completed. Making a chain stitch first and then turning the work allows space to begin work on the next row. The chain stitch is counted as the first single crochet stitch.

Figure 9. Below is a completed swatch of single stitch.

Skip the next stitch so as not to have two stitches coming from the first stitch on the completed row. Then single crochet in each stitch across the row to the end, working through the top two loops of each single crochet stitch. Be sure that there are an equal number of stitches in each row.

Always keep the thumb and third finger near the working area and remember to point the crochet hook down when pulling the loops through. Work several rows for practice. To correct errors, take off the loop that is on the hook and pull out the necessary stitches. Then replace the loop on the hook and proceed. To fasten off the work, crochet to the end of the row and cut the thread, leaving an end of approximately 4 inches. Pull the loose end through the loop on the hook to lock off the stitches.

Figure 10. The half double crochet stitch begins with a completed chain. Loop thread over the hook (A), draw a loop through the third chain (B), wind another loop (C), and draw a loop through the three loops on the hook (D).

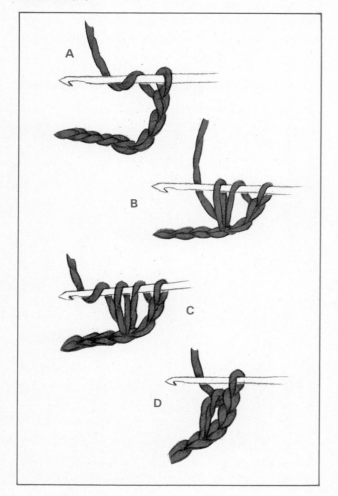

HALF DOUBLE CROCHET STITCH (hdc)

Once again, work from a chain stitch foundation. To work a half double stitch, hold the thread and hook as previously explained. Wrap the thread over the hook one time, then place the hook into the third chain from the hook and pull a loop through (see diagram). There are now three loops on the hook. Lay the hook in front of the loose thread, bring yarn over hook (yarn over), and pull another loop through all three of the loops on the hook (follow illustration). One half double crochet stitch has been worked: continue to work one half double crochet stitch in each stitch across the chain.

Turn work and chain two to count as the first half double crochet stitch for the next row. Continue across, working half double crochet stitches in each stitch across row. The last stitch of the row should be placed in the turning chain of the previous row. Maintaining the proper count (one less stitch than the original chain), work several rows for practice. (NOTE: In the second row, after chaining two stitches to turn, the chain comes directly on top of the last half double crochet stitch. This chain two counts as the first stitch of the new row. Put the first half double crochet on top of the second stitch from the end of the previous row.)

Figure 11. Shown is a swatch of half double crochet.

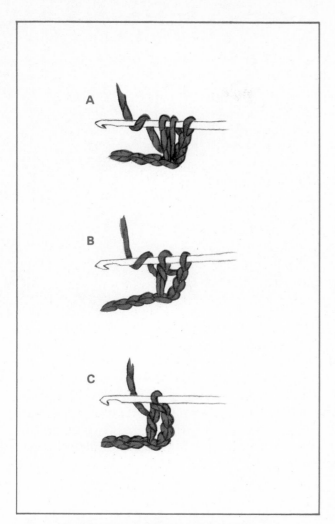

Figure 12. Work the double crochet stitch from a chain. First form three loops (A), as in Figure 10. Pull one loop through the other two, yarn over (B), and repeat, creating a double stitch (C).

DOUBLE CROCHET STITCH (dc)

To work the double crochet stitch, hold the thread and hook as explained previously and work off a row of chain stitches. Wrap the thread over the hook one time, and place the hook into the fourth chain from the hook (do not count the stitch on the hook as one chain). Pull a loop through, forming three loops on the hook. Lay the hook in front of the loose thread, yarn over, and pull another loop through the first two loops on the hook. There are now two loops left on the hook. Yarn over and pull another loop through the last two loops on the hook. This is a double crochet stitch.

Work several rows for practice. Turn work and chain three to count as the first double crochet stitch for the next row. (Note: In the second row,

after chaining three stitches to turn, the chain comes directly on top the last double crochet stitch. This chain three counts as the first stitch of the new row. Put the first double crochet on top of the second stitch from the end of the previous row.)

Figure 13. Pictured is a sample of double crochet.

TREBLE CROCHET STITCH (tr or trc)

As before, make a chain. Begin a treble crochet stitch by wrapping the thread over the hook twice. Place the hook into the fifth chain from the hook. (See drawing. Do not count the stitch on the hook as one chain.) Pull a loop through. There are now four loops on the hook. Lay the hook in front of the loose thread, yarn over, and pull another loop through the first two loops. There are now three loops left on the hook. Yarn over again and pull another loop through the next two loops on the hook. There are two loops left on the hook. Yarn over and pull another loop through the last two loops on the hook. This is one treble crochet stitch. Work one treble crochet stitch in each chain across the row, then chain four and turn the work around to begin next row.

On the next row, work a treble crochet stitch in each stitch across the row. The chain four after turning counts as the first treble crochet stitch.

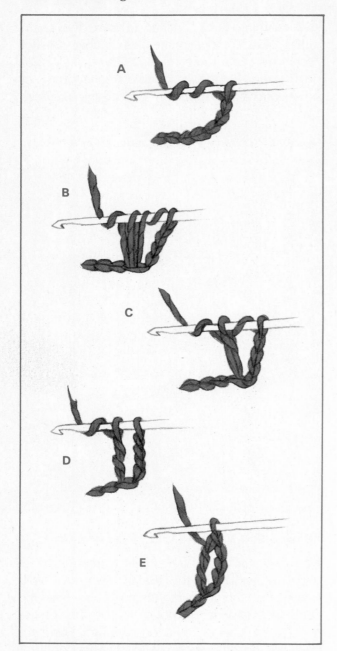

Figure 14. The treble crochet stitch begins with a chain and two loops over the hook (A). Pull a loop through the fifth chain and put yarn over (B). Pull loops through as in double crochet (C, D). When complete (E), treble crochet will have three stitches.

Work several rows, maintaining the stitch count. (NOTE: In the second row, after chaining the four stitches to turn, notice that the chain comes directly on top of the last treble crochet stitch worked. Because this chain four counts as the first stitch of the new row, do not put another stitch through this stitch. Put the first treble crochet stitch on top of the second stitch from the end of the previous row.)

Figure 15. The swatch above is treble crochet.

SLIP STITCH (sl st)

A slip stitch is a very small stitch. To work it, make a foundation chain and insert the hook into the second chain from the hook. Yarn over the hook and pull a loop through the loop on the hook. This is a slip stitch. Work a row of slip stitches across the chain.

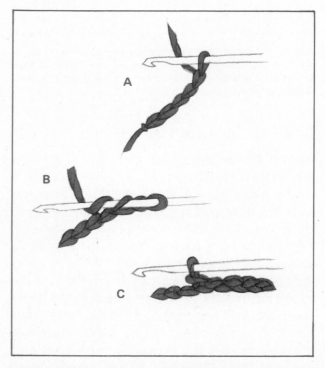

Figure 16. The small slip stitch is also worked from a finished chain (A). The hook is placed in the second chain with yarn over the hook (B). Pull the loop through, forming slip (C).

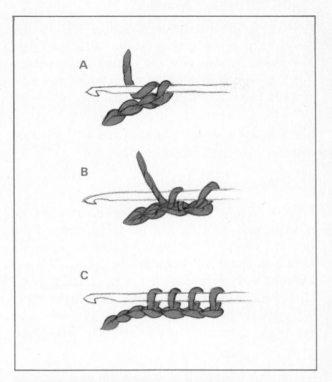

Figure 17. In the first step of an afghan stitch, begin as shown (A). The hook is then placed under the top strand of second chain with yarn over hook. Yarn is drawn through to create loops (B, C). Repeat until the loops equal the number of chains.

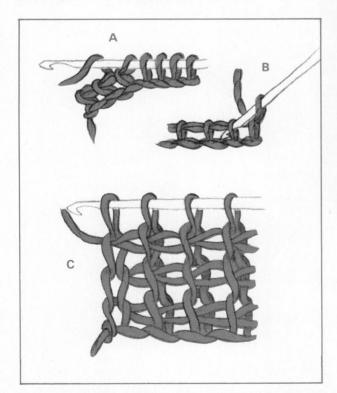

Figure 18. For the second step of the afghan stitch, draw yarn first through one loop, then the next (A). Repeat, ending with one loop on hook (B) to begin next row. Work several rows (C).

Figure 19. Pictured is a swatch of afghan crochet.

AFGHAN STITCH

Unlike other crochet stitches, this stitch requires two steps to complete one actual row. Chain a row of 18 stitches, then begin Row 1 of afghan stitches as follows. Skip the first chain. * Insert hook under top strand only of next chain, catch yarn, and draw it through chain. There are now two loops on the hook. Repeat from * to end of chain. There are now as many loops on the hook as the number of chains — this is the first step toward completion of the afghan stitch.

For the second step, draw yarn through the first loop only; * draw yarn through two loops. Repeat from * to end of row, ending with one loop on hook. *This is the first loop of the next row.* Study this row and note that there is a series of upright or vertical stitches. These are called bars.

The first step of the second row is as follows. Always skip the first bar because the first loop is already on the hook. * Insert hook through the next bar, and draw yarn through. There are now two loops on the hook. Repeat from * to the end of the row. The second half of each row is worked the same as the second half of Row 1.

Remember, when working the afghan stitch, the work is never turned. One works over, then back from the same side. Always begin the second half of a row by drawing the yarn through one stitch only and then through two at a time. The last stitch remaining is always the first stitch of the next row; always skip the first bar when starting a row. Always work with exactly the same number of stitches as were in the original chain.

CRO-HOOKING PROCEDURES

Using the cro-hook needle, chain desired length using color A. Work from right to left. Insert hook in the second chain, yarn over, pull up the new stitch, and hold it on the hook. Continue across the row, holding all the stitches on the hook. There should be one less new stitch than the number in the starting chain.

Slide all the work to the other side of the needle and turn. Loosely tie in color B. Yarn over, pull through one stitch, yarn over, and pull through two stitches. Work off all stitches across row by yarn over and pulling through two stitches.

For Row 4, work from color B, right to left; insert hook in last stitch made, yarn over, pull up new stitch, hold it on the hook, and work across row, holding all stitches on hook. Slide work to opposite end of the needle and turn. Pick up color A and repeat as in Row 3 from yarn over, pull through one stitch.

Remember that when cro-hooking, two skeins of yarn are being used. Two rows are worked from one skein. Work then slides to the other end of the needle, is turned, and the next two rows are worked with the second skein. The yarn never needs to be cut; two rows are worked with the first skein, starting and ending on the same side; then two rows are done with the second skein, starting and ending on the opposite side. Pick-up rows are worked from right to left. The last row is worked left to right.

Since this is a stretchy type of crochet, it is best first to work a swatch to check the gauge.

HAIRPIN LACE STRIPS

Hold a hairpin fork in the left hand with the rounded part at the top and the prong points at the bottom. Tie a loop of yarn around the fork and knot it in the center between the prongs. Always keep the yarn at the back of the work. Insert a crochet hook in the knot and make one chain stitch. Remove the hook from the chain loop and turn the fork to the left — the yarn will pass around the

Figure 20. Shown (below) is a hairpin fork, with the work evolving into a hairpin lace strip. The result of this technique is a section of delicate lace.

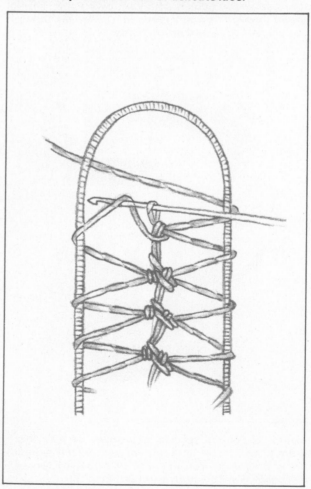

right prong. Then, with the crochet hook, pick up the dropped chain stitch loop in the center. Insert the hook under the top front loop to the left of center and work a single crochet stitch, thus: yarn over and pull through loop on hook, yarn over and draw through two loops on hook. Remove the hook from the loop and turn the fork to the left. With hook, pick up the dropped single crochet loop and insert hook under the last top front loop to the left of center. Work a single crochet stitch and repeat procedure from point of removing hook from single crochet loop. Work until the required number of loops have been made. Break the yarn, leaving about 3 inches at the end. Pull through the last loop to secure.

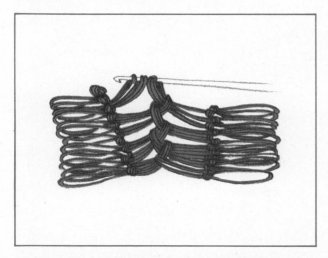

Figure 21. To connect two hairpin lace strips (above), use a simple type of cable joint, being careful not to twist the strips while working. Sew the loops at the end with matching yarn; bind securely.

Always keep the metal bar on prongs at the bottom to prevent the work from slipping off. When the fork prongs are filled with loops, remove the bar and slide off all but the last few loops. Then replace the bar and continue working the strip to the desired length. For example, when instructions call for a strip of 15 loops, be sure to make 15 loops on the left prong and 15 loops on the right prong before fastening off and removing from the fork.

To join two strips together, place them side by side. The left strip will be referred to as A and the right strip as B. With a crochet hook, pick up the first three loops of strip A. Then, pick up the first three loops of strip B and pull the B loops through the three A loops that are already on the hook.

There are now three B loops on the hook. Pick up the next three loops of A and pull through the B loops already on the hook. Continue on to the end of the strips; picking up three loops from one then three loops from the other and pulling through until the two strips are joined. This forms a cable-like joining between the strips. Be careful not to twist the strips when joining them. At the end of the strip, sew the remaining three loops to the center cable with matching yarn to prevent pulling out.

In order to prevent a possible slanting appearance to the finished article, alternate the pick up of the first three loops as follows. Make a third strip and slip it from the fork with the crochet hook. Pick up the first three loops of the third strip and pull the first three loops of strip B through the three loops of the third strip on the hook. Follow this procedure all the way across unless otherwise indicated in particular instructions.

WORKING AN ACCURATE STITCH GAUGE

When crocheting any kind of garment, it is wise to work a swatch to acquire a 4-inch gauge, which is usually the most accurate. Using the hook size suggested in the pattern, make a chain equal to the number of stitches required for a 4-inch piece. Then, the appropriate number of the stitch being worked should be crocheted onto the chain. For example: a gauge of 4 double crochet stitches equals 1 inch, so 16 double crochet stitches would be crocheted on the 4-inch chain.

Next, block the sample by wetting it with cold water and laying it on a towel. Stretch it out width-wise, making the edges straight and even. Next, work with the length so that it does not stretch more in one direction than the other. Press the gauge with the palm of the hand to get rid of excess water, and set aside to dry. When it is completely dry, measure out 4 inches and count the number of stitches across. If the swatch is not the expected size, work another one with a different size hook. Write down the before and after blocking measurements and the size hook used. The width of the swatch is more important than the length. A gauge correct in width is usually correct in length. If not, rows can be added or subtracted to adjust the length.

*Figure 22. A crocheted scarf (above) is a simple and popular project. This pattern,
designed by Barbara O'Brien, can be done quickly and inexpensively.*

CROCHET ABBREVIATIONS AND SYMBOLS

beg: beginning	lp: loop	sl st: slip stitch
CC: contrasting color	MC: main color	sp: space
ch: chain	pat: pattern	st: stitch
dc: double crochet	rep: repeat	sts: stitches
dec: decrease	rnd: round	tog: together
hdc: half double crochet	sc: single crochet	tr: treble or triple crochet
inc: increase	sk: skip	yo: yarn over

Projects You Can Do

The projects described here represent a crochet project, a cro-hook project, and a hairpin lace project. Read through them first to decide which is appealing to you. None of these projects is difficult or requires a great deal of materials.

SPORT SCARF

Materials needed for this project, designed by Barbara O'Brien of Malden, Mass., are: one 4-ounce skein of knitting worsted and a size K or 10½ crochet hook. Gauge: 4 dcs = 1 inch.

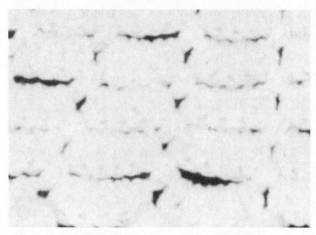

Figure 23. Shown above is a detail of the finished sport scarf.

First Side

Chain 22 loosely.

Row 1: Sc in the 6th ch from hook, * ch 3, skip 3 ch, sc in the next ch, repeat from * twice, ch 3, sc in the last ch, turn. This should make 5 lps.

Row 2: Ch 3. Working under the chain of the first lp, make 2 dcs, 3 dc in each of the next 3 lps, 2 dc in the last lp, 1 dc in the stitch at the end of the row. (This last stitch will keep the edges straight.) Now there are five groups of 3 dc each.

Row 3: Ch 3, sc in the space between the first and second group, *ch 3, sc in the space between the next two groups, repeat from * twice, ch 3 sc in the last dc, turn. Repeat Rows 2 and 3 alternately 11 times.

Row 26: Ch 3, 3 dc in the first lp, 4 dc in each of the next 3 lps, 3 dc in the last lp, and 1 dc in the stitch at the end of the row.

Row 27: *Ch 4, sc in the space between the next two groups, repeat from * 3 times, ch 4, sc in the last st. Repeat Rows 26 and 27 alternately three times.

Row 34: Ch 3, 4 dc in the first lp, 5 dc in each of the next 3 lps, 4 dc in the last lp, 1 dc in the last st.

Row 35: *Ch 5, sc in the space between the next 2 groups, repeat from * 3 times, ch 5, sc in the last st. Repeat Rows 34 and 35 alternately three times.

Row 42: Ch 3, 5 dc in the first lp, 6 dc in each of the next 3 lps, 5 dc in the last lp, 1 dc in the last st.

Row 43: *Ch 6, sc in the space between the next two groups, repeat from * 3 times, ch 6, sc in the last st. Repeat Row 42 once, fasten off.

Second Side

Attach yarn to outside edge of scarf, on the other side of the starting chain. Ch 3, 2 dc in the first lp, 3 dc in each of the next 3 lps, 2 dc in the last lp, 1 dc in the st at the end of the row, turn.

Starting with Row 3, work to correspond with the first side.

Tassels

Make six tassels for each end of the scarf. Wrap yarn eight times around a piece of cardboard 4 inches wide. Cut at one end. Cut another piece of yarn 8 inches long and pull this piece through scarf at the place where the tassel will be tied. Lay the eight strands across this piece and tie tightly in the center. Fold the strands over and tie with another piece of yarn about 1/2 inch from the top; trim evenly.

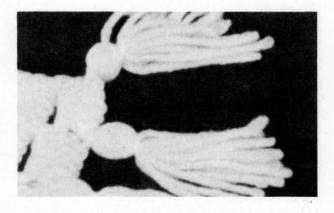

Figure 24. The tassels (above) of the finished sport scarf are easily made and attached.

Figure 25. Designed by Boye Design Studio, this lovely cro-hook baby afghan is easy to make and needs a minimum of material. Before fringing it measures 26" by 29".

CRO-HOOK BABY AFGHAN

Materials needed for this project, designed by Boye Design Studio, are: a size K cro-hook; a size K crochet hook; four 4-ounce skeins, 4-ply knitting worsted; two 4-ounce skeins MC; and two 4-ounce skeins CC. Finished size: 26 x 29 inches before fringing.

Row 1: MC — Using crochet hook and MC, ch 100.

Row 2: MC — Change to cro-hook, insert in 100th ch. Insert cro-hook in next ch, yo pull up new lp, hold on hook, * insert hook in next ch, yo pull up new lp. Rep from * across row for 100 lps.

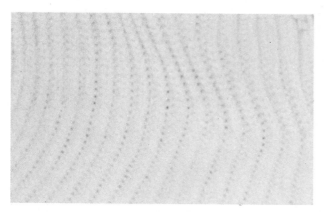

Figure 26. A detail of the baby afghan (above) shows careful workmanship.

Row 3: CC — Slide all work to other end of hook, turn. Attach CC, yo with CC, pull through 1 lp of MC, * yo pull through 1 lp of CC and 1 lp of MC. Rep from * across row. Work off all lps of MC, ending with 1 lp of CC. This becomes first lp for next row.

Row 4: CC — *Do not turn work.* Work right to left. * Insert hook in next ch, yo pull up new lp, hold on hook. Rep from * across row for 100 lps.

Row 5: MC — Slide all work to opposite end of hook, turn. Yo with MC, pull through 1 lp of CC, * yo pull through 1 lp of MC and 1 lp of CC. Rep from * across row working off all lps of CC ending with 1 lp of MC. This becomes first lp for next row.

Row 6: MC — *Do not turn work.* Work right to left. * Insert hook in next ch, yo pull up new lp, hold on hook. Rep from * across row for 100 lps.

Row 7: CC — Slide all work to other end of hook, turn. Yo with CC, pull through 1 lp of MC, * yo pull through 1 lp of CC and 1 lp of MC. Rep from * across row, work off all lps of MC ending with 1 lp of CC.

Row 8: CC — *Do not turn work.* * Insert hook in next ch, yo pull up new lp, hold on hook. Rep from * across row for 100 lps.

Rep Rows 5-8 for 29 inches or to desired length. End with Row 5 and all lps worked off. Cut yarn. With crochet hook, work yarn ends smoothly into blanket.

Finishing

Use crochet hook and CC. Insert hook in corner sp, ch 3.

Step 1: *† yo, insert hook in same sp, yo pull through. Rep from * 3 more times, yo pull through 8 lps, yo pull through 2 lps, ch 2 †. Rep † to † in same corner sp. Ch 2.

Step 2: Sk 3 sps, rep Step 1 from † to †.

Step 3: Rep Step 2 across side ending sk 4 sps.

Step 4: Rep steps 1 through 3 on remaining three sides.

Step 5: MC — Insert hook in corner sp, ch 3.

Step 6: Rep Steps 1 through 4, putting a group of yo sts in every sp. Do not sk any sps.

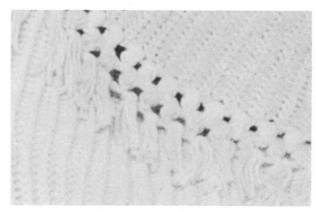

Figure 27. The fringe on the baby afghan (above) may be attached on three sides or on all four.

Fringe

Wind both MC and CC yarn five times around a piece of cardboard 3½ inches wide. Cut at one end and tie yarn into each chain space around three sides of blanket. (Leave one side of blanket without fringe to be placed next to baby's chin.)

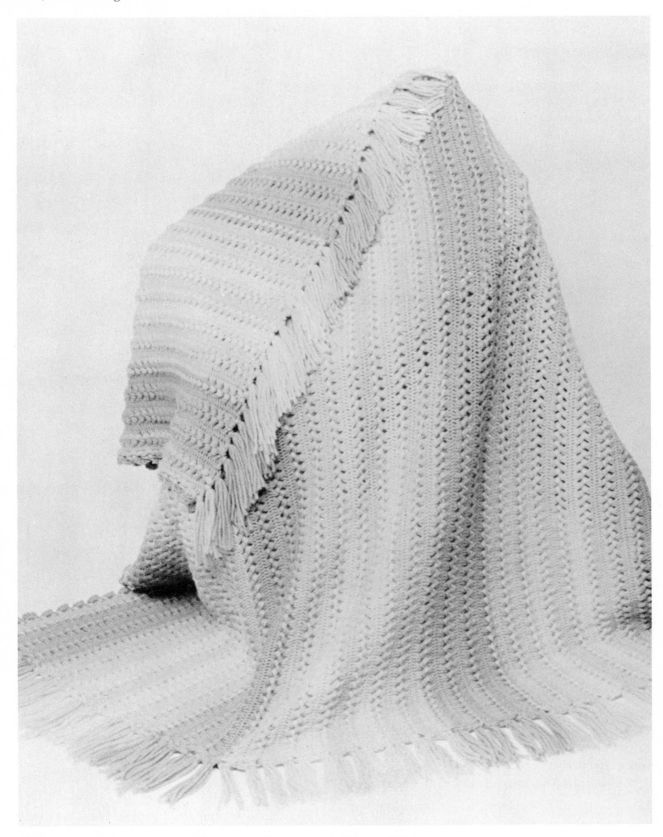

Figure 28. This beautiful lace afghan (above), designed by Dorothy Bradford, would be a treasured gift. Even a beginner can make it.

HAIRPIN LACE AFGHAN

This project, designed by Dorothy Bradford for Scovell Manufacturing Company, measures approximately 54 x 72 inches, including the fringe. Materials needed for this project are: 4-ply knitting worsted in 4-ounce skeins (5 skeins of A, 3 skeins of B, 4 skeins of C, and 3 skeins of D); a 3-inch metal hairpin fork; a size 4 crochet hook; and a size 9, 10-inch plastic afghan hook. Gauge: approximately 4 stitches = 1 inch.

Following the basic procedures for making hairpin lace, make 12 strips of 297 loops each with A; 8 strips of 297 loops each of B; 9 strips of 297 loops each of C; and 6 strips of 297 loops each of D.

Joining Strips

Following the general instructions under "Basic Procedures" for assembling hairpin lace strips, proceed as follows. Starting with center strip 1 (color C), pick up the first 3 lps. Then pick up first 3 lps of strip 2 (color D), and pull through the 3 color C lps on hook. Pick up next 3 lps of strip 1 and pull through the 3 color D lps on hook. Con-

tinue to end of strips, alternating the pick up of lps first from one strip then the other. With matching yarn, sew the last 3 lps to end of strip.

Now pick up the first 3 lps of strip 3 (color C), and cable to strip 2 (color D). Pull 3 lps through 3 lps to end of strip, fastening last 3 lps with matching yarn. Pick up the other first 3 lps of strip 3, then first 3 lps of strip 4 (color B), and pull through. Cable all strips tog in like manner. Always start at the same end of work so that all cable joinings will lie in the same direction. After all 35 strips have been cabled tog, finish off the two long sides by pulling 3 lps through 3 lps.

With color A, work a shell edge as follows. Attach yarn in back lp of first st, * work a shell of 1 sc, 3 dc, and 1 sc in back lp of next st, fasten with a sl st in back lp of next st, and repeat from *.

Figure 30. Fringe (above) makes an attractive finish to the afghan project.

Fringe

Cut yarn in 11-inch lengths and knot four strands of corresponding strip color in end lps, one on each side of crocheted center of every strip. Trim evenly to finish about 4 inches wide. Place afghan right side down on a large flat surface and steam-press lightly with a damp cloth between the iron and the afghan.

Figure 29. A detail of the hairpin lace afghan (below) reveals its strong yet delicate texture.

Figure 31. Use your crocheting skills for other projects, such as a purse (left).

Figure 32. Another simple crocheting project is this versatile vest (right).

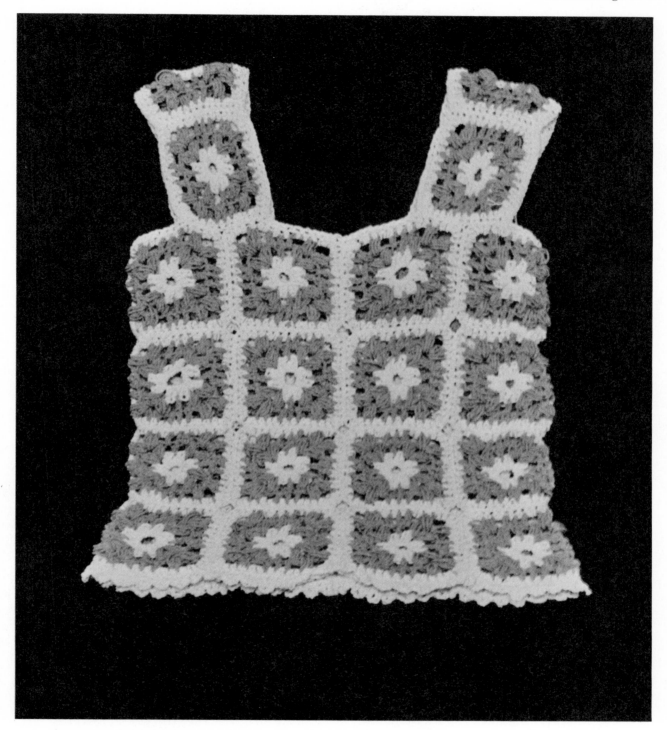

Figure 33. A fancier, flowered vest (above) makes a wonderful gift for a girl or young woman.

For Additional Reading

Blackwell, Elizabeth, **A Treasury of Crochet Patterns,** Scribner, 1971.

Dawson, Mary M., **A Complete Guide to Crochet Stitches,** Crown, 1972.

Mathieson, Elizabeth Laird, **The Complete Book of Crochet,** World Publishing, 1946.

Taylor, Gertrude, **America's Crochet Book,** Scribner, 1972.

Throughout the ages, crafts work of many kinds has been part of the human impulse toward artistic expression, even in everyday objects. In this painting from the Flemish school (*left*), Jan Vermeer portrayed the crocheting of lace, a typical home craft of the 17th century. (*Courtesy, The Louvre, Cliché des Musées Nationaux.*) Many forms of crafts, modern and traditional, contribute to the overall effect of the striking contemporary room (*below*) in the Jaoul House, Neuilly, France, designed by the modern architect-designer Le Corbusier. (*Courtesy, The Museum of Modern Art.*)

Candlemaking, once a practical craft necessary to daily life, has developed from the ancient tallow candles used thousands of years ago to these amusing decorative candles that can be made by the home crafts worker. (Courtesy, Lee Wards.)

Candlemaking

When the invention of electricity replaced candles as the prime source of light, candle making became a beautiful and creative art.

Candles date back to the first civilizations. Egyptians placed candles in their tombs, and their drawings depicted cone-shaped candles held aloft in dishlike holders. The Greeks left many candlesticks in Crete which date from about 3000 B.C.

The Romans had both tallow and wax candles. Tallow candles were called "dips"; the tallow was rendered from beef or mutton suet. The process of making dips was simple, but tedious. Several strands of yarn, serving as the wick, were dipped into the melted fat and allowed to cool. The dipping and cooling processes were repeated alternately until the desired thickness was reached. Wax candles or "tapers," made of beeswax, were produced by repeatedly pouring melted beeswax over a suspended wick and removing any unevenness in the finished candle by rolling it over a hard surface. Beeswax tapers were so costly that only the wealthy could afford them. Thus, dips made of tallow were the most common source of lighting. The common folk used a rushlight, consisting of a reed stripped to the pith and dipped in oil.

Figure 1. This tin and wood candle mold (opposite) is from a nineteenth-century Shaker community in Canterbury, New Hampshire. (Courtesy, The Henry Francis du Pont Winterthur Museum.)

Figure 2. Large candle molds such as this were useful during the mid-1800s when candles where the main source of lighting. (Courtesy, The Henry Francis du Pont Winterthur Museum.)

Candle making was exclusively a domestic project for many years, but, with the growth of medieval town life, it became a specialized craft. In the large cities of Europe, guilds of chandlers — one for tallow and one for wax — were set up in the thirteenth century. These were designed to maintain the distinction between the two candle types. The chandlers went from house to house making candles. In the fifteenth century, a Monsieur de Brez of Paris invented the candle mold. This was important only to tallow chandlers because beeswax could not be molded satisfactorily.

The emergence of modern candles began in the nineteenth century. The first improvement was by a French chemist, M. E. Chevreul, who proved that fats were composed of fatty acids and glycerin. These components, when separated under pressure, produce palmitic and stearic acids, the substance of the superior stearin candle. From this beginning, new processes for producing pure candle stock appeared in rapid succession. The next important ingredient was *spermaceti*, which was derived from the oil in the head cavity of the sperm whale. This produced a candle with superior illuminating power, but the candle was extremely brittle. This brittleness was corrected by the addition of beeswax.

The successful production of paraffin wax in 1850 was of great importance. By 1855, paraffin was being profitably produced in England, Europe, and the United States. Discovery of petro-

Figure 3. Tapers were made in this tin candle mold, which dates back to the mid-nineteenth century. (Courtesy, The Henry Francis du Pont Winterthur Museum.)

leum in the United States in 1859 made possible the economical production of paraffin. Its disadvantage — a low melting point — was overcome by combining it with stearic acid. This composite material was soon used in most candle production.

The modern candle-making machine evolved from Joseph Morgan's machine of 1834. This was the first which permitted continuous wicking and ejection of molded candles by movable pistons. These machines can produce up to 1500 candles an hour. For certain specialized purposes, tallow "dips" are still produced. Beeswax and taper candles are still produced in the same way as they were in the fifth century, the major difference being that a machine now dips thousands of candles at a time instead of two by hand.

Candles have always been popular in both spiritual ceremonies and aesthetic functions. Though candles no longer are needed for illumination, they are valued for their soft light and beauty.

Basic Equipment And Supplies

The relatively few materials needed to begin candle making are readily available from a variety of sources. For the best selection and the newest ideas, the hobby craft store is a good place to start. Most major department stores have a craft section which includes candle supplies, as well as a large variety of kits to choose from. Large craft stores which have a mail-order service are also a

good source. A complete kit can also be found in a large drug store, dime store, discount variety store, or toy store.

WAX

The first item to obtain is the wax. Always use slab wax which has been produced for candle-making purposes. This is sold in 11-pound blocks and will make approximately four quart-sized candles. Do not use grocery store paraffin because the melting point is too low.

The differences in wax are the hardness and the melting temperature. (The latter is the temperature at which the finished candle will melt while burning.) Low-grade wax will melt at temperatures of 125° F to 133° F. This type of wax has a limited use, such as candles for glass containers. Medium-grade wax melts at 136° F to 148° F. This is the most easily obtained type and is ideal for molded candles, sand candles, and novelty candles. The highest grade of wax melts at 155° F and is used for sculpting and hot wax baths.

The uniqueness of a candle begins with three basic items — the individual design, the scent, and the dye — which can be mixed together in hundreds of combinations. Stearic acid is used to improve the quality of the candle.

DYES

There are many types of candle dyes. The easiest to find and to use are liquid color or concentrated and colored cubes of wax. As a last resort, crayons can be used, but they tend to settle, re-

Figure 4. Supplies should be systematically arranged before work is begun. A block of wax, glass molds, wicks, and various oils, chemicals, and perfumes are among the supplies shown here.

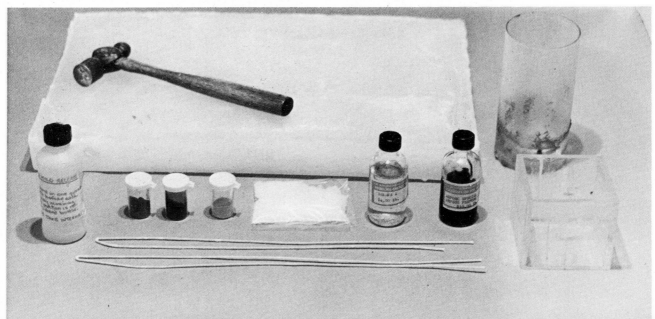

sulting in a candle of various shades. They also may smoke and sputter while burning. Do not use food coloring because it will not mix with the wax. When using cubes, start with one cube, drop it into the melted wax, and stir. Test the color by dropping a small amount of colored wax into a small dish of cold water. If liquid dye is used, add a few drops to the hot wax, stir, and test the color in the same way.

Interesting effects can be obtained by mixing colors for candles. By keeping in mind a few simple rules and by using the accompanying color chart, and endless variety of colors can be achieved for candle designs.

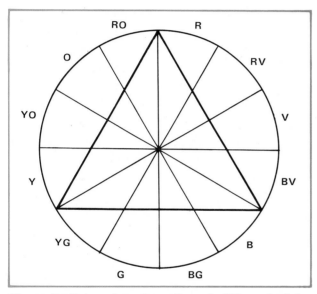

Figure 5. Color chart key: R—red, RV—red violet, V—violet, BV—blue violet, B—blue, BG—blue green, G—green, YG—yellow green, Y—yellow, YO—yellow orange, O—orange, RO—red orange.

Remember that color can always be added but that it cannot be removed. Begin, therefore, by adding just a little of the darker color; then, obtain the desired shade by adding additional color a little at a time. To tone down a color, add a tiny amount of the color that is opposite the one being used on the color chart. Again, remember to work very slowly, adding only very small amounts of color at a time.

To use the color chart, find the shade the candle is to be. For example, blue and red make purple. If, however, the candle is to be red-violet, begin adding a little more red until the desired shade is achieved.

SCENT

Candle scent, available in both liquid and tablet form, has an oil base, and mixes well with wax. Perfume can also be used so long as it has an oil base. A half ounce of scent is adequate for 2 to 3 pounds of wax.

There are two ways the scent may be added: either to the melted wax just before pouring or by soaking the wick in the scent. For a stronger scent, use both methods.

STEARIC ACID

Stearic acid increases the melting point of the candle and makes it harder. This is obviously beneficial in hot weather when candles tend to droop or bend. The acid also makes the candle more opaque and intensifies the color. Stearine or stearic acid is added to the melted wax — use about three tablespoons per pound of wax. Never use stearine in glow candles (candles in glass containers) or hot wax baths because its opaque quality will keep light from shining through.

WICK

The wick must fit the candle: a wick too small will sink into the candle and burn out; a wick too large will smoke and drip excessively. The larger the diameter of the candle, the larger the wick has to be. A woven cotton wick is the type used in all candles. When the wick is to be inserted from the top of a finished candle, the wick must first be dipped in melted wax several times until stiff. Then, heat an ice pick and make a hole down the center of the candle. Insert the stiffened wick into the hole and then fill it with melted wax. A small-sized wick is essential for thin candles up to 1¼" in diameter, a large size is for candles 1¼" to 4" in diameter. Several wicks may be inserted in oversized candles, such as sand candles.

MOLDS

Candles can be made in commercially produced molds or from objects around the house. Candle molds are made from metal, plastic, or rubber. Metal is the most durable, and many classic designs are available. Plastic comes in many novelty shapes, and in two halves which have to be clamped together. Rubber comes in one piece with a slit in the side that is sealed before pouring. Other molds which may be used are: ceramic

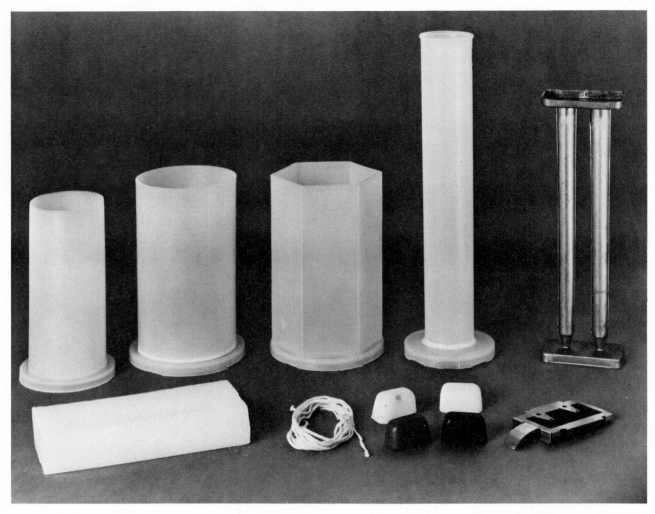

Figure 6. Different sizes and shapes of plastic and metal molds (above) are a useful addition to the candle maker's supplies.

Figure 7. Equipment for melting wax can include everyday household items (left) such as old coffeepots, a hot plate, a candy thermometer, and a cookie sheet.

plaster, milk and cream cartons, juice cartons, any prewaxed cartons or hard plastic containers, gelatin molds, and sherbet or drinking glasses. All of these molds should be first treated with a mold release such as a spray silicone. Pouring temperatures of wax also vary according to the type of mold that is being used: metal mold, 190° F to 200° F; plastic and rubber, 145° F to 150° F; cardboard, 145° F; and glass, 170° F.

MELTING EQUIPMENT

A few pieces of simple equipment and a stack of newspaper are all that is necessary to create a candle. Most of the necessary equipment is around the house. Begin by assembling the following items: (1) double boiler or melting pot and a pan; (2) candy thermometer; (3) pouring container (an old seamless coffee pot is perfect); (4) hobby knife or paring knife; (5) ice pick; (6) long knitting needle; (7) pencil; (8) pot holders; (9) electric hot plate (or the stove); (10) cookie sheet or aluminum foil; (11) stirring spoon with a long handle; and (12) floral clay.

Basic Procedures

The art of candle making is very easy to learn. Once the basic steps are mastered, experimentation and variation are endless. Each candle is an original because the craftsman selects the color, shape, scent, and decoration. Making the first candle from a slab of white wax is a new, exciting art form to be tried by every hobbyist. If any attempt proves unsatisfactory, just melt the candle down and start over again. There is no need for costly mistakes in candle making.

Begin by covering the work area with newspaper. Assemble all the required equipment and supplies.

PREPARING THE WAX

Break the slab of wax into small pieces by placing the wax in a sack such as a pillowcase and hitting it with a hammer. Melt the wax in a pot over boiling water to the temperature required for the mold being used. Do not get water in the wax. Check the temperature of the wax with a candy thermometer. When the wax has reached the correct melting temperature, add stearic acid (if desired). Stir this with a wooden spoon or dowel.

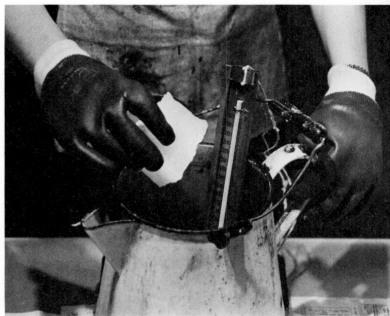

Figure 8. The slab of wax is broken into smaller pieces with a hammer and then added slowly to the melting pot (above). The mold to be used determines the temperature, which should be measured with a candy thermometer (below).

Figure 9. When the wax is melted, transfer it to another pot for mixing (above left). Stearine or stearic acid, which comes in powdered form, can then be added as a hardener. Add stearine to the liquid wax and mix well (above right).

Figure 10. Liquid color, one of the easiest candle dyes to use, is added a few drops at a time (top left). Test the color by dropping a chunk of wax in cold water (top right). Scent can be added to the liquid wax (below left); or used to saturate the wick, or both. Mix it thoroughly with the liquid wax (below right).

Add color dye and add scent. Bring wax to correct temperature before pouring.

PREPARING THE MOLD

Be sure the mold is clean. Use the appropriate mold release and wipe away the excess. Thread the wick through the closed end of the mold. Cut the wick, making sure there is plenty of extra at both ends. Pull the wick taut and, with floral clay, seal over the wick and around the hole on the outside of the mold. This will prevent the hot wax from seeping out. Be sure that the mold sealer is flat enough to allow the mold to rest evenly. Turn the mold right side up. Pull the wick taut and tie it around a pencil lying across the top of the mold. Make sure the wick is in the center of the mold.

POURING THE WAX

Place the mold on a cookie sheet or similar item. Pour about 1/4" of wax at the correct temperature to seal the wick hole. Let this set for a half hour. Hold the mold at an angle and, using a pot holder,

Figure 11. The first step in preparing the mold is to clean the inside thoroughly and spray on silicone mold release (above left). The mold release is needed so that the candle can be removed from the mold in one piece. Cut the wick to fit the mold, but leave an extra allowance at either end (above right). Thread the wick through the bottom of the mold; then pull it taut and wrap around a stick or pencil (below left). To prevent wax seepage, seal the base of the mold (below right) around the hole made for the wick.

Figure 12. Pour wax into the mold. Begin with a layer about ¼ " thick to seal the wick hole. After that layer sets, hold the mold at an angle and pour the wax slowly down the side.

pour the wax into the mold slowly and carefully. Let the wax slide down the sides of the mold so that no air bubbles form. Fill the mold to the desired height and save at least one cup of wax to fill the cavity left by shrinkage. Make sure the mold is perfectly level while the wax cools.

FILLING THE WELL

After approximately one hour the wax on top of the mold will begin to cool and cloud to the correct color. This is the time to start filling the well.

Insert a knitting needle into the warm candle near the wick two or three times to relieve pressure caused by wax shrinkage. Be careful not to insert the needle all the way to the bottom of the mold. Reheat the left-over wax and pour it into the cavity which has formed. Do not fill the well beyond the first pouring, or it will stick to the sides and be difficult to remove from the mold. Left-over wax should be poured into a separate container to cool because it can be used again. Never leave it to harden in the melting pot.

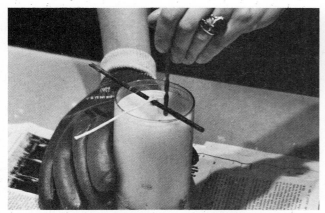

Figure 13. When the candle has partially cooled, use a long, narrow object to make a hole, or well, near the wick (top left). Then fill the well with reheated wax (below left). To save the leftover wax for reuse, pour it into a separate container (above). Do not allow it to harden in the pot.

MATURING THE CANDLE

Let the candle cool for at least eight hours at room temperature. Remove the floral clay and loosen the wick on both ends of the mold. Turn the mold upside down and let the candle slide out. If it does not slip out of the mold, place it in the freezer for 15 to 30 minutes. Do not strike the mold because this dents it for any further use.

Figure 14. Untie the wick from the stick or pencil after the candle has thoroughly hardened (left). Then cut off the wick to the desired length (right).

Figure 15. Remove the candle from the mold with care: turn the mold upside down and let the candle ease out (left), so that the two pieces are separated without damaging either (right).

Figure 16. The final step is to remove seam lines from the candle by cutting them away with a knife and then polishing the candle with a cloth.

Figure 17. This charming "gingerbread house" candle illustrates one of the many variations possible with molded, dyed candles. (Courtesy, Lee Wards.)

FINISHING TOUCHES

Remove the seam lines from the candle with a hobby knife or paring knife. A nylon stocking is excellent for polishing the seam line and removing blemishes. Cut the wick to the desired length, and the candle is ready to use or decorate further.

SAFETY PRECAUTIONS AND OTHER HELPFUL HINTS

Candle wax is very similar to cooking oil. It is flammable but, with certain precautions, accidents need not occur.

1. Always melt wax over boiling water either in a melting pot placed in a water-filled pan or in a double boiler. Heating wax directly over an open flame is hazardous. If wax is heated over water, the temperature will not exceed 212° F and no problems will develop. Wax will not boil but will start to smoke if it is too hot.

2. Do not exceed 260° F when melting candle wax. This will cause the wax to burn, will ruin the mold, and will cause the color to be uneven.

3. Never pour wax directly over an open flame.

4. Never pour wax over or in the sink because it will clog the plumbing.

5. When pouring a candle, always place the mold on foil or on an old pan in case the mold should leak. Place this on a newspapered surface.

6. Never leave hot wax unattended.

7. Hot wax can cause burns on the skin. If this happens, run cold water over the burned area so the wax will harden and peel off. Treat as a regular burn.

8. NEVER pour water on a wax fire, as it will cause the fire to spread. To extinguish a fire in a pan, turn off the heat and cover the pan with its lid. Always keep baking soda handy, as it will extinguish a wax fire. Do not move pan or lift lid until pan is cold to the touch.

9. Always slip chunks of wax into hot wax — never drop them.

10. Always pour left-over wax from the melting pot into shallow pans. Then clean the pot with paper towels.

11. Always use a candy thermometer to check the temperature of the wax.

12. Pour wax at 175° F. If the temperature is lower, the candle will look dull and pitted because air bubbles do not have a chance to escape. Pouring wax higher than 175° F will create steam bubbles.

13. Mold seams can be removed with a spatula and buffed with a nylon stocking.

Projects You Can Do

The fulfillment in candle making is achieved by using the imagination to create a unique candle. The basic process of making a candle is relatively easy. The various candles described in this section can be made with a minimum investment of work, time, and money. Keep in mind that these projects are just starting points for an endless assortment which can be designed and made.

ICE CUBE CANDLES

1. Make a pillar candle 2" x 7" with a metal mold as described in "Basic Procedures." Make sure that the wick will burn only up to 2" in diameter. This will allow the ice cube decoration to remain intact. Additional materials that are needed are cracked ice cubes and a metal mold, 4" x 7", square or cylindrical.

2. Prepare the work area.

3. Prepare the wax as described earlier.

Figure 18. The interesting effects achieved in the ice cube candle explain why this technique has become so popular with home craftsmen.

4. Prepare the mold. Then place the 2″ x 7″ candle in the center of it. Its wick will serve as the wick for the entire candle.

5. Pour a small amount of wax (1/2″) in the bottom of the mold to secure the center core candle.

6. Place cracked ice cubes around the center core to a depth of approximately 3″.

7. Pour hot wax to within 1/2″ of the top of the ice. After waiting a minute for the wax to harden slightly, continue placing ice and pouring wax until reaching the top.

8. Let the candle cool at room temperature for at least three hours.

9. After removing the candle from the mold, turn it on all sides so that all the water escapes. It may be necessary to use a knitting needle to release some of the trapped water.

10. Be sure to dry the mold thoroughly so that it will not rust.

Variations of the Ice Cube Candle

1. Use a tapered candle the same height as the candle, instead of the 2″ x 7″ center core suggested above. (The tapered candle will allow the ice cube design to burn; the 2″ x 7″ will not.)

2. Instead of ice cubes, fill the outside of the mold for the basic 2″ x 7″ candle with sea shells or beads. If, when the candle is removed from the mold, the shells or beads are embedded too far in the wax, run a butane torch over the outside of the candle until the desired effect is achieved. Be sure to work on a surface that is covered with many layers of newspaper.

Figure 19. This candle was decorated in three stages with seashells. Note that the shells on top were placed first. Wax overlaps the shells to some extent to hold them in place; excess wax is removed when the candle is thoroughly dry.

SAND CANDLES

In addition to the basic equipment, a fairly large box filled with at least 8″ of clean, damp sand is needed. For a thick crust of sand on the finished candle, pour the wax at 200° F. For a thinner crust of sand, pour the wax at 150° F. For larger candles, embed driftwood or branches into the sand before pouring the wax.

1. Prepare work area.

2. Prepare the wax: break it into small pieces and melt it to the desired temperature (150° F or 200° F).

3. Add stearic acid, dye, and scent, following directions in "Basic Procedures."

4. Prepare the sand mold. First, spoon out the sand to the desired shape (vases, pots, or bowls may also be pressed into the sand). Then, press

three holes of equal depth into the bottom of the sand to form a footed candle. Use fingers or an article such as an ice pick handle. Do not go through to the bottom of the box.

5. To pour the wax, hold a tablespoon near the bottom of the sand mold and slowly pour the wax into the spoon until the bottom of the mold is covered. This will prevent an indentation in the bottom of the sand.

6. After the candle has set for an hour, reheat the wax to the melting point and fill the well following the directions in "Basic Procedures."

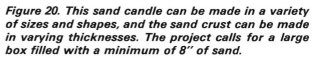

Figure 20. This sand candle can be made in a variety of sizes and shapes, and the sand crust can be made in varying thicknesses. The project calls for a large box filled with a minimum of 8″ of sand.

7. Heat an ice pick and insert the wick or wicks in position after the candle has matured for at least an hour (an additional hour after the filling of the well).

8. The candle chould be left to mature at least eight hours at room temperature.

9. With *great* care, lift the candle from the sand. Wash off the excess sand with cold water. (Note: It is a good idea to wash the candle outside to avoid getting sand all over the house or down the drain.)

Variations of the Sand Candle

1. Add small pebbles or small sea shells to the sand and pour the wax at the higher (200° F) melting point.

2. After the candle has matured, add chips of dye to the top of the candle. Shave off extremely small parts of the color dye chips — either the same color or various colors. Place the shavings on top of the candle and, with a butane torch, very lightly melt them into the wax just enough so that the color starts to bleed.

3. Make clusters of candles. Instead of one indentation in the sand, make connecting indentations. This type of sand candle makes an excellent hanging candle.

4. Make stepping stone candles. Make the indentations at various levels and connect them. Try using driftwood and tree branches to connect the various levels.

5. Trim the candle around the edges with dried flowers or small ceramic animals. These will look like miniature wildlife scenes, reflecting pools, or whatever else the craftsman wishes to create.

6. Place a piece of aluminum in the sand mold and pour the melted wax into the aluminum foil. This will produce a very glossy candle. For a more interesting candle, try using different colors of wax. If using different colors, make sure that each layer hardens completely before pouring or the colors will run together.

BABY ANIMAL CANDLES

For this project, the following materials are needed: (1) plastic molds (hollow toys will do); (2) one medium block of wax; (3) candle color or box of child's wax crayons; (4) scent (optional); (5) wick — height of mold plus 1½"; (6) masking tape; and (7) melting pan, knife, and nylon stocking.

1. Prepare the mold by first cutting a hole in the bottom to allow for pouring.

2. Lay the wick across the center of the mold and secure at the bottom with a piece of masking tape.

3. Close the mold and tape along all sides to insure tight closure.

4. Set the mold upside down in a secure position. One easy way to hold a mold in place is to fill a small box with sand and push the mold in it until it will stay upright.

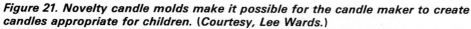

Figure 21. Novelty candle molds make it possible for the candle maker to create candles appropriate for children. (Courtesy, Lee Wards.)

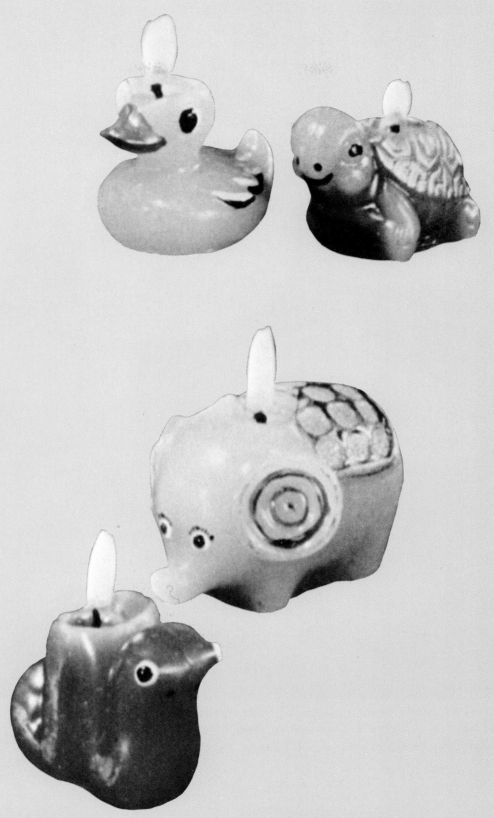

Figure 22. By following the steps in the project, the candle maker can make any of these colorful and appealing baby animals. (Courtesy, Lee Wards.)

Figure 23. Only the candle maker's imagination limits the variations in design and mood that can be achieved in candle making. Everything from "smilies" to Volkswagens can be expressed in wax. (Courtesy, Lee Wards.)

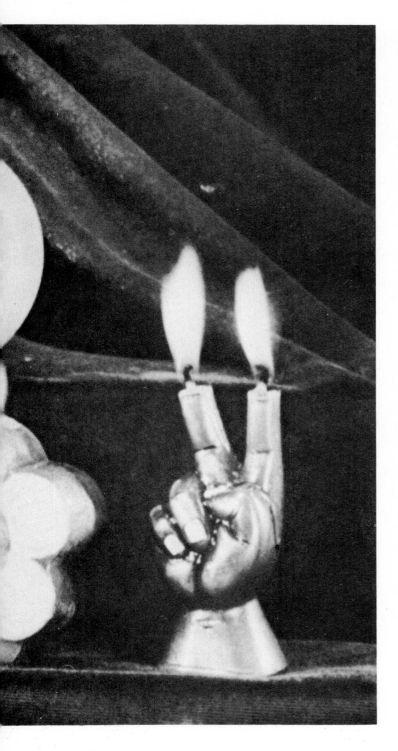

5. Place the wax, a small amount of the color desired — shaving or chipping makes it melt more easily — and the scent, if desired, in the melting pan. Place the melting pan in heated water until the wax and color are melted and are ready to pour. **Do not** leave the hot wax unattended and do not exceed 200° F.

6. Pour the wax into the mold and allow to cool. During the cooling process the wax may shrink, and it may become necessary to add a small amount of molten wax to completely fill the mold.

7. When using more than one color, remember to allow each color layer to harden before pouring the next color.

8. When the wax is completely cool, remove the candle from the mold. If necessary, trim excess wax with the knife from the line where the mold was joined together. Using the nylon stocking, polish the candle until it has a smooth, shiny surface.

9. Trim the wick, if necessary.

For Additional Reading

Feder, Carol, **The Candlemaking Design Book,** Watts, 1974.

Newman, Thelma R., **Creative Candlemaking,** Crown, 1972.

Schutz, Walter E., **Getting Started in Candlemaking,** Collier Books, 1972.

Strouse, Susanne, **Candlemaking,** Sterling, 1968. †1

Scrap Art

Scrap art is a delightful way of transforming trash into treasures.

For hundreds of years man has used worn-out materials in various ways. Completely worn-out garments, for example, were cut into pieces and woven into rugs or made into the beautiful patchwork quilts which are seen today in many museums. Modern technology has resulted in the development of many new products for the home. Trash cans often contain such items as ice-cream sticks, colored or clear glass bottles, plastic containers, cigar boxes, tin cans, odds and ends of fabric, ribbon, paint, and nail polish. All of these things can be used in scrap craft.

Church groups, clubs, and camps hold bazaars and sell such handmade items as pot holders, neckties, and aprons made from scraps of fabric; toys and dolls from old containers or socks; Christmas tree ornaments from scraps of felt; and rugs, quilts, and pillows from worn-out garments. Articles utilizing plastic, including wreaths and toys made from plastic bags and toys and plant holders made from plastic containers, are also sold.

Many craftsmen have created original works of art from attractive boxes or containers. And bags, banks, toys, and vases are but a few examples of the items that can be made from discarded plastic.

The ancient art of mosaic is usually not thought of in relation to scrap art. However, today, mosaic designs are made from many materials, including such food items as croutons, beans, and rice. The appearance of an ordinary box or bottle top can be transformed into an attractive gift simply by covering it with a mosaic design.

Scrap, of course, also includes much of the material discarded from factories. Many of these materials, such as scraps of metal, fabric, and wood can be purchased or obtained from metal companies, fabric mills, or lumber mills.

Figure 1. An automobile carburetor and a car radio were the scrap materials combined inventively by Suzanne Peters to create this "Atomic Man." (Courtesy, Collection of Dr. and Mrs. Charles Turk.)

pletely dry, trim all the loose threads. Then, spread glue around all the edges and press the yarn in place.

If a styrofoam ball is used for the inside of the

making a pillow. Tie the ends securely.

Spread some glue inside the chair across the bottom. Place the ball or pillow inside the chair and press it in place.

Common Terms Used In Scrap Art

Baste: to sew long, temporary stitches.

~~Curl: to curl the edges of tip with long-nosed~~

Projects You Can Do

Scrap materials usually bring to mind items due for discard, unusable materials, or empty containers. The dictionary describes scrap as "small

Rinse the inside of the eggshell with water; then blow again to remove the water. Set the eggshell, small end down, in an egg carton to drain and dry. Eggshells should be thoroughly dry before they are cut to prevent warping and formation of mildew.

Cutting the Egg

The egg has two layers. The outside layer is hard like porcelain; the inside, soft like chalk. To keep the egg from cracking while cutting, paint the entire shell with white glue and let dry.

Cutting a Hole for a Figure. (1) With a pencil, sketch an opening of the desired size on the eggshell. The hole must be large enough to allow a small figure to be placed inside the egg. (2) Use small manicure scissors to cut an opening along the pencil line. (3) Cut around the pencil line, taking small cuts with the middle part of the scissors.

Don't worry about jagged edges — they can be covered. If the egg cracks, apply one coat of white glue to both the inside and the outside of the shell.

Cutting an Eggshell in Half. An eggshell can be cut horizontally or vertically in half. Score lines gently with a razor blade and cut through.

Cutting a Door and Placing Hinges. (1) With a pencil, sketch an opening of the desired size on the eggshell. Use a razor blade to cut out this "door." (2) Place the hinge on the door so that the ridge at which the hinge bends is along the edge of the door. Trace around the hinge and along the edge at the bend of the hinge (this will be a notch). (3) Place the hinge on the egg so that the ridge is along the edge of the hole (or "doorway"). Trace around the hinge and along the edge at the bend of the hinge as before. (4) Cut out rectangular notches in the door and the egg for the hinge. Use manicure scissors and snip into the edge of the shell. (5) Place the hinge into the notch on the egg. Glue hinge to egg with cement glue (epoxy) and allow to dry for several hours. Avoid getting glue into hinge. Glue hinge to door and allow to dry for several hours.

Trimming the Egg

Gather trim — pearls, jewels, sequins, gold-silver braids (preferably with adhesive backing), velvet, or scraps of lace. Some braid has loops which can

be filled with small beads. To fill braid with beads, apply a bit of glue to each loop and, using tweezer, place a pearl on each loop. Then, place a line of glue next to the beads for another type of braid. Place the ends of the braid at the top or the bottom of the egg so they are not noticeable. Beads which have already been strung are particularly easy to apply. Allow the glue to dry.

Miniature figures can be placed inside the egg. They can either be glued or attached to a small piece of white styrofoam which has been placed inside the egg. Grass or angel hair can be used to cover the styrofoam. The figures can be used to create scenes which tell a story or depict an historical event. These are particularly apropos for holiday gifts and displays.

Decorated eggs may be mounted on a base. This base can be plain or decorated with many of the same ornaments used for the egg.

STYROFOAM CRAFTS

Rather than discussing general procedures for working with styrofoam, the reader is referred to the "Projects You Can Do" section of this article. Several specific methods of working with styrofoam are described.

BEADCRAFT EMBROIDERY

Embroidery with beads involves threading the beads on cord or string and holding the beads together as a design. Use a needle to fasten the beads to a prepared backing. Embroidering on loosely woven fabric is easier than on closely woven material.

The threads or lines in the fabric act as a guide for keeping the stitches straight. If using plain material with no guides, add lightly colored chalk lines. Use beads with large holes in case the thread must pass through the hole several times. The type of bead is very important; on projects which will be laundered, use only glass, plastic, or ceramic beads — never wooden ones. Detergent will cause the wood finish to flake. Use thick wool yarn.

Learning the Stitches

The *running stitch* is the basic stitch. Thread a needle with a polyester thread and knot one end.

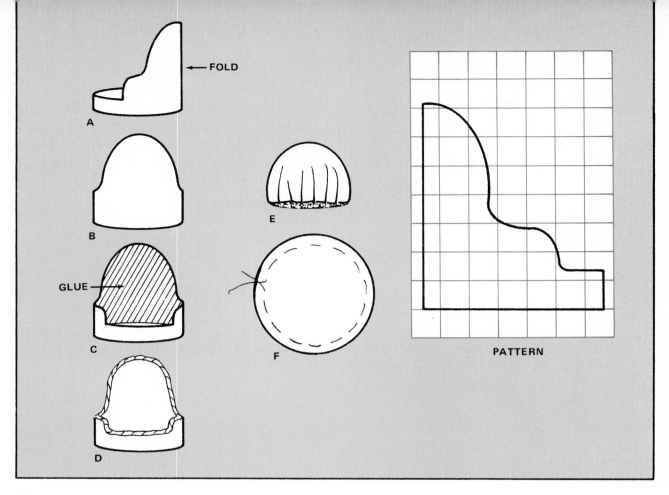

Figure 3. Tape the pattern in several places to the outside of the container (A). The lower edge of the pattern should be placed on the bottom edge of the container (B). Make any adjustments in the pattern size, and cut out the chair form. Pin the pattern to the fabric, cut the material, and glue on (C). After covering the inside and outside, glue on yarn around the edge (D). To cover the seat, cut a circle from the fabric. To cover a styrofoam ball, make slits around the edges of the circle (E); to cover a wad of steel wool, sew a running stitch around the edges (F).

container around pattern, leaving the bottom in place.

Pin the pattern on the fold of the material, centering the design. Cut out fabric for the inside of the container. Cut an identical piece for the outside of the container.

Assembling

Spread glue around the sides and back of the inside of the container; do not spread glue on bottom. Place one of the fabric pieces, right side out, over the glue and press it in place. Spread glue around the outside of the container and press the second piece of fabric in place. Be sure all edges are glued securely. When the chair is completely dry, trim all the loose threads. Then, spread glue around all the edges and press the yarn in place.

If a styrofoam ball is used for the inside of the chair, cut a small section off the bottom so that it will lie flat. If stuffing such as steel wool is used, use a wad large enough to fit the inside of the chair.

To cover a styrofoam ball, cut out an 8″ circle of fabric. Spread glue over the top of the ball and center the fabric on the ball. Press in place. Make slits around the fabric, leaving about 3½″ uncut across the center. Glue the slit pieces in place to cover the ball.

To cover a wad of steel wool or other stuffing material, cut out a 10″ circle of fabric. With needle and thread, sew a running stitch 1/4″ from the edges, leaving 4″ ends of thread. Place the wad inside the circle and draw the ends together making a pillow. Tie the ends securely.

Spread some glue inside the chair across the bottom. Place the ball or pillow inside the chair and press it in place.

Figure 4. A plastic gallon container, fabric, and ribbon were used to make this drawstring bag. It makes a useful carryall for beach gear, hair rollers, or sewing supplies.

DRAWSTRING BAG

Materials

Materials for this project are: (1) plastic gallon container, such as is used for milk or bleach; (2) 1/2 yard solid and 1/2 yard checked material; (3) needle and thread; (4) lightweight cardboard; (5) safety pin; and (6) 2 yards of 3/4" gros-grain ribbon.

Cutting

If the plastic container has a handle, cut around the container below the handle with scissors or a sharp knife. If there is no handle, cut the container to a depth of about 10" or 12".

Making Pattern

Place the container on a piece of cardboard. Draw a line around the bottom to make the pattern. Cut out the cardboard, allowing an extra 1/2" *outside* the line. This 1/2" allowance will be the seam. Measure around the outside of the container to determine its perimeter. Write the value for the measurement on the pattern.

Cutting Fabric

Use the cardboard pattern of the bottom to cut out one piece of the solid color and one piece of the checked fabric. The solid color will be used to cover the outside bottom of the bag; the checked fabric will be the bottom lining.

Divide the perimeter measurement in half and add 1" for seams; this is the new width. From solid color, cut out two pieces measuring the new width and 2½" in length. Next, cut two pieces of the checked fabric measuring the new width and 14½" in length (cut fabric on pattern line). These four pieces will be the outer sides of the bag.

Cut two pieces of checked fabric measuring the new width and 16" in length for lining the sides of the bag.

Assembling

Determine the center point of the two bottom pieces and mark two opposite edges of each (see illustration). These marks indicate placement of the two side seams. Set the bottom pieces aside.

With right sides together, join one of the checked pieces for the outside (measuring the new width and 14½" in length) to a solid piece (measuring the new width and 2½" in length) along the width in a 1/2" seam (see illustration). Do the same thing with the other outside pieces. Press all seams flat. With right sides together, join the sides of the two sections using 1/2" seams: start at the solid color and stitch to within 3" of the top (see illustration). Do not stitch the ends. Knot the threads to secure both ends of each seam. Starting at the top edge, stitch a 1/2" seam for 1¾". Knot the threads as before, and press the seams flat. The 1¼" opening that remains will be the casing for the drawstring (or ribbon).

Turn the completed side section wrong side out. Match the two side seams with the two marks made previously on the solid color bottom section (it should also be wrong side out). Baste the side section to the bottom; stitch the bottom to the side section with a 1/2" seam. Turn the bag right side out and place it over the plastic container.

With right sides together stitch the remaining two pieces of checked fabric with 1/2" seams. *Do not leave an opening.* Knot threads and press seams flat. Turn the completed lining section wrong side out. Match the two side seams with the two marks on the remaining bottom section (also wrong side out). Baste as before and stitch the bottom to the side section with a 1/2" seam. Place the lining inside the container, matching seams of lining and those of the outside of the bag.

Turn under the upper edge of the outside of the bag 1/2"; do the same with the upper edge of the lining. Pin the lining to the outside of the bag,

baste, and stitch 1/8" from the edge. Sew another seam 1" below, and a third seam 1½" below that (stitch across the pattern line).

Cut the ribbon into two one-yard lengths. Attach a safety pin to the end of one length and thread it into the casing and around the bag. Stitch the ends of the ribbon and arrange it so that the stitching does not show. Do the same thing with the other length or ribbon at the opposite opening. Pull both ribbons to close.

Figure 5. To begin the drawstring bag, make a pattern for the bottom pieces 1½ " larger than the container (A). Mark opposite sides of these pieces for seam placement (B). Measure the perimeter of the container and cut out the side pieces of the bag (C). Sew together pieces of solid and checked fabric for the outside (D). Repeat, then sew the two outsides together, starting at the bottom and ending 3" from the top (E). Now make the ribbon casing by stitching down 1¾ " from the top (F). Attach the bottom (G). Make the lining, then sew it to the outside pieces and make seams for the ribbon casing. Use a safety pin to thread the ribbon through the casing (H). Sew ribbon ends together and pull the seam to the opposite side (I). Repeat for the second ribbon (J).

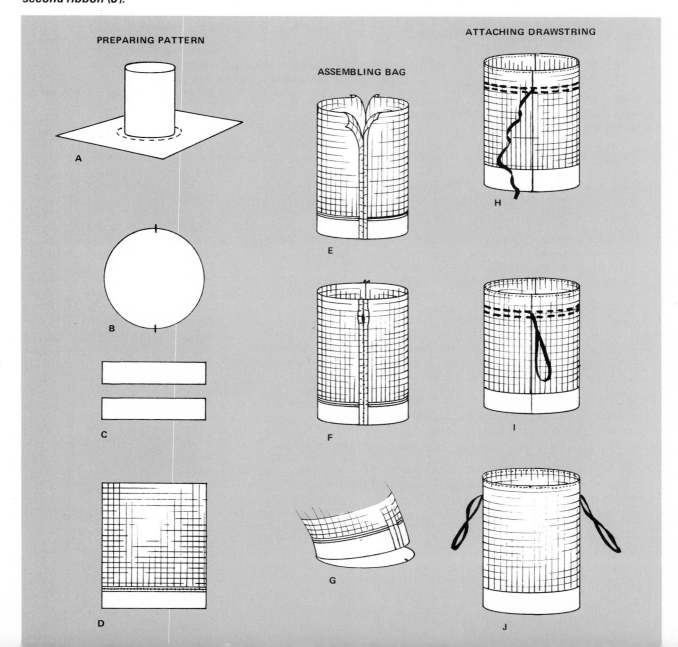

PREPARING PATTERN

ASSEMBLING BAG

ATTACHING DRAWSTRING

A

B

C

D

E

F

G

H

I

J

Figure 6. This finished bureau box (above) was covered with corduroy and trimmed with braid and velvet ribbon.

BUREAU BOXES

Materials

Materials needed for this project are: (1) any can approximately 3¼″ to 4″ in diameter and about 1½″ to 2″ deep (such as a tuna fish can); (2) scissors; (3) glue; (4) trimmings; (5) fabric or felt; (6) heavy cardboard; and (7) a pencil.

Cutting

Wash can thoroughly. Using the lid as a pattern, draw a circle on heavy cardboard. Again using the lid as a pattern, draw a circle on a piece of fabric for the inside bottom of the can. Discard lid. Cut out the cardboard circle, allowing an extra 1/8″ all around the *outside* of the circle. For the top of the can, use the cardboard circle as a pattern and cut out two circles of fabric, allowing an extra 1″ by 1¼″ for a hinge on one side of each circle, as shown in the accompanying illustration. Measure the depth of the container and cut out two strips of fabric long enough to fit around the outside and inside of the can.

Assembling

Spread glue on the inside bottom of the can. Place the first fabric circle (same size as lid) over the glue and press in place. Place glue around the inside of can and press a strip of fabric in place, trimming it to fit. Set second strip aside.

For the cover, spread glue on each side of the cardboard circle and press the two fabric circles in place, matching the hinges. Glue the hinges together. Place the lid on the top of the container and glue the hinge to the side of the can. Allow the hinge to dry in place. Glue the second strip around the outside of the can, placing the strip over the hinge.

Trim the can with braid, sequins, beads, or as desired. Loose covers can be made by omitting the hinge or cans can be left uncovered.

Figure 7. In making the bureau box, use a can as a pattern for the inside bottom lining (A). Make a cardboard pattern for the top, allowing a rectangular end for the hinge, then cut two pieces of fabric from the pattern (B). After attaching the hinged top (C), cover the inside and outside surfaces of the can (D and E).

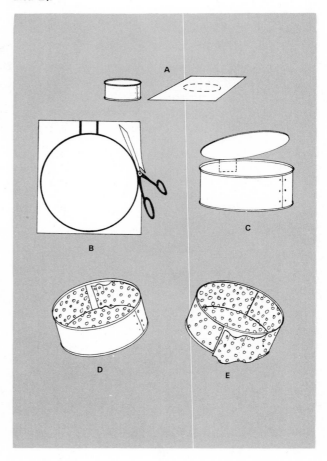

Figure 8. These decorated cans are handy containers for jewelry, coins, or paper clips. They can be left open (left) or covered with a loose lid (center). The outside can be trimmed with fancy braids, ribbons, beads, and sequins (right).

Figure 9. A plastic half-gallon container for ice cream was used to create a container for buttons or sewing equipment (above). The sides and top are decorated with cut-out fabric floral motifs and satin ribbon.

BUTTON OR SEWING BOX

Materials

Materials needed are: (1) a half-gallon plastic ice cream container with cover; (2) glue; (3) tracing paper; (4) pencil; (5) manicuring scissors; (6) 1/4-yard print cotton fabric or chintz; (7) 1 yard of 5/8" satin ribbon; (8) needle and thread; and (9) damp paper towels.

Cutting

Place a piece of tracing paper over the cover and sides of the cover and trace it. Cut out pattern. Pin pattern to the fabric, center the design, and cut it out. Cut out enough motifs or flowers from the fabric to cover most of container.

Assembling

Before gluing, spread glue on the back of a scrap of fabric and allow it to dry. The glue should saturate the fabric but not stain it.

Spread glue on the cover and press the round piece of fabric in place, using a damp paper towel. Spread glue on the backs of the motifs and press them in place around the container.

Trimming

Measure the circumference of the container below the cover and cut the ribbon 1/2" longer. Place a small amount of glue on the ribbon at the ends and at the center; press the ribbon in place around the container.

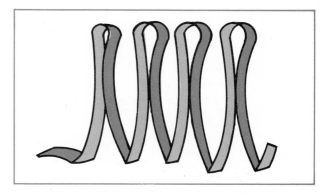

Figure 10. Make a candy ribbon bow to decorate the box by cutting ribbon ends on the diagonal, arranging the ribbon in four equal loops, and gathering them with a thread.

Figure 11. This striking wall hanging was made by covering a board with wood grain contact paper and mounting pieces of tin, wire and buttons. Old tin can lids can be cut and curled to make flower petals.

SCULPTURED WALL HANGING

Materials

Materials needed for this project are: (1) tin can lids in various sizes and colors (silver, gold, or bronze) for flowers; (2) tin shears; (3) heavy work gloves; (4) tying wire; (5) coat hangers or heavy wire; (6) pliers; (7) masking tape; (8) buttons with shanks for flower centers — preferably gold, silver or bronze; (9) long-nosed pliers; (10) hammer; (11) thin nail; (12) aluminum foil or foil pie plate; (13) wood, plywood, heavy cardboard, or fiber board for background; and (14) 1 yard of contact paper in simulated wood tone (if heavy cardboard or fiberboard is used).

Cutting Flowers

Remove lids from cans (use an electric can opener if possible), opening the end of can which is without imprinted markings. Place a lid on a board, and, using the hammer and the thin nail, punch two holes in the center of each lid approximately 3/8" apart.

There are many ways by which lids can be cut with tin shears to form flowers. Invent designs or try the following.

1. Cut a lid into four sections to within 3/8" of the center. Then divide the lid into eight sections by cutting between quarters. There should be about 3/4" left at the center (see accompanying illustration).

2. Cut a lid into two sections; cut to within 3/8" of center. Then divide each half into three sections. There should be about 3/4" left at the center.

3. Cut a lid into eight sections as above, then cut between each section again, making cuts slightly shorter than the previous ones.

4. Make four cuts on a slant (see illustration), cutting into a lid about 3/4". Then make two more cuts in each section, turning the lid and keeping the cuts on a slant.

5. Cut a lid into four sections.

6. Cut a lid into 16 sections, then cut again between each section. The last cuts should be slightly shorter than the original ones.

7. Cut a lid into 4, 8, 16, or 32 sections, but cut only 1" into lid.

Curling Edges of Flowers

Using gloves, place long-nosed pliers over one edge of a cut section and roll the edge toward the center on a diagonal (see illustration). Roll opposite edge. Edges may also be rolled under, of course, or one edge over and one edge under.

Assembling Flowers

Use two or three lids for each flower. Draw a double strand of tying wire through the shank of a button (see illustration), then draw one end through a hole in the top lid and through the corresponding hole of the second and third lids. Draw the other end of the wire through the remaining holes. Twist wire tightly to fasten. Assemble the other flowers in the same manner.

For leaves, cut large ovals from aluminum foil or from a foil pie plate.

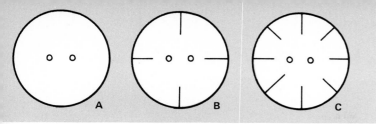

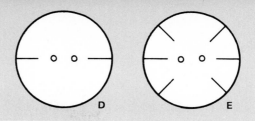

Figure 12. To make a "flower" from a tin can lid: punch two holes about 3/8" apart in the center (A). Cut the lid into four sections (B). Divide each quarter in half to make eight equal parts (C).

Figure 13. Another type of "flower" can be made as follows: cut twice across the diameter of the lid to within 3/8" of the center (D). Then divide each section into three parts, a total of six cuttings (E).

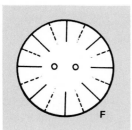

Figure 14. For a third type of "flower" (F), divide the lid into quarters, then into eighths, and finally into sixteen equal segments. The last eight cuttings should be slightly shorter than the others.

Figure 15. Start a "flower" by making four ¾" slanted cuts into the lid (G). Turn the lid and make eight additional slanted cuts (H). Be certain that the slanted cuts are all made in the same direction.

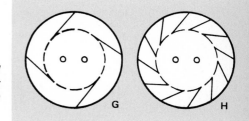

CURLING EDGES

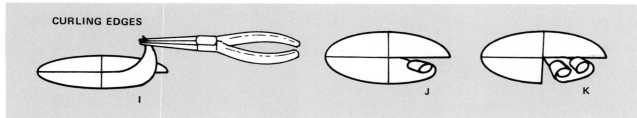

Figure 16. To curl the edges of the "flowers," place pliers over the edge of one of the sections (I). Roll the pliers on a diagonal to curl the tin (J). Place the pliers on the other edge and curl in the opposite direction (K).

Figure 17. To attach the button center to the flower, draw a strand of tying wire through the button shank (L). Then thread the wire through the holes in the lids (M) and secure the wire.

ASSEMBLING FLOWERS

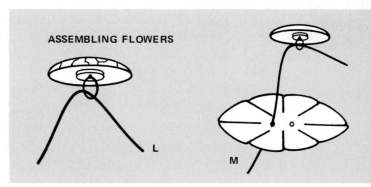

Assembling Wall Hanging

Select wood, plywood, heavy cardboard, or pressed fiber board for the background, and cut it to the desired size. Smooth all rough edges. If a wooden board is used, stain it the desired color and shellac or varnish. If plywood, cardboard, or pressed fiber board is used, cover carefully with the contact paper.

Cut several lengths of heavy wire from coat hangers; bend and curve as shown in the illustration. Place one of the wires on the board for a stem. Mark the board at the points at which the wire is to be attached (two points for each stem). With a hammer and the fine nail, make the holes in the board. Twist tying wire around the coat hanger,

insert both ends of tying wire through the punched holes, and tape to back.

After several stems are attached to the board, attach flowers as follows: make a hole at the top of a stem or where desired and bring both ends of tying wire from flower to the back of the board. Tape the ends. Glue leaves where desired.

Make a loop by cutting a length of wire and folding it in half. Attach picture hanging hooks on opposite sides and run wire through them.

To make a floral arrangement with tin flowers, assemble flowers and leaves on stems and arrange the assembled flowers in a low bowl. Cut the stems to different lengths and use glue to attach the leaves to the stems.

AFGHAN

This afghan is made from scrap fake fur which can be purchased from a fabric mill by the bag or in short lengths. Other usable fabrics include scrap corduroy and woolen or other warm fabric. The finished size of the afghan will be 56" by 72".

Materials

Materials needed for this project are: (1) fake fur; (2) scissors; (3) needle and thread; (4) lightweight cardboard for pattern; (5) colored pencils or marking pens; and (6) sewing machine (optional). The afghan can be made reversible by using squares of the same fabric, a lightweight blanket, or any other warm material as a backing.

Cutting

Draw an 8" square on cardboard and cut it out. If material is in small pieces, use a smaller square. Do not cut fur into too small pieces, however, because it will be difficult to work with. Using the pattern and a colored pencil, draw an 8" square onto the back of fabric and cut it out. It is not necessary to place the pattern on the grain of the fabric: a bias cut will not show or make any difference in assembling. If corduroy is used, however, be sure to place pattern on the line of the fabric.

The afghan shown requires 63 squares; it is 7 squares wide and 9 squares long. If the afghan is to be reversible, make 126 squares. Colors should blend.

Assembling

Sort squares according to color. (Afghan can be made with a different color combination on each side if desired.)

Select nine squares for the first row. Baste them together on the wrong side about 1/2" from the edge. (An alternate method is to place the squares side by side and cross stitch them together.) Use a pencil or marking pen to write 1T on the wrong side of the first square in this row. On the floor, lay out squares for the next row. Be sure that the colors blend and that the same colors are not next to each other. Baste the squares as before and write 2T on the wrong side of the top square. Make five more rows, each time selecting colors

Figure 18. This afghan was made from different colored squares of fake fur. Any type of fabric and color combination can be used. The afghan can be backed with a blanket if it is to be reversible.

that complement the previous row; mark the top square of each row on the wrong side.

Sewing

Stitch the squares of the first row together, taking about a 1/2" seam. Remove basting. Sew the remaining rows. Baste row 1T to row 2T. Sew the two rows together. Lay the seam open to prevent too much bulk. Baste row 3 to row 2 with 3T at the top; join the remaining rows.

If the afghan is to have a backing of the same fabric as the front, repeat the sewing steps above. If backing of a different fabric is to be used, cut the fabric to the same size as the afghan. To join front and back, place right sides together, baste, then sew around three sides and half the fourth, leaving an opening for turning. Turn right side out. Turn under the seam allowance on the open edges and pin. Using a strong double thread, sew the opening together using tiny stitches.

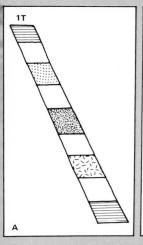
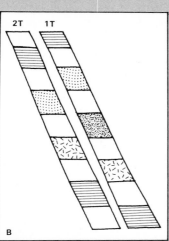
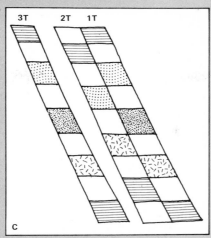

Figure 19. To assemble the afghan, use a cardboard pattern to cut squares of material, and stack the pieces according to color. Baste together nine squares of material (left). Mark the top of the strips, and alternate the colors in the next row of squares (center). Assemble the rows so that the same colors are not placed side by side (right).

Figure 20. The plastic pin box and pieces of old jewelry were decorated with rice for a mosaic effect. The rice was glued to the surface areas and arranged with a toothpick. Then the design was painted.

MOSAIC BOX AND JEWELRY

Materials

Materials for this project are: (1) old earrings, bracelets, rings, or pins with missing stones (for the jewelry project); (2) any small box of plastic or cardboard (for the box project); (3) short-grained rice (do not use minute rice or wild rice); (4) glue; (5) toothpicks; (6) clear nail polish; (7) watercolors or tempera paint; and (8) a small brush.

Covering a Box

Spread a small amount of glue, about the size of a penny, on the center of the top. Drop a few grains of rice onto the glue. Using a toothpick, arrange the grains of rice into the shape of a small flower. Make a second flower close to the first. Add additional flowers and glue, placing the grains of rice so as to fill in the space within each flower as much as possible. Make as many flowers as desired. Glue a few grains of rice around the flowers for leaves. Allow the design to dry for about 10 minutes. Carefully paint the flowers and leaves. (Flowers that are to be white need not be painted.) When the flowers are dry, add a background by spreading a small area with glue and pushing rice as close as possible around design until the entire top of the box is covered. Cover the sides of the box top with glue and rice in the same manner.

Allow rice and glue to dry for a few minutes, then paint the background, pushing paint around rice to cover. Allow the paint to dry for at least one hour. Paint the mosaic design with a coat of clear nail polish, being careful not to disturb the paint. Wait 10 minutes and then add a second coat.

Making Mosaic Jewelry

Use old jewelry with missing stones — preferably with an area about the size of a dime or penny. Fill in the spaces with glue and rice or remove additional stones and make a completely new design. Paint rice as desired, then brush with two coats of clear nail polish.

Figure 21. An assortment of gift boxes can be made with shirt cardboard and wrapping. The boxes can be constructed to the desired size and covered with paper.

GIFT BOXES

Materials

Materials needed for this project are: (1) shirt cardboards, 8″ x 14″; (2) cellophane or masking tape; (3) rubber cement; (4) gift wrapping paper; and (5) scissors.

Making the Pattern

Determine the box size by following these rules: (1) all sides of the box must be the same depth; (2) the top of the box should be 1/16″ larger on all sides than the bottom; and (3) the sides of the top are usually shorter than those of the bottom.

The following are instructions for the top and bottom of a box, the bottom of whose measurements are 3½″ x 5½″ x 1¼″. For the bottom, draw a line across the 8″ dimension of the cardboard 1¼″ from the lower edge (see accompanying illustration). Measure and draw another line 3½″ above the first, then a third line 1¼″ above the second. Cut the cardboard across the last marked line. Measure and mark a vertical line 1¼″ from the edges of the right and left sides — the width between these lines should be 5½″ (see illustration).

Using the back of a pair of scissors and a ruler, score all lines by pressing the scissors lightly over them. The impression or groove left in the card-

board makes it easy to fold. Take care not to cut or scratch the cardboard. The scored side will be the wrong side of the box.

For the top, measure and draw a line across the 8″ dimension of cardboard, 1″ from the lower edge. Draw another line 3⅝″ above the first, then draw a third line 1″ above the second. Cut the cardboard across the last marked line. Now draw a vertical line 1″ from the right edge and another line 5⅝″ from the first and another 1″ from the second. Cut off the remaining cardboard. Cut out the corners marked X on the illustration for both top and bottom. Score all lines. Do not assemble the box at this time; use it as a pattern for the wrapping paper.

To measure for the wrapping, place the bottom of the box on the wrong side of a piece of wrapping paper; with a pencil, lightly draw a pattern around the box, remove the box. Now measure and mark a 1/2″ margin around the outside of the pattern on the wrapping paper. Carefully cut out the paper on these last lines. Clip the corners and cut out each corner marked X on the illustration. Repeat this procedure for the top.

Turn up the sides of the bottom and the top of the box along the scored lines. With masking or cellophane tape, join the corners on the outside of the box.

Wrapping the Box

Place the wrapping paper over the bottom of the box and glue the 1/2″ margin at the top of two sides opposite each other. Glue the notched pieces at these sides to the outside of the box. Now, fold back the notched pieces of wrapping paper of the remaining two sides and tuck them in. Glue the remaining 1/2″ margins to the inside of the box. Cover the top of the box in the same way.

Diagrams are given for two other boxes: (1) a 4″ x 4″ x 1/2″ box requires one sheet of cardboard 8″ x 14″; (2) a 5″ x 11″ x 1½″ box requires two sheets of cardboard 8″ x 14″.

Figure 22. Assemble the cardboard gift boxes following steps A through L (right). Also shown are various sizes and dimensions for the boxes themselves.

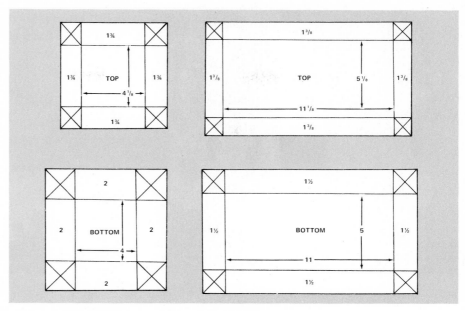

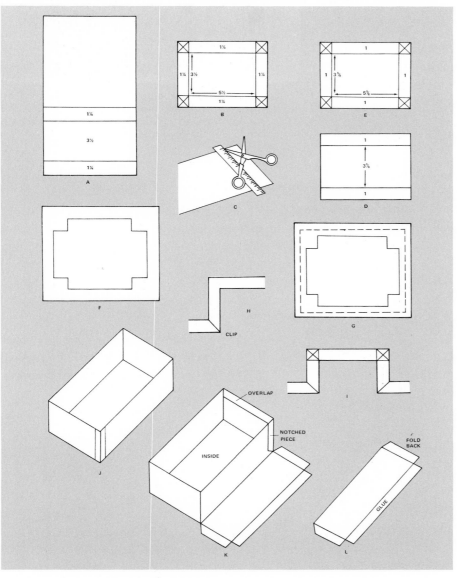

Figure 23. These Tiffany style vases are inexpensive to make. Paint small section with different colors of nail polish, and outline the areas with liquid lead (left) or a black marking pen (right).

TIFFANY VASES

Materials

Materials needed are: (1) plastic liquid detergent bottles; (2) various shades of nail polish; (3) liquid lead; (4) permanent black marking pen; (5) sharp scissors or knife; (6) cotton swabs; and (7) nail polish remover.

Preparing Bottle

Be sure the outside of the bottle is completely clean. Use the marking pen to draw a line around the bottle at the desired height. Cut out a hole in the top of the bottle and widen it until the line is reached. Carefully cut along line.

To Make a Vase Having a Large Pattern

With the permanent marking pen, outline large areas on the bottle as shown. Use different shades of nail polish (colors can be mixed) to fill in the areas. If the polish is thick, it should cover the bottle with one coat. If thin, allow the bottle to dry completely, then apply a second coat. Blot any runovers with a cotton swab dipped in nail polish remover.

With liquid lead, carefully outline each area and across the top and bottom of the bottle.

To Make a Vase Having a Small Pattern

With the permanent black marking pen, outline small areas around the bottle. Start at the bottom and fill in each area with different shades of nail

polish, using two coats if necessary. Cover an area 1" wide around the bottle at a time. Allow it to dry completely and then go over every outline again. Be careful to make the lines as even as possible and to completely fill in the corners. Fill in areas for another inch and repeat procedure. Continue to the top of bottle, ending with a solid line of black at the upper edge.

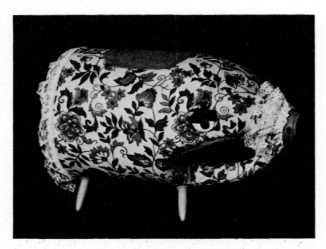

Figure 24. The finished piggy bank is supported by plastic corn cob holders. When the bank is filled, the coins can be removed by unscrewing the bottle cap.

PIGGY BANK

Materials

Materials needed for this project are: (1) bleach or fabric softener bottle; (2) 1/2 yard of print fabric; (3) 1 yard of lace; (4) scraps of white, black, and gold felt; (5) glue; (6) four corn holders; and (7) thin wire.

Preparing Bottle

Wash and dry bottle thoroughly; replace cap. Place handle down. With scissors or knife make a 2" slit on the top back of the bottle (see accompanying illustration).

Cutting Fabric

Cut a 13" x 20" piece of print fabric. If the circumference of the bottle is more or less than 20", cut fabric accordingly.

Assembling

Place glue along the long edges of the fabric. Start at the slit and wrap the fabric around the container, ending at the slit; 1" of fabric should extend over the rounded end (bottom of the bottle). Slit the 1" extension, about every inch, and glue the slits so that they overlap and are flat.

Cut 4" slits in the fabric at the neck end of the bottle about every 2" and glue so that they overlap and are flat. Glue the fabric under the handle as well as possible; it will be covered later. Cut a strip of fabric the length of the handle and wide enough to completely cover it; glue the strip in place. Glue strips of fabric to cover any bare spots. From the print fabric, cut out a circle 7" in diameter and glue it to the rounded end (bottom) of the bottle.

Cut out a piece of gold felt 5" x 3½". Round off each corner and glue the felt to the indentation above the handle.

For the snout, cut out a 1¾" circle of felt and glue it over the cap. Slit the edges, fit, and glue flat. Cut out a 3/4" strip of gold felt and glue it around the sides of the cap. Cut two tiny circles from black felt and glue these to the front of the snout for nostrils.

Assemble the eyes as follows: cut out two 1" circles from white felt. From black felt, cut out two small circles for pupils and glue them to the white circles, slightly off center. Then cut a 3/4" strip of black felt 1¼" long. Cut fringe at one side. Glue one eye to each side of the bottle about 3" from the snout and 1/2" up from gold section. Glue fringe for eyelashes over eyes.

To make the ruffles, cut two pieces of lace, each about 12" long. With needle and thread, gather the straight edge and place it around the face about 1/2" from the snout; tie the threads under the handle. Gather and tie a second ruffle around the snout. Glue another piece of ruffle (without gathering) around the bottom of the bottle as shown.

Cut out a piece of gold felt and round off the corners. Cut a 2" slit in the center. Glue the felt over the slit at top of back.

For the tail, cut two pieces of gold felt each 3/4" x 5" in length. Sew the two pieces together by hand 1/4" from one long edge. Cut thread and fasten. Sew by hand 1/4" from first seam. Trim edges slightly. Draw a 10" piece of medium-weight wire through the remaining 1/4". Punch a small hole in the back of the bottle and push the uncovered end of the wire into the hole. Twist wire to curl. Insert the corn holders as legs.

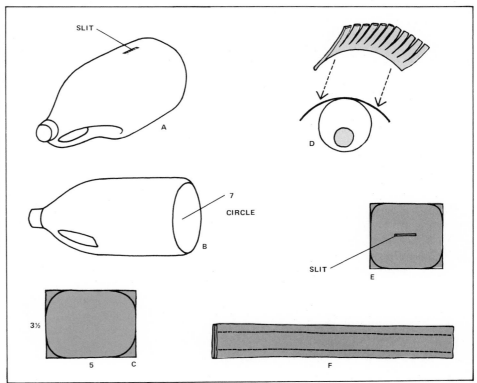

Figure 25. To make a piggy bank, cut a slit on the side of a bottle (A). After the sides of the bottle are in place, glue a circle of print fabric to the bottom (B). A rounded piece of felt is glued above the handle (C). Make each eye from a circle of white felt. Cut small circles from black felt for the pupils (D). Cut a rounded piece of gold felt with a slit in the center (E), and place the felt over the slit in the bottle. Use two pieces of felt and wire for the tail (F).

RAG DOLL DOOR STOP

Materials

Materials needed for this project are: (1) one-gallon plastic bleach bottle; (2) 1/2 yard of blue cotton fabric; (3) 1/2 yard of red gingham; (4) pair of pink socks for a small child; (5) man's white handkerchief about 16" square; (6) scraps of red, white, and black felt; (7) 1 yard of narrow elastic; (8) two 1/2" buttons with shanks; (9) 16" of heavy wire; (10) cotton for stuffing arms; (11) styrofoam ball about 3" in diameter for head; (12) one 1/4" wide wooden dowel or heavy knitting needle to support head; (13) 45 yards of yellow worsted knitting yarn; (14) glue; (15) masking tape; (16) sand; (17) red, white, blue, and yellow thread; and (18) one 8" x 10" cardboard.

Cutting

Cut a 10" x 28" piece of the blue fabric for the skirt. Cut a piece of gingham 16" x 25" for the blouse and bottle covering. Cut two pieces of gingham 4" x 10" for the sleeves.

To make the arms and head, cut the foot of the sock above the heel and cut the leg 5" from the top edge (see illustration). Cut leg of sock lengthwise into two pieces, or, if the width of the sock is very small, use as is.

To make the apron, cut the handkerchief into one piece 6" long and the width of the handkerchief; two pieces 2" long and the width; two pieces 1¼" long and the width; and one piece 3½" long by 3¾" wide (see illustration). A piece of the remainder of the handkerchief will be used for a triangle for the head.

Sewing

Join the short ends of the blue fabric with a 1/2" seam. Turn under 1/4" at lower edge and pin. Then, turn under 1/4" again and sew hem. Turn under 1/4" at upper edge and pin. Turn under and sew a 1/2" casing for the elastic at the upper edge: start and end 1/4" from the seam. Cut elastic to 24". Draw it through the casing and tie the ends in a knot. Do not cut the elastic. Set skirt aside. Place a large wad of cotton under the handle of the bottle and tape it in place. This is to fill out the bust.

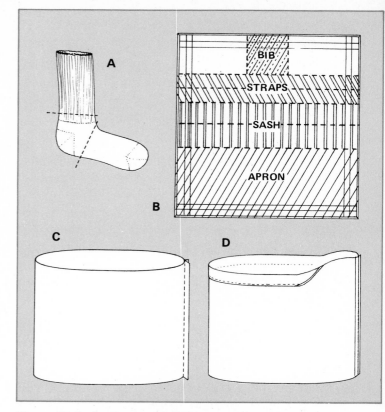

Figure 26. *To begin the ragdoll door stop, cut the top and toe portions of a ribbed sock to make the arms and head of the doll (A). Divide and cut a 16" square handkerchief to make the apron sections (B). Join the ends of the blue skirt fabric and sew a ½" seam (C). Then, sew a 3/4" hem at the lower end (D). Make a casing at the top for the elastic.*

To sew the blouse and bottle covering, join the wrong sides of the two short ends of the 16" x 25" piece of gingham with a 1/2" seam. Sew a 1/2" casing at the upper and lower edges (as on the upper edge of skirt). Draw elastic (without cutting) through the casing at the upper edge and draw together tightly, leaving about 1" at the center to fit over the opening of the bottle. Tie the ends of the elastic at this end of the gingham and cut off the extra elastic. Place the gingham, right side out, over the bottle. Draw elastic through the casing at the bottom edge of the gingham and draw it tightly over the bottom of the bottle.

To make the sleeves, sew the wrong sides of the short ends of the sleeve pieces together with a 1/2" seam. Make a 1/2" casing at both the upper and lower edges (as on the upper edge of skirt). Draw elastic through the casings; fasten it tightly at the upper edge and loosely at the lower edge. The lower edge will fit over the arm; the upper edge will be fit over a wire.

To make the apron, take largest piece of apron

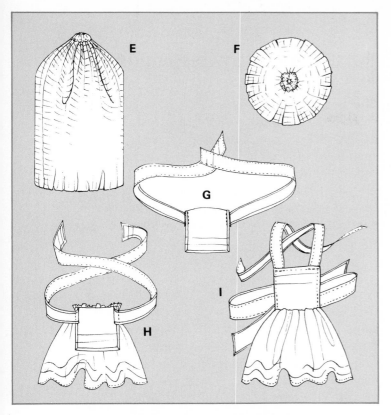

Figure 27. Place the checked fabric over the bottle. Draw a piece of elastic through the upper casing at the top of the bottle (E) and through the lower casing on the bottom of the bottle (F). Use the cut up handkerchief to make the apron. Sew the sash ends to the bib. (G) and attach the bib to the apron (H). Sew the straps to the bib (I) and finish the raw edges.

Figure 28. Cover a styrofoam ball with the toe portion of the sock. Make the eyes and mouth by cutting the shapes from felt and gluing them to the face. Use strips of yarn to make the hair (J). For the arms, fold the two top portions of the sock in half and sew a seam down the edge and across the bottom of each (K). Push a piece of wire through the sides of the bottle (L). Attach the shank of a button to each of the wire ends (M). Wrap a strip of cotton around the wire and button (N), and secure it with masking tape.

fabric (6"); it is already hemmed on three sides. Sew a running stitch across the fourth edge, drawing in the apron to about 4" in width. Turn under and sew a 1/4" hem on each 3½" side of the bib. Set aside. Turn under and sew a 1/4" hem on each long edge of straps and sashes. With right sides together, sew an end of the sash to each side of bib. Now place the right side of the bib to the right side of the apron. There should be about 1/2" of sash at each side of the bib. Sew a seam across the upper edge of the apron. Now sew a strap to each upper end of bib, placing right sides together. Make a 1/4" hem at each end of straps and sashes and at upper edge of bib.

Assembling

Place skirt over bottle. Place apron over front of skirt. Draw sashes to back of bottle and tie a bow. Draw straps around top of bottle and tie a bow.

Head

Draw toe section of sock over styrofoam ball for head. Gather sock at lower edge with needle and thread. Cut lips out of red felt and glue in place. Cut two small circles out of white felt for eyes. Cut two tiny circles out of black felt and glue to center of white. Glue eyes to face.

Insert wooden dowel or knitting needle into bottom of head. Set head aside.

Arms

Fold each piece of sock in half lengthwise right sides together and sew a seam down one side and across the cut edge. Turn right side out. Punch a small hole through the fabric and bottle at each side about 1½" down from the opening. Push wire through the bottle so that it extends at each side. Push the tight end of a sleeve over each wire and push sleeve up close to bottle. Draw the end of wire through the shank of a button and fold back the wire so that the arms are about 5" long. Twist end of wire so the button cannot slip. Wrap a strip of cotton around button and wire and wrap with masking tape to hold together. Draw arm covering (sock top) over covered wire. Pull loose end of sleeve over arms.

For a door stop, fill the bottle with sand and push the wooden dowel into the sand so that the head is firm.

Hair

Cut out a 1/2" slit in the 8" x 10" piece of cardboard 1" down from one long edge and 1" in from the side edges (see illustration). Wind yarn over the cardboard 100 times. Push strands over the slit. Machine sew across the slit; sew back and forth several times. Remove strands from cardboard (cut cardboard at slit). Sew or fasten with straight pins the stitched end of yarn across the back of the head. Divide loops into two groups. Draw a strand of yarn through each group and tie tightly. Draw one group to top of head and sew or pin to head. Twist once, then sew or fasten with pins. Cut a small triangle from the remainder of the handkerchief and pin to top of head; hem edges if necessary.

Figure 29. The bottle is filled with sand to provide the necessary weight to hold a door open. A dowel rod is inserted in the styrofoam ball and pushed into the sand to hold the head erect.

BUTTERFLIES 'N FLOWERS MEMORY BOX

The beauty of the memory box is that it can be made from anything — some seashells from the beach, dried flowers from the garden, all the mementos of a happy experience. Memory boxes reflect the personality of the maker and so no two are alike. The one shown here is made from purchased materials, but almost every item might be substituted for something else. The idea is to give imagination a free rein.

Materials

Materials for this project are: (1) memory box, 8" x 10"; (2) wild oats, 3 stems; (3) yarrow, 2 stems; (4) large star flowers, 8 stems; (5) mini star flowers, small bunch; (6) butterflies, 4 prints (2 pairs exactly alike); (7) owl; (8) duck; (9) turtle; (10) rabbit foot; (11) walnut stain; (12) 2" cork-like base, 5 pieces; (13) hemp cord, 18"; (14) adhesive clay, 6"; (15) chenille bee; and (16) silicone glue.

Preparation

Stain the box and the wooden holding strips with the walnut stain. Bind the small bunch of mini star flowers together with a piece of thread. Tie the piece of hemp cord over the binding and make a bow. Trim the ends of the flowers so that the bunch is about 3" long. Now very carefully cut out the butterflies. Be sure there is no white left around the edges. Use the silicone glue to glue the bodies of the butterflies together so that they

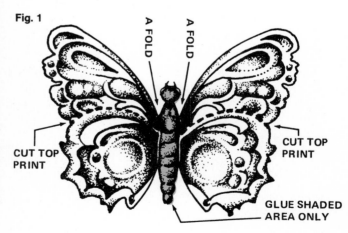

Fig. 1

A FOLD
A FOLD
CUT TOP PRINT
CUT TOP PRINT
GLUE SHADED AREA ONLY

Figure 30. Carefully cut out two pairs of butterflies for use on the memory box. Cut the top pair of wings of each butterfly close to the body for a more realistic effect.

Figure 31. Memory boxes can be arranged with purchased materials or personal treasures and momentos collected over the years. The display can be arranged so that it portrays a specific theme.

are alike on front and back. When thoroughly dry, bend the wings up toward the body. A more realistic effect can be obtained by cutting the wings of the top print apart as far as the body so that they resemble two sets of wings.

Assembling

The sections are numbered vertically so that sections 1, 2, and 3 are the small spaces on the left and 4 and 5 are the larger sections on the right.

Section 1. In a 1" piece of the cork-like base pierce small holes on the top. (A toothpick does a fine job.) Dip the ends of the rabbit foot in glue and place in the holes. Apply adhesive to the bottom of the cork-like material and place it in the lower right corner of the section. Apply adhesive to the bottom of the owl and place it in the middle of the left hand side of the section.

Section 2. In another small piece of the cork-like material, make more holes as in Section 1. Again, dip the stems in glue and place the large star flowers in the material. Place in the lower left corner and hold in place with adhesive. Apply glue to the back of the body of the butterfly and position against the back of the box. (Lay the box flat to help keep the butterfly in place.)

Section 3. Break the cork-like material into a strip which is about the width of the section. It should be about 1/2" high. Place against the back of the section and hold in place with adhesive. Position the yarrow in the middle left of the strip. Apply adhesive to the bottom of the duck and place in the right hand corner of the section.

Section 4. Apply glue to the back of the mini star flower bouquet. Position at any angle in about the center of the back of the box. (Again, laying the box on its back is helpful here.) Place glue on the back of the body of the butterfly and secure in the upper right hand corner of the section at a downward angle. Glue the chenille bee to the bottom lower left of the section.

Section 5. Repeat the directions for Section 1, but substitute the turtle for the owl and the wild oats for the rabbit foot.

Dry for at least 24 hours. Clean the glass and, making sure none of the materials extends past the dividers, place the glass on top of the dividers.

Fasten holding strips in place, being careful not to break the glass.

For Additional Reading

Benson, Kenneth R., **Creative Crafts for Children,** Prentice Hall, 1958.

Comstock, Nan, **McCall's Golden Do-It Book,** Golden Press, 1967.

Gilbreath, Alice, **Spouts, Lids and Cans,** William Morrow, 1973.

Pflug, Betsy, **You Can,** Van Nostrand Reinhold, 1969.

Sattler, Helen Roney, **Kitchen Carton Crafts,** Lothrop, Lee & Shepard, 1970.

Boutiquing

Boutiquing is a craft which deals with a wide array of decorative elements, such as painted eggs, styrofoam, and beads.

The egg is one of the oldest symbols known to man. Throughout history, men have used it to represent the universe, and practically all cultures have put the egg to decorative and ornamental use. In 988 A.D., the Europeans developed a batik method — a wax resist technique — for decorating eggs. As the wax resist was applied, the egg was dipped into various dyes. The wax was then removed and the dyed design remained on the egg. Unusual beaded eggs originated with the Sudanese in Africa, and jeweled eggs were commissioned by a one-time emperor of Russia as gifts for his wife. The Russians filled their eggs with colored crystal to symbolize day and night: darker jewels to represent the disappearance of the sun; and lighter jewels, the daylight. Indeed, many ornate pieces which decorated the boudoirs of wealthy European and Russian noblemen are now displayed in museums throughout the world.

Figure 1. This lovely Christmas tree is created by the careful placement of pearls, sequins, and gold filigree in a styrofoam base.

Figure 2. This beaded bag (above) was made by an Indian craftsman, probably a Plains Indian. (Courtesy, Field Museum of Natural History, Chicago.)

Figure 3. Two creations of the 19th-century jeweler Carl Fabergé are the Kelch Hen Egg (below left) and the Chanticleer Egg (below right). (Courtesy, the FORBES Magazine Collection, New York.)

The egg is also a symbol of rebirth and fertility. Easter eggs represent the new life that returns to nature in the spring. The custom of exchanging eggs was established in ancient times: the early Christians of Mesopotamia were the first to use eggs as gifts for Easter. According to legend, the Persians believed that the earth was hatched from a giant egg. Thus, they painted eggs in spring colors, as did the Egyptians. These ornamental eggs were often given as gifts and were considered very valuable.

Beadcraft, another aspect of boutiquing, is almost as old as civilization itself. Ancient usage of the bead can almost be used to chart the ages of man. Beads, identified as belonging to the Neolithic period, have been discovered by archaeologists. Egyptian artisans were using beads as early as 4000 B.C. American Indians used beads for money as well as for ornaments on clothing, belts, moccasins, and tomahawks. Today there is a fascinating variety of round, square, convex, concave, and carved beads.

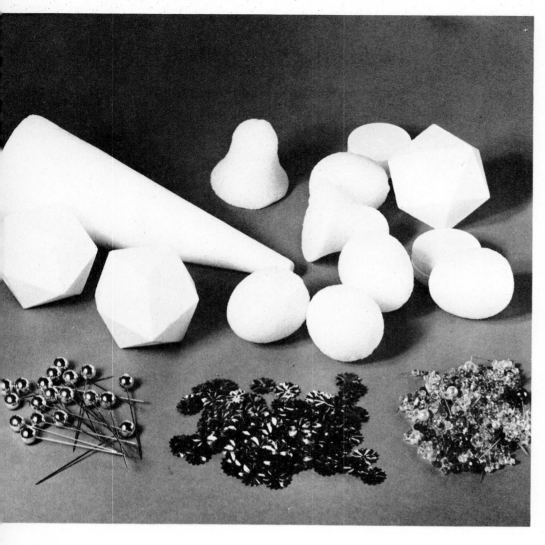

Figure 4. Styrofoam, which may be bought in many shapes, can be imaginatively adorned with pin-in decorations and "jewels."

Basic Equipment And Supplies

Following are separate lists of materials for eggery, styrofoam crafts, and beadcraft.

EGGERY

Several kinds of eggs can be used for boutiquing. Obviously, the most common are chicken eggs. Double-yolk chicken eggs and duck, goose, and turkey eggs may also be used — these are available from hatcheries or farms. Other suggested materials, depending upon the type of project undertaken, are: (1) diamond dust for adding sparkly effects to surfaces; (2) white or cement glue; (3) gold braid, gold paper lace, and gold leaf (available in sheets); (4) hinges, available in various sizes, for holding egg pieces together; (5) miniature ornaments such as pearls, beads, ribbons, and sequins; (6) acrylic paints; (7) straight pins; (8) sharp knife or single-edge razor blade for scoring eggshell; (9) manicure scissors; (10) darning needle and thread; (11) toothpicks; (12) colored pencils; (13) plaster of Paris; (14) paint brushes; (15) masking tape; (16) shellac; (17) egg cartons; and (18) paper towels.

STYROFOAM CRAFTS

Styrofoam is a widely used craft material. Lightweight and waterproof, it is available in almost any shape, from cones and blocks to sheets.

Styrofoam can be cut with a sharp knife or punctured with a pencil point or soldering iron. Pieces can be joined with glue, pins, or toothpicks.

Supplies necessary for working with styrofoam are: jewels, fabric, sequins, straight pins, braid, and ribbons for decorating the ornaments; and

Figure 5. This eye-catching anniversary "egg tree" utilizes twig branches, plastic grass, and a plastic goblet or dish. Photographs are mounted on styrofoam backings and hung from the branches.

scissors, pencil, paper, brush, and glue for tracing patterns. For flocked ornaments made with styrofoam balls, the following additional materials are suggested: designer yarns, tinsel, and gold and silver thread.

BEADCRAFT

Part of the fun of beadcraft lies in collecting interesting beads. Thrift and antique shops can be valuable sources; old costume jewelry can be dismantled and the parts used in new and original ways. Of course, beads can always be purchased. There are several kinds available including cut, faceted, flower, lined, opaque, translucent, seed, spacer, and vertebrae beads.

Other supplies necessary for beadcraft are beadcraft thread and wire, bead pins, dental floss, elastic yarn, flower wire, glue, pliers, ruler, and T-pins.

Basic Procedures

The procedures for the three crafts discussed here will be described separately.

EGGERY

Use large white eggs. Carefully wash and dry the eggs, and allow them to warm to room temperature.

Emptying the Eggshell

Hold an egg in one hand over a bowl. At one end of the egg make a small hole, approximately 1/4" in diameter, with a hat pin and take away the small pieces of shell right around the hole. Make a second hole a bit larger at the opposite end. Place the mouth over the small hole and blow the contents of the egg out of the larger hole into the bowl. (The contents can be cooked and eaten.)

Rinse the inside of the eggshell with water; then blow again to remove the water. Set the eggshell, small end down, in an egg carton to drain and dry. Eggshells should be thoroughly dry before they are cut to prevent warping and formation of mildew.

Cutting the Egg

The egg has two layers. The outside layer is hard like porcelain; the inside, soft like chalk. To keep the egg from cracking while cutting, paint the entire shell with white glue and let dry.

Cutting a Hole for a Figure. (1) With a pencil, sketch an opening of the desired size on the eggshell. The hole must be large enough to allow a small figure to be placed inside the egg. (2) Use small manicure scissors to cut an opening along the pencil line. (3) Cut around the pencil line, taking small cuts with the middle part of the scissors.

Don't worry about jagged edges — they can be covered. If the egg cracks, apply one coat of white glue to both the inside and the outside of the shell.

Cutting an Eggshell in Half. An eggshell can be cut horizontally or vertically in half. Score lines gently with a razor blade and cut through.

Cutting a Door and Placing Hinges. (1) With a pencil, sketch an opening of the desired size on the eggshell. Use a razor blade to cut out this "door." (2) Place the hinge on the door so that the ridge at which the hinge bends is along the edge of the door. Trace around the hinge and along the edge at the bend of the hinge (this will be a notch). (3) Place the hinge on the egg so that the ridge is along the edge of the hole (or "doorway"). Trace around the hinge and along the edge at the bend of the hinge as before. (4) Cut out rectangular notches in the door and the egg for the hinge. Use manicure scissors and snip into the edge of the shell. (5) Place the hinge into the notch on the egg. Glue hinge to egg with cement glue (epoxy) and allow to dry for several hours. Avoid getting glue into hinge. Glue hinge to door and allow to dry for several hours.

Trimming the Egg

Gather trim — pearls, jewels, sequins, gold-silver braids (preferably with adhesive backing), velvet, or scraps of lace. Some braid has loops which can be filled with small beads. To fill braid with beads, apply a bit of glue to each loop and, using tweezer, place a pearl on each loop. Then, place a line of glue next to the beads for another type of braid. Place the ends of the braid at the top or the bottom of the egg so they are not noticeable. Beads which have already been strung are particularly easy to apply. Allow the glue to dry.

Miniature figures can be placed inside the egg. They can either be glued or attached to a small piece of white styrofoam which has been placed inside the egg. Grass or angel hair can be used to cover the styrofoam. The figures can be used to create scenes which tell a story or depict an historical event. These are particularly apropos for holiday gifts and displays.

Decorated eggs may be mounted on a base. This base can be plain or decorated with many of the same ornaments used for the egg.

STYROFOAM CRAFTS

Rather than discussing general procedures for working with styrofoam, the reader is referred to the "Projects You Can Do" section of this article. Several specific methods of working with styrofoam are described.

BEADCRAFT EMBROIDERY

Embroidery with beads involves threading the beads on cord or string and holding the beads together as a design. Use a needle to fasten the beads to a prepared backing. Embroidering on loosely woven fabric is easier than on closely woven material.

The threads or lines in the fabric act as a guide for keeping the stitches straight. If using plain material with no guides, add lightly colored chalk lines. Use beads with large holes in case the thread must pass through the hole several times. The type of bead is very important; on projects which will be laundered, use only glass, plastic, or ceramic beads — never wooden ones. Detergent will cause the wood finish to flake. Use thick wool yarn.

Learning the Stitches

The *running stitch* is the basic stitch. Thread a needle with a polyester thread and knot one end.

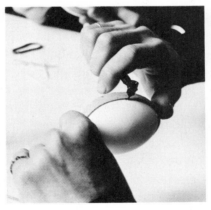

Figure 6. To make these exquisite Ukrainian eggs (A), dip the heated stylus tip into beeswax (B), then draw the design, using a rubber band for control in making parallel lines (C). Add additional decoration freehand (D). The first dye (E) should be the lightest; when the egg is dry, draw lines that are to remain light. After the final dye, let the egg dry, melt the wax over a flame (F), then carefully wipe the wax off.

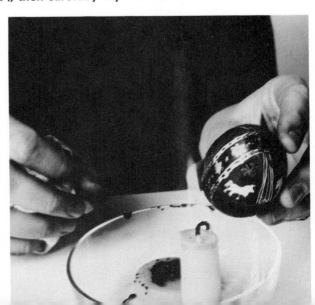

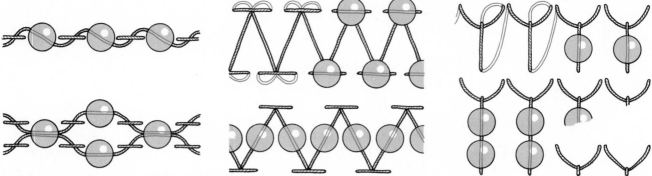

Figure 7. The basic stitch in beadcraft embroidery is the running stitch (left). Use a winding thread under each stitch to hold the bead. A chevron stitch (center) can be done with one thread, doubled back halfway on the underside running stitches. A Y-stitch (right) begins with a loose, arc-like stitch, fastened by a stitch from underneath for the tail.

Bring the needle from the wrong side of the fabric backing to the right side. Slip a bead onto the needle and go back through the wrong side again, pulling the thread until the bead lies flat. This is one running stitch. The stitches should be neat and evenly spaced, but space between stitches can be longer or shorter than the stitches themselves. The beads will not slide around on the thread if the running stitches are close together and the beads are large enough to fill in the spaces.

The *chevron stitch* looks like two parallel rows of running stitches with a third thread winding between rows. The stitch is made with one thread on two parallel lines (see illustration). Practice a few times using embroidery floss, then string some beads to determine the desired placement.

The *Y-stitch* looks like the letter "Y" and is very easy to make. Variations of this stitch depend upon the length of the stem of the Y. Follow the diagram to learn the stitch. The Y-stitch makes an interesting border.

Projects You Can Do

PLASTER OF PARIS EASTER EGGS

Materials

The materials needed are: dry, empty eggshells; plaster of Paris; small brushes; acrylic paints; masking tape; clear shellac; needle; and bottle caps or disposable plastic cups to use as egg holders.

Making and Painting Plaster Eggs

Chip out a small hole at both ends of each of sev-

eral eggs, and blow out the contents of the eggs into a bowl (see under "Basic Procedures"). Then wash out and dry the shells. Enlarge one of the holes in each egg by chipping away some of the shell. Place the eggshells in the egg cups with the chipped-out holes facing up. Mix plaster to a creamy consistency, following the manufacturer's directions. Pour the plaster slowly and carefully through the chipped-out hole in each eggshell.

Fill the shells to the top and allow a few days for drying. When the plaster is set, gently tap the egg against a hard surface and peel the shell away. If necessary, sand the plaster egg until it develops a smooth surface. Paint the eggs. Apply two or three coats of a light color, allowing each coat to dry before applying the next. After paint is dry, apply two or three coats of shellac.

JEWEL-LIKE MOSAIC EGG

Materials

The materials for this project are: dry, empty eggshells; six or eight colors of enamel paint; small brushes; colored sequins; round, colored 1/16" beads on thread; match sticks; egg carton; large needle; and white glue.

Preparation of Eggs

With a darning needle, pierce a small hole in the small end of each egg and a larger hole at the opposite end. Blow out the contents of each egg, then wash out and dry the shells (see under "Basic Procedures").

Work with the smaller end of the egg up. Copy

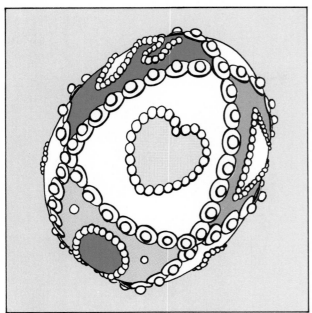

Figure 8. Pictured above is the finished mosaic egg project, ready for display.

symmetrical designs quarter by quarter: first on the front of the egg, then on the back, joining the lines at the sides. Use bright colors for filling in one-color areas on the top and bottom of each egg. Let each color dry before starting another. Use eight colors on each egg. When drying the egg, place a match stick in one of the holes and push the other end of the match stick into the lid of the egg carton. After half of the egg has been enameled and is dry, repeat the process on the other half.

Using a large needle, draw a line with clear-drying glue on an area where threaded beads are to go. Lay the beads on the glued lines, and hold them in place so that they do not slip while the glue dries. Cut off any excess threaded bead and glue the last bead to the egg. Place glue over all beaded areas to make sure they are secure. Glue sequins on the design lines and over the holes of both eggs. Glue a single bead in the center of each sequin.

LACQUERED EGGS

Materials

Materials needed for this project include: dry, empty eggshells; dried moss; small, dried flowers; delicate fern fronds; clear glue; acrylic paints and soft brushes; small sponge; bowl; egg carton; and paper towels.

Preparing the Eggs

Select such materials as dried flowers, moss, and fern fronds. Create a design and lightly trace it onto the egg. Brush glue on eggshells to fit design. Moisten fingers to pick up materials; place them on the glue. Place all petals and cover the holes at each end of the egg. Moisten a sponge and squeeze it in a paper towel until the towel is damp. Press the towel gently against the materials until they are affixed to the shell; remove excess glue. Place the egg in the egg carton until the glue dries. Repeat the steps to attach any remaining materials to the shell. Let the design dry for several days.

Coat the egg with an acrylic varnish, applying it to half the egg at a time. Apply three coats, brushing each coat in a different direction.

Figure 9. This lacquered egg (above) is decorated with dried flowers, leaves, and moss. These materials should be thoroughly dried before they are glued to the egg.

Figure 10. For the styrofoam balls project, use fabric, sequins, ribbons, and beads for decoration. Fabric and ribbon are glued to the ball, then the beads and sequins are secured with pins.

STYROFOAM BALLS

Materials

Materials needed for this project include: styrofoam balls; pencil and paper; scissors; fabric; clear-drying glue; pins; braid; and jewels, sequins, and beads.

Decorating the Ball

Trace a pattern of a section of the ball on paper, cut out the pattern, and pin it to the fabric. Cut out the fabric around the pattern and glue the fabric section to the ball. After the material is glued, pin each end of the section to the ball with a straight pin to secure it. Repeat the procedure, adding fabric sections all around the ball. (The ball will have alternating areas of styrofoam and fabric.) Then, glue thin braid at the edges of each fabric section. Fill in areas of the braid with sequins and beads, using pins to attach them. Designs can be added between the fabric sections using sequins, pins, pearls, or jewels. Finally, cut a piece of braid for hanging the ball. Overlap the ends to form a loop. Glue the ends together and pin them into the braid and ball.

STYROFOAM CENTERPIECE

The centerpiece — consisting of a snow scene with several buildings, a small girl, and small artificial evergreen trees — is constructed of styrofoam, cardboard, and various trims.

Materials

The materials needed for this project are: one styrofoam circle 17" in diameter; one styrofoam circle 13" in diameter; one styrofoam block 5" x 5" x 3"; one styrofoam ball 5" in diameter for the arch at the top of the block; one square styrofoam column about 6" tall; one styrofoam cylinder about 5" tall; styrofoam slabs; two styrofoam balls from which onion-shaped domes will be made; a small styrofoam ball for head; cardboard; wrapping paper; scissors; knife; spoon; felt-tip pens; clear-drying glue; trims; artificial snow; and tiny evergreen trees.

Constructing the Centerpiece

Glue the 13" circle on top of the 17" one for the base. Glue the 5" x 5" x 3" block of styrofoam to the center of the base. Cut the 5" ball in half and

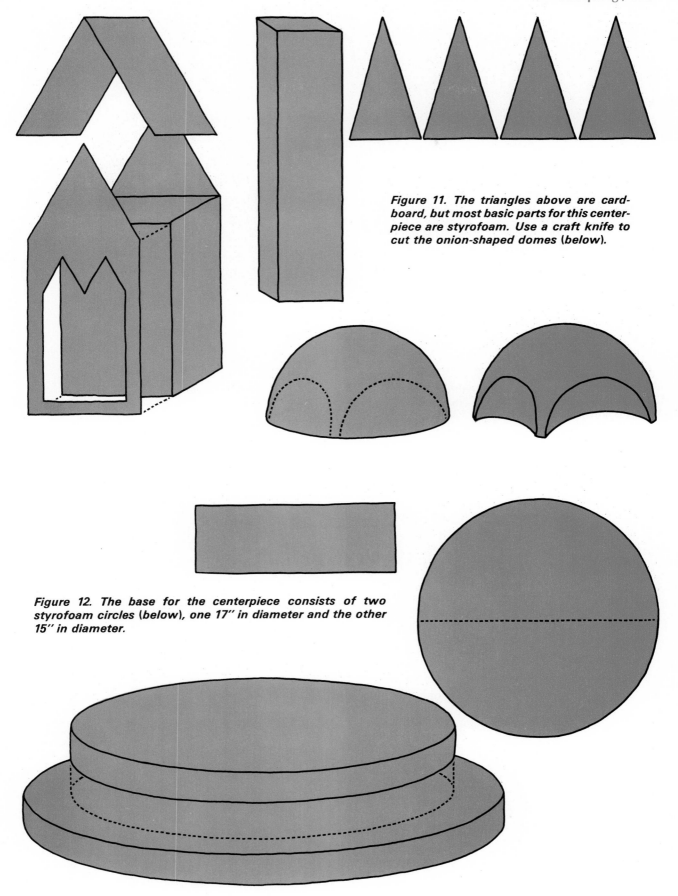

Figure 11. The triangles above are card-board, but most basic parts for this center-piece are styrofoam. Use a craft knife to cut the onion-shaped domes (below).

Figure 12. The base for the centerpiece consists of two styrofoam circles (below), one 17" in diameter and the other 15" in diameter.

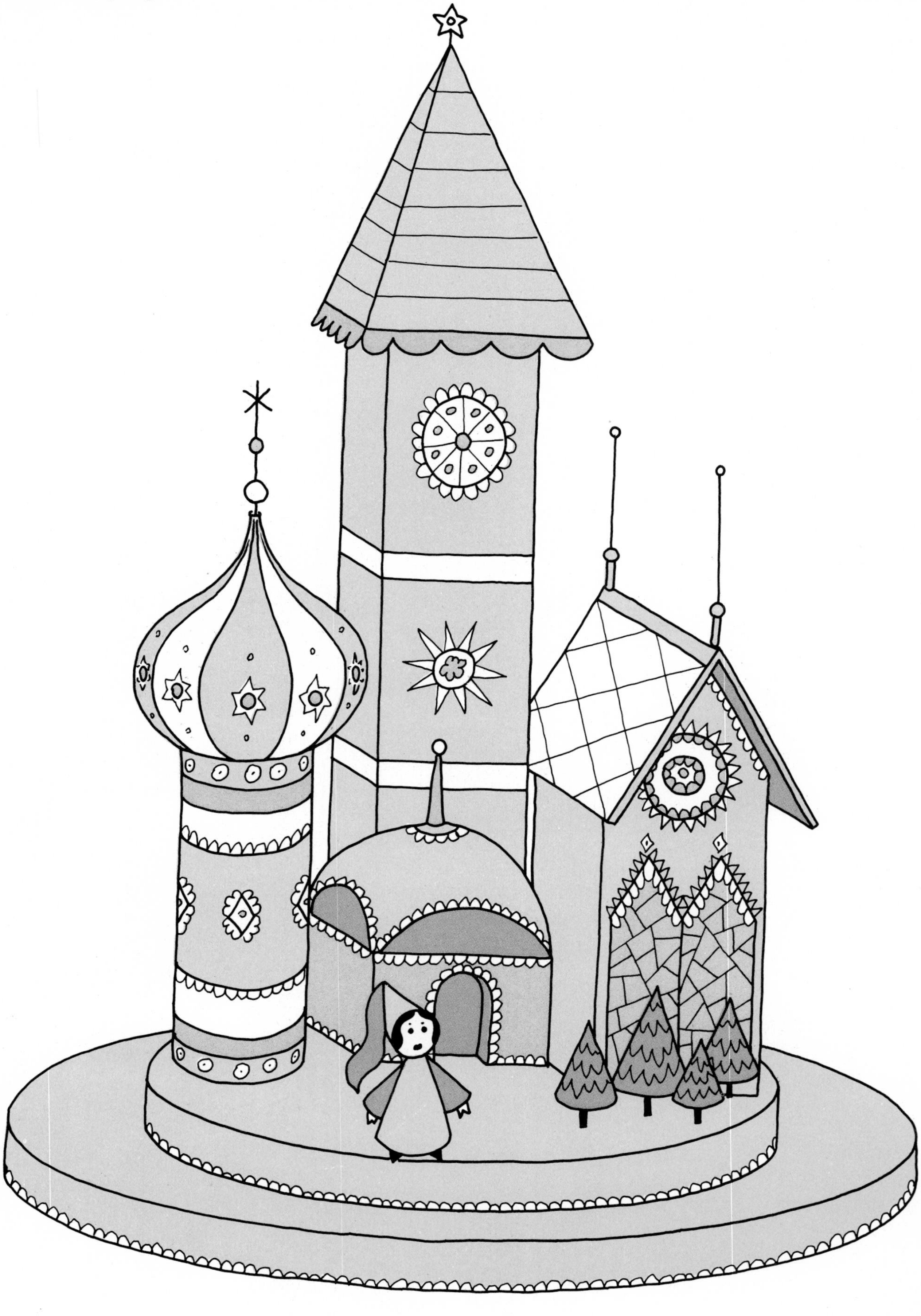

scoop it out to form arches (see illustration); glue this piece to the top of the square block. Glue the square styrofoam pillar behind the arched structure. For the top of the pillar, cut four triangles measuring 2″ on each side from cardboard and glue them together (see illustration). Glue this piece to the top of the square pillar. To the left of the arched structure, glue the 5″ cylindrical pillar. Using a knife, fashion two onion-shaped domes from the two styrofoam balls (see illustration). Glue one dome to the top of the cylinder. For the remaining building, cut and glue styrofoam slabs as shown in the illustration. Glue the remaining onion-shaped dome top to this building. Trim the pillars, buildings, and domes with braids and beads as desired.

To make the little girl, cut a circle about 5″ in diameter from wrapping paper. Fold the circle in half and roll it into a cone. Glue the ends together to make the dress. Make the sleeves the same way using circles 3″ in diameter. Glue the sleeves to the dress. Glue a small foam ball to the top of the dress for a head; paint in facial features. For the hat, roll several strips of wrapping paper, glue together, and trim with scissors to a point; glue feathers made with colored felt pens to the hat. Glue the girl to the base.

Add artificial snow and tiny evergreen trees to complete the scene.

STYROFOAM FLOCKED ORNAMENTS

Materials

Materials required for this project include: styrofoam ball, designer yarn in several colors, thin cord, gold and silver braid, white glue, straight pins, pencil, and tinsel.

Preparation of Ornament

Make an outline of the desired design on the foam ball. Glue gold and silver cord over the lines.

Figure 13. Artificial snow and miniature evergreen trees are used as finishing touches on the styrofoam centerpiece (left). The little girl's dress is made of wrapping paper; her head is a small foam ball, with the facial features painted on. The hat can be decorated with feathers.

Cut the various colors of yarn into 1″ lengths, keeping the colors separated. Spread glue over the part of the ball which is to be flocked with one of the colors. Paste the 1″ pieces of yarn to the glued area of the ball, covering it completely. Repeat the procedure with the other colors.

To enhance the appearance of the ornament, make the following tassel.

1. Cut a piece of cardboard 4″ x 2″ and wrap tinsel or yarn around the 4″ side about 30 times.

2. Put a 7″ thread under the wrap (see illustration) at one end and tie a knot to hold the wrap together. This end will be the top of the tassel.

3. At the other end, cut the wrap free from the cardboard. Trim the bottom if necessary.

4. Cut a 12″ piece of yarn. Wrap this length tightly around the top of the tassel several times. Tie the ends and clip off the extra yarn.

5. Pin the top of the tassel to the ornament.

STYROFOAM EASTER EGG

Materials

Materials required for this project are: (1) a styrofoam egg; (2) sequins; (3) clusters of tiny artificial flowers; (4) single tiny artificial flowers; (5) small oat pearls; (6) small faceted beads; (7) appliqué flowers; (8) bunny or some other Easter figure; (9) narrow velvet ribbon; (10) straight pins; (11) hatpin; (12) scissors; (13) knife; and (14) white glue.

Cutting the Egg

Cut the egg lengthwise with the knife so that one piece is larger than the other. Using the knife, scoop out a cavity in the larger piece big enough for the figure. The smaller piece will be used for the base.

Decorating the Egg

1. Begin decorating the egg by placing sequins and small faceted beads around the cavity. However, leave some space between the cavity and the sequins and beads for the placement of flowers. Use straight pins to position the sequins and beads.

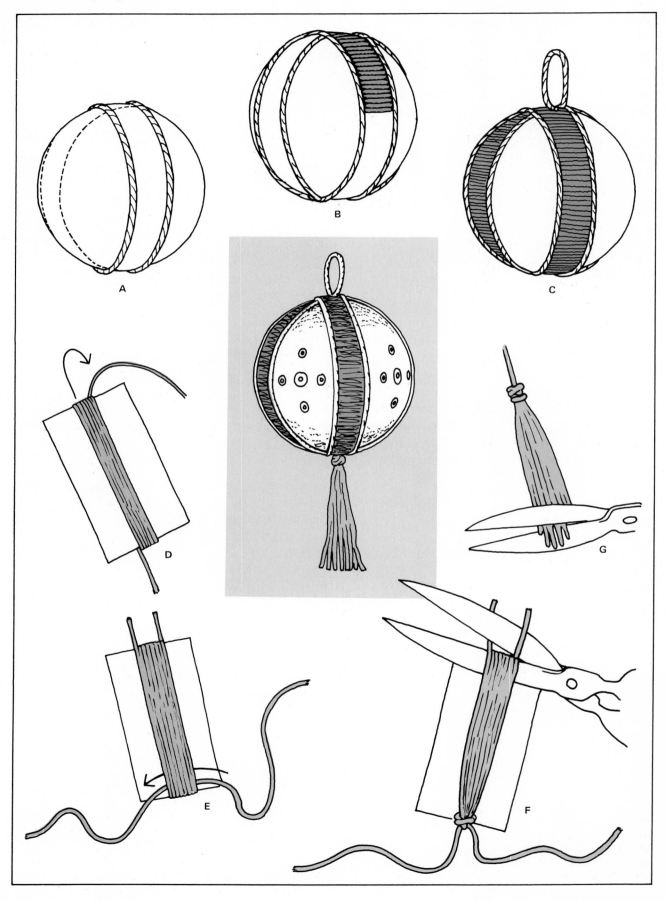

A

B

C

D

E

F

G

2. Insert clusters of tiny flowers into the egg between the cavity and the sequins and beads and also inside the cavity.

3. Place the figure inside the cavity. If the figure cannot be inserted into the styrofoam, glue it in place.

4. Fill in any empty spots around and inside the cavity with the single tiny flowers.

5. Cut a length of the velvet ribbon for a bow. Glue a faceted bead on a straight pin, and pin the bow to the top of the egg.

6. Cut a length of velvet ribbon for around the front of the egg, and pin it in place. For a more decorative effect, glue an oat pearl on the head of each pin before inserting it through the ribbon.

Decorating the Base

1. Arrange appliqué flowers around the base about halfway between the top and the bottom. (Leave enough space at the center of the top for the egg.) Secure the flowers by inserting a straight

pin with an oat pearl attached through the center of each flower.

2. Cut a length of velvet ribbon for around the bottom of the base. Pin it in place with straight pins to which oat pearls have been attached.

3. Insert clusters of tiny flowers around the base, and fill in empty spots with single flowers.

4. Insert the hatpin into the flat part of the base and out the top. To make the base level, push the end of the hatpin into the styrofoam.

5. Press the egg onto the protruding end of the hatpin. To make the decoration more stable, place glue on the hatpin and at the points where the egg will touch the base before pressing the egg onto the hatpin.

EMBROIDERED LEATHER HANDBAG

A plain handbag or change purse can benefit from an embroidered and beaded design. Use an old leather handbag at home for practice, or buy one with no decoration. Use a smooth leather rather

Figure 14. To make styrofoam flocked ornaments, follow text directions and steps A-G in the diagram (opposite).

Figure 15. On the right is the pattern for a beaded and embroidered handbag. Be sure to use a thick needle for sewing on leather.

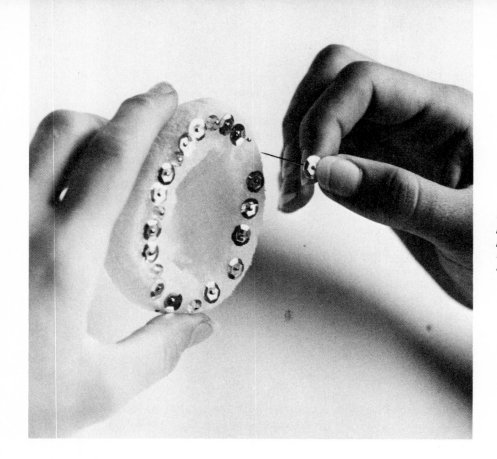

Figure 16. For the Easter Egg project, decorate the prepared styrofoam egg by pinning sequins and beads around the cavity (left).

Figure 17. Continue decorating by placing tiny flower clusters between the sequin decorations and the inner part of the egg (left).

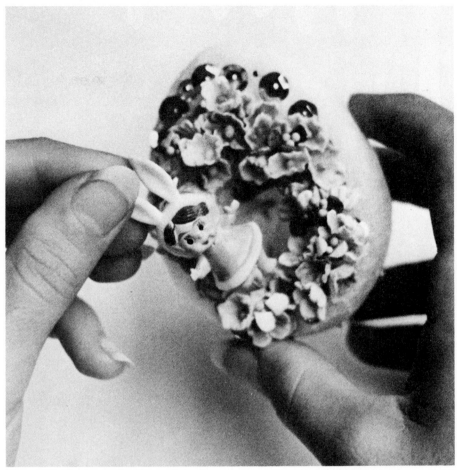

Figure 18. Now put the figure into the decorated cavity of the egg (above). Add additional flowers as needed.

Figure 19. Attach a bow made from narrow velvet ribbon to the top of the egg.

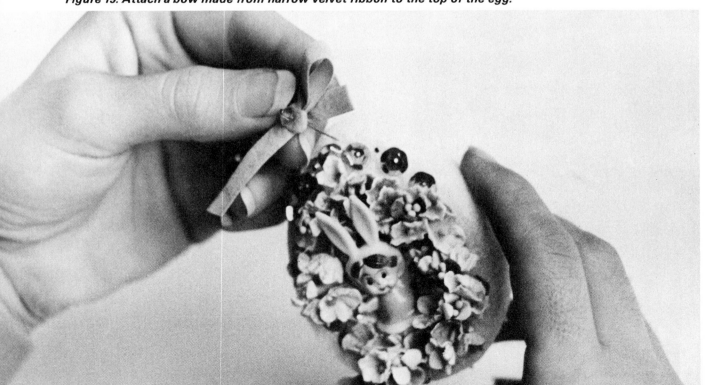

Figure 20. Attach a length of velvet ribbon to the top of the egg and wind it around the front.

Figure 21. To decorate the base, arrange and pin appliqued flowers.

Figure 22. After adding clusters of flowers and pinning velvet ribbon around the bottom, insert a hatpin through the base.

Figure 23. Attach the decorated Easter Egg to the base by pressing it onto the end of the hatpin.

Figure 24. Embroidered beadwork decorates this handsome evening bag (above). The embroidery for this bag is time-consuming but well worth the effort, considering the price of a purchased bag of this type.

than suede. Sewing on leather requires a heavy-duty needle with a large eye. When the needle goes through the leather, the eye will make a hole larger than the thread, and the thread will go through without any problem. Use buttonhole twist when sewing on the leather. It is strong, has a sheen, and comes in a variety of colors.

To make embroidered decorations, follow the steps suggested in *Beadcraft Embroidery* under "Basic Procedures." For leather decorations, use a sharp knife and carefully cut out leather circles of the desired size. Glue and stitch the desired pattern.

For Additional Reading

Barth, Edna, **Lillies, Rabbits, and Painted Eggs,** Random House, 1962.

Glick, James E., **Boutique Eggs and Ornaments,** Mission Viego, California, 1973.

Hofsimde, Robert, **Indian Beadwork,** 1958.

Newall, Venetia, **An Egg at Easter,** Indiana Univ. Press, 1971.

Purdy, Susan, **Festivals,** Lippincott, 1969.